PRINCES OF THE EARTH

SUBCULTURAL DIVERSITY IN A MEXICAN MUNICIPALITY

by BARBARA LUISE MARGOLIES

a special publication of the American Anthropological Association
number 2

Copies of this title and other titles from the American Anthropological Association may be ordered from:
American Anthropological Association
2200 Wilson Boulevard, Suite 600
Arlington, VA 22201
Telephone: 703.528.1902
Fax: 703.528.3546

http://www.aaanet.org/publications/Books-and-Monographs.cfm

To my parents
June and Albert Margolies,
for their many years of encouragement

CONTENTS

Maps and Drawings

Photographs

FOREWORD

This book focuses on a single municipality of central Mexico, but it is more than an ethnographic study. The author describes the situation and feelings of the people of San Felipe with a rare sensitivity. At the same time she shows with considerable documentation, much of it in the words or writings of the people themselves, how the Mexican Revolution has affected the countryside. The experience of this revolution and the Mestizo society it was supposed to have produced has been much debated recently in academic circles. Moreover, the Mexican, American and Cuban revolutions represent differing styles which are of immense importance, intellectually, socially and politically throughout Latin America. We feel therefore that this book is a timely contribution in the best anthropological tradition of using the particular to illuminate the general.

David Maybury-Lewis
SPECIAL EDITOR

—photo by B. L. Margolies

princes of the earth

PREFACE

Mexico experienced a revolution in 1910, but it was many years before its repercussions were felt in rural regions peripheral to the principal drama. Some scholars have argued that the Mexican Revolution is dead; yet it has lived on for sixty years in the rhetorical eulogies borrowed and reiterated by the post-revolutionary government. While the Revolution totally shattered the caste-like, tightly structured society of the nineteenth century and imbued Mexicans with an optimistic nationalism, a large sector of the society has not shared proportionately in the modern gains of the new Mexico. This underprivileged sector has generally been identified as Indian and distinguished from the non-Indian–or Mestizo–by a grinding poverty and separate culture. In an analysis of why "Indians" continue to exist in a nation ideologically committed to the minimization of cultural, social and economic differences, many scholars have resorted to the "culture of ethnicity" explanation: the Indian has existed in relative isolation and only recently been admitted to the "national society"; his conservatism and traditionalism in the face of disrupting influences are the roots of his imperviousness to change. Unless the Indian abandons his basic cultural assumptions, he will persist as a marginal participant in national life. This explanation, hidden behind the masks of such euphemisms as "dualism," "pluralism," and "image of limited good," often slights determinants inherent in the wider society–the social and economic inequities perpetuated by the national polity.

Princes of the Earth is the study of a rural municipality and its relationship to Mexico as a nation; it is a study of the local sectors of the national society at selected points in history–the late nineteenth and early twentieth centuries, the two decades succeeding the Revolution when its basic goals were institutionalized, and the present period. This community has always formed a viable part of the nation, although events which were precipitated outside its boundaries have reverberated locally with predictable sluggishness. While in other parts of the nation, local social sectors form part of a class society, this community has not completed the transformation from a caste-like to a class society, differentiated solely on the basis of socioeconomic factors. Here the factor of ethnicity still pays a predominant role in stigmatizing the Indian segment of the local society. Only by analyzing the relationships between the Indian and both his non-Indian neighbors and the wider society, can one understand why an Indian group should continue to exist. This study is not an exhaustive ethnographic description of either Indian or non-Indian culture. Indians and non-Indians share basic cultural traditions, but participate differentially in the national society. Differential participation, rather than resulting from cultural conservatism or traditionalism, has been the consequence of a policy of exclusion on the part of the national polity. Only with the removal of presently existent social and economic injustices, can the underprivileged take their place in a veritable class-structured nation.

This study is based on data collected from June 1969 to July 1970 in the municipality of San Felipe del Progreso. My first field trip to San Felipe, however, was in 1967 when I was given a summer fellowship by the Institute of Latin American Studies of Columbia University. I wanted to test the subcultural typology of Wagley and Harris (1965), particularly the Town subculture. The carriers of Town subculture–upper-class townspeople–were among the least known groups of Latin America and provided "the key to the problem of the relationship of Peasant subcultures to lines of national political and economic integration" (1965:54). My first problem was finding a town, an equivalent of our county seat, where different subcultural groups lived in close proximity.

Professor Fernando Cámara, my summer advisor, suggested the highlands of Mexico State. He was directing an urgent anthropology project which included the Mazahua Indians of central Mexico. The Mazahua peasants had had continual contact with their non-Indian neighbors since the early colonial period and were tied to the national life through their dependence on the provincial center. Neither they nor their Mestizo neighbors had been systematically studied.

After visiting several towns with Professor Cámara, I chose the small town of San Felipe del Progreso, eighty-seven miles north of Mexico City. The town had fewer than 1000 inhabitants, but was the seat of one of the largest municipalities in the country. The town had passed its economic apogee and was now an administrative center. Founded by wealthy landowners who commuted between country estate and townhouse, it was now an obscure county seat where people worked hard to lead respectable lives. There was obviously a great distance between the people who lived in the once baronial houses of the town and the peasants from the satellite villages who frequented the town.

During my four months in San Felipe, I traveled extensively in the municipality, met village officials, and became acquainted with many town families. I told people I wanted to learn about their history and customs. After a summer of mutual observation, I wrote a brief article on the rural elite (1969) and decided to do a complete ethnographic study of the distinct subcultures.

My return to San Felipe in 1969 was relaxed and pleasant compared to my first nervous field trip. People knew me. I had passed the point of explaining my presence and answering curious questions. The López family invited me to live with them and introduced me to their relatives, friends and *compadres*. They treated me as one of the family and softened my entry into town life. In the company of Carolina Moreno, my assistant, I had friendly access to village homes. The Moreno family had migrated from the village of Jalpa and had extensive contacts both in town and village. They helped me over the "letters of introduction" phase which only disconcerted villagers.

My unit of analysis was the entire municipality, not just a single village or the town. I had to define the subcultures and delineate their institutional networks. I suspected that each group had distinct institutional networks which overlapped with the corresponding networks of the other groups. All this seemed an impossible task. Alone, I would have to "learn" several cultures in a regional community with almost 90,000 inhabitants and some 150 settlements. During my first month, I tried to define my project more precisely and did "busy" but necessary work. I mapped the town and its four barrios, took a complete census of the town and a sample census of the barrios (the barrios alone had 5000 inhabitants). I had complete information on household composition, work and migration history, education, marriage, etc. I gradually realized that what I had first perceived as subcultural differences were actually gradations on a socioeconomic scale. San Felipeños subjectively perceived two "ethnic" groups. Objectively, the similarities between these two groups were far more striking than the differences. But San Felipeños magnified the differences and had stereotypic concepts of Indian and Mestizo culture which were no longer viable. To understand why "ethnicity" obscured class relations I had to analyze each group's position in the larger society through time. My final orientation was more structural-functional than descriptive; I concentrated on a diachronic study of changing ethnic relations (economic, political and religious) in the context of the national social system.

I relied heavily on participation and observation. I attended political meetings, fiestas, inaugurations and markets, joined pilgrimages, audited classes, witnessed local litigations, farmed and worked as a census taker. Aside from my formal notes and tapes, I kept a detailed running diary of the day's events, conversations, and miscellanea. I cross-indexed the diary as I went along; later, it was one of the most valuable sources of "fresh" material.

The local community was highly stratified and diversified and no one person was familiar with all aspects of local culture. I therefore worked with various tutors on a regular basis. Don Ernesto and Don Fidel reconstructed the local history of the hacienda and the agrarian movement; Don Rubén taught me the formal and informal structure of religious activity; Guillermo López explained the intricacies of municipal government; and the Ruíz family described crops and yields. Other townspeople and villagers filled in gaps and verified my information. I visited ex-hacendados and former residents of San Felipe in Mexico City; they spoke of the past, their motives for leaving San Felipe, and their present circumstances. From the beginning my rapport with these persons was excellent. They spoke freely and took me under their tutelage with pleasure. The more they knew of their specialty, the more they spoke, almost with a personal pride in demonstrating their knowledge.

Every week I spent a day or two in a different village. I generally introduced myself to village officials when they were in town on business, or migrant townspeople introduced me to their village relatives. I had a long list of memorized questions that would give me a composite view of the village life. Several villages I returned to many times and I spent a month in La Ciénega, living in the local schoolhouse.

I also worked extensively with archival materials. I consulted the Archivo General de la Nación for data on eighteenth-century land tenure. The Municipal Archives dating from the 1860s were an excellent source of information on nineteenth-century land tenure, local industries, racial and occupational classifications, and the agrarian reform. My information on colonial ethnic relations is based on research in the parish archives, while the private archives of the hacienda San Onofre documented the step-by-step destruction of the agrarian estate.

Before I left San Felipe, I formally interviewed 100 families in the town and barrios. I selected families which represented distinct positions along the socioeconomic scale and collected quantitative data on diet, possessions, land ownership, crop yields, agricultural practices, expenditures, political and religious participation, and social mobility. This data is incorporated into the study.

This study would not have been possible without the long sponsorship and invaluable guidance of Dr. Charles Wagley. To Dr. Conrad Arensberg, I am grateful for his numerous suggestions and for teaching me anthropology as a comparative science. To Professor Fernando Cámara, who introduced me to Mexican anthropology and offered the resources of the Museo Nacional de Antropología e Historia, I am particularly indebted. My fieldwork was financed by a National Institute of Mental Health Field Research Training Grant and the preparation of the manuscript by a National Institute of Mental Health Research Fellowship.

I also wish to thank my mother, June Margolies who edited the manuscript, and my husband Graziano Gasparini who tempered my judgment with advice based on years of academic experience in Latin America.

To the people of the municipality of San Felipe del Progreso, I am grateful for their openness, patience and affection. They treated me as a "first cousin" for sixteen months and introduced me to their way of life. The López family invited me into their home and this study could not have been completed without the help of the late Don Ernesto López. He was extraordinarily knowledgeable about San Felipe, the Revolution and Mexico, and was an astute and kind teacher.

1

"THE DISINHERITED"

It is in the twentieth century that the long struggle for social vindication, rooted in the colonial past, is again re-emerging.
–Stanley and Barbara Stein [1970]

In 1966, the Ethnography Department of the National Museum of Anthropology in Mexico City initiated an urgent salvage program–Rescate Etnográfico Nacional–to compile data on relatively unstudied rural groups. The major foci of the project were "Indians" and "isolated communities" (Cámara 1965); the underlying assumption was that Indian groups would rapidly disappear due to "the intensity and rhythm of cultural and social change" engendered by urbanization and industrialization (Cámara 1965:99; 1966:7). It was also assumed that Indians were culturally distinct, although only the remnants of an original culture persisted, alternated with modifications from the colonial period and the "influence of non-Indian cultural complexes of the national period" (1966:1).

I joined the program in 1967 with the intention of studying the Mazahua Indians of the northwestern part of Mexico State. Before entering the field, I reviewed archival and secondary sources in a fruitless attempt to reconstruct an "original culture." Our knowledge of the pre-Columbian Mazahuas is founded totally on a legendary perspective. It is evident, however, that numerically the Mazahuas composed an insignificant ethnic group, and were linguistically differentiated from other groups. The Mazahuas participated in the general population movements of Central Mexico and were exchanged between the more powerful nations as trophies of war. They never attained independent political unification and were the product of a cultural mosaic shared with contiguous groups in which ethnic idiosyncrasies were blurred. With their incorporation into the Aztec empire as vassals, the Mazahuas were increasingly subordinated; they were placed under the jurisdiction of Nahua speaking caciques, appointed by "the lords of Mexico for the protection and conduct of the natives" (Codice Mendocino 1937, Folios 17, 18), and more pertinently, for the purpose of both suppressing revolt and collecting and forwarding tribute payments. Well before the Spanish conquest, the Mazahuas were complacently manipulated and exploited by alien subjugators; they had neither the distinctive culture nor ethnic solidarity of their more illustrious compatriots.

My first impressions of the Mazahua Indians were formed in the Museum. According to official sentiment expressed by the staff, the ethnography presented in the museum is "a fundamental part of Mexican reality" (Bernal 1968:175). Despite brief references to Indians in their actuality–cash cropping,

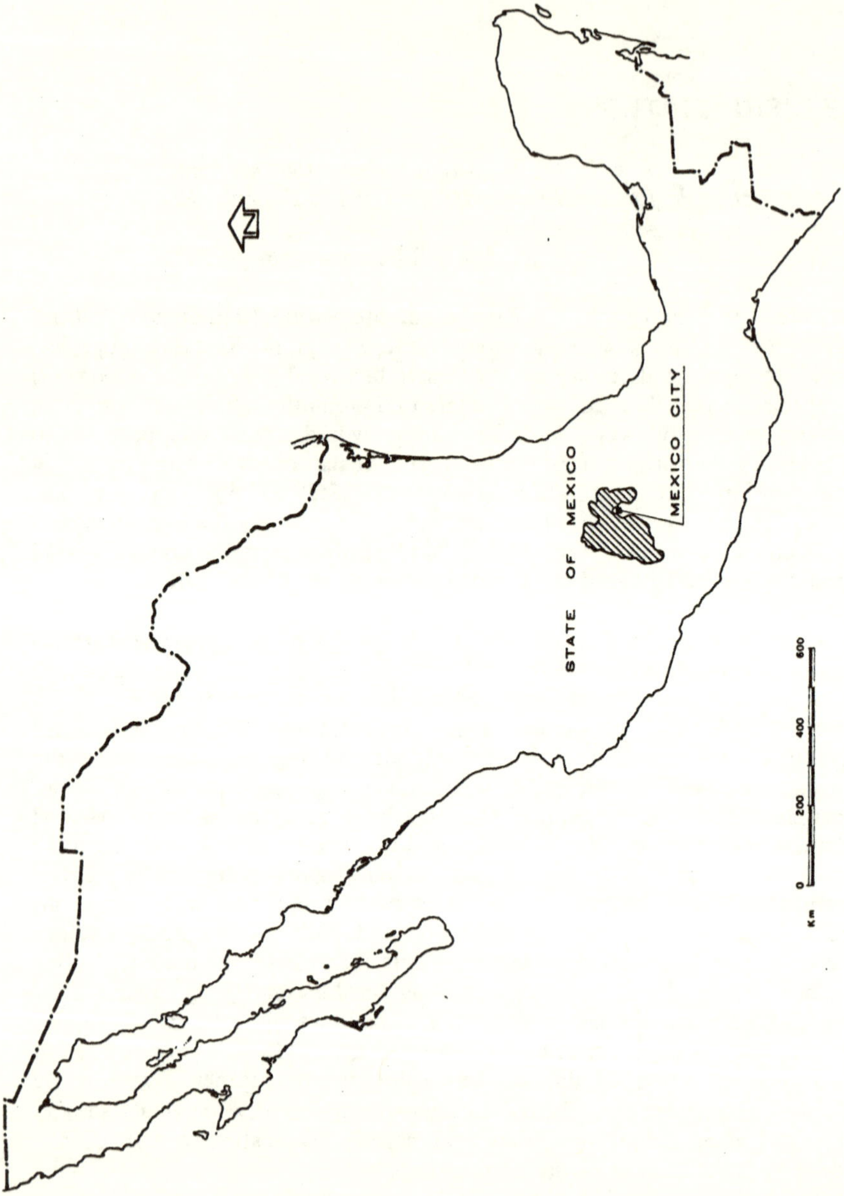

STATE OF MEXICO

MEXICO CITY

Km 0 200 400 600

N

Mexico

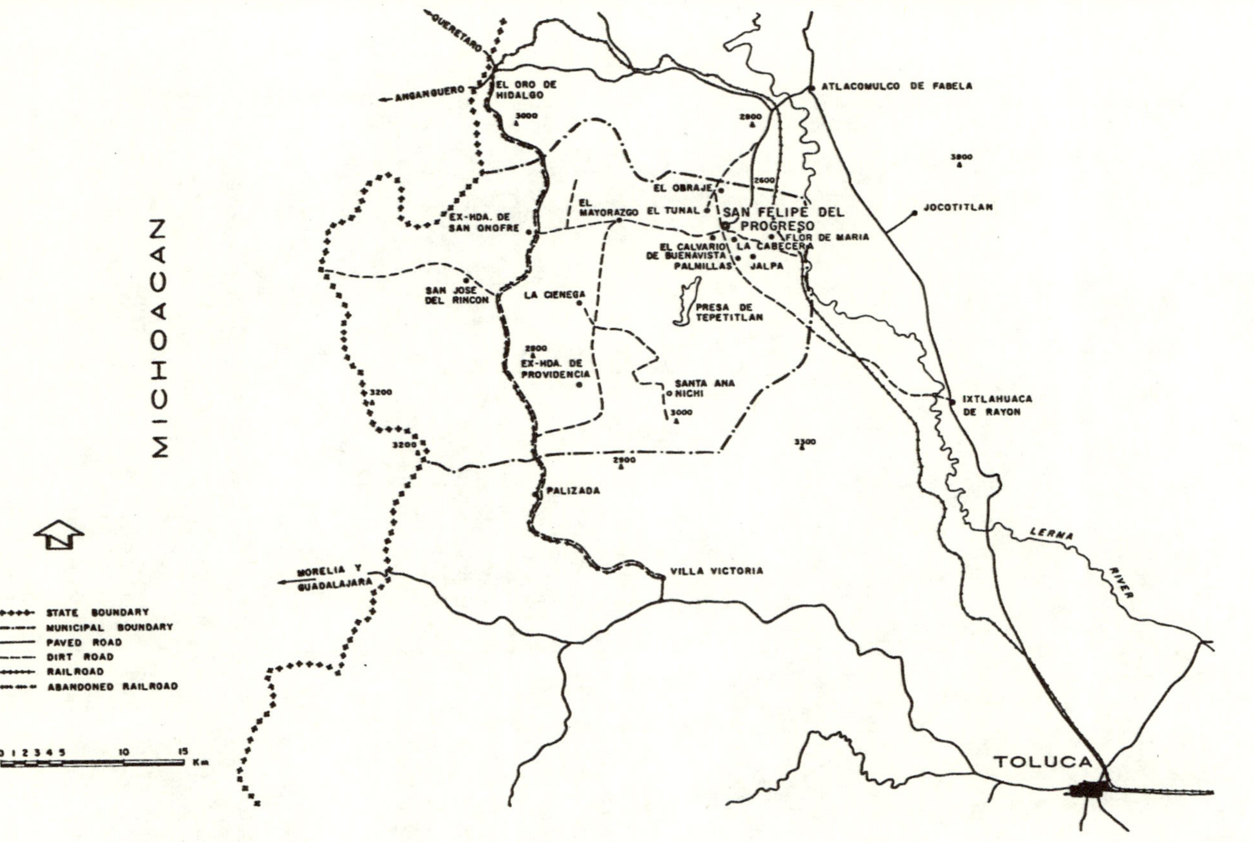

Municipality of San Felipe del Progreso

—photo by Graziano Gasparini

a typical town street

—photo by B. L. Margolies

a typical village house, with barley drying on the roof

educational institutions, communications and social interaction beyond place of origin which have resulted in greater participation in the "national life"–the ethnographic situation of Mexico continues to be presented as though Indians constituted a coagulum petrified by cultural peculiarities which distinguish them from non-Indians:

> Some four million Indians live isolated in small hamlets, forming part of the rural Mexican population. They continue to cultivate their fields of maize, chile, beans, and squash, while weavers and potters develop their arts and crafts. The government is in the hands of the old men and progressive young men, while their present life remains bound more to the past and the supernatural [Bernal 1968:174].

The sparse section on the Mazahuas conforms admirably to this postulate. The scenographic mounting of Mazahua culture consists of various "folk" elements of an Indian way of life: a freshly painted and immaculate family oratory decorated with flower motifs and doorless so that the visitor can see the elaborate ritual offerings of their religious cult, which is labeled an *exact replica* of an actual chapel; a mannequin clothed in a finely woven woolen skirt and an intricately embroidered tunic; examples of Mazahua looms, Mazahua musical instruments, Mazahua ceramics and Mazahua technology.

I naively expected to find these characteristic expressions of Mazahua culture in the field. My first contact with the Mazahuas occurred in the municipality of San Felipe del Progreso. I had been forewarned of its rusticity, its spiritual distance from Mexico City and its lack of amenities that suggested respectable city life. I arrived in the municipal seat on a Sunday, at the height of a busy market attended by Indians from the interior. It was superficially obvious that for each person who spoke Mazahua, there were several who did not, and no one was garbed in the costumes that had formed a prominent part of the Museum's exhibit. After a few weeks it was also evident that there were minor vestiges of a family chapel—perhaps a dozen families in a sample of ten villages possessed an oratory inherited from their parents and virtually abandoned—but none of the other elements facilely associated with Mazahua culture, ranging from musical instruments to digging sticks, were either uniquely Mazahua or even in general use. Later, it became apparent that these people were neither encapsulated in their past nor totally bedazzled by religious cults. Indeed, they considered Mazahua a language which for practical purposes should best be forgotten; they *never* associated "Mazahua" with "indígena," and while acknowledging their Indian ancestry, consistently identified themselves as farmers, peasants, Mexicans or the poor. The major single desire expressed by these people was to overcome their past and forget the customs that symbolized this past.

The Museum, as well as other institutions, compound their disservice to the so-called Indian groups by presenting the Indian through the mask of scenographies that create an illusion scarcely relevant to reality. Much as in a wax museum where one can relive former events or contemplate fusty personages, the Indian is rendered in timeless permanency and Indian material culture is depicted as though it were ever enduring.

The Indians, themselves, are exalted as "disinherited princes" (Ideario 1970:160), an allusion to the aristocracies which culturally and politically dominated pre-Columbian Mexico and were irrevocably shattered by the "civilizing" Spanish conquest. The traumatization suffered during three centuries of infra-human exploitation was a disinheritance not only from the land, but also from the most elemental human conditions. Indian culture was not simply modified; it was deformed. From the level of "indígena," autonomous and autochthonous, the Indian plummeted to the level of "indio," occupying the lowest caste position in a colonial society structured to benefit and privilege the dominators. In addition to the deprivations associated with his low status, he suffered a more insidious derogation:

> the degradation of arrogating a self-image which was little more than a reflection of a European world view equating racial inferiority with Negro, Indian, or Mestizo. Consequently, their backwardness was explained as a fatalism derived from innate and ineludable characteristics, of laziness, of lack of ambition, of tendency to lechery, etcetera [Ribeiro 1969:103].

The systems of exploitation juridically condoned by the colonial government were abandoned in the nineteenth century, but exploitation was subsequently perpetrated under the fetters of regional wardships (agrarian estates) which were not annihilated until they crumbled under the pressures of the Revolution. The disinherited Indian was reimbursed with a semblance of his land and ideologically incorporated into a new Mexican society. He lost many of the characteristics which distinguished him as Indian, but continued to occupy the lowest status position in Mexican society.

This book focuses on the Indian and his changing status under the aegis of the hacienda agrarian system, during the revolutionary but halting process of land distribution, and since the institutionalization of revolutionary principles. The Indian was and is a part of Mexican society; in order to understand his variant historical roles as caste member, peon and peasant farmer and the various

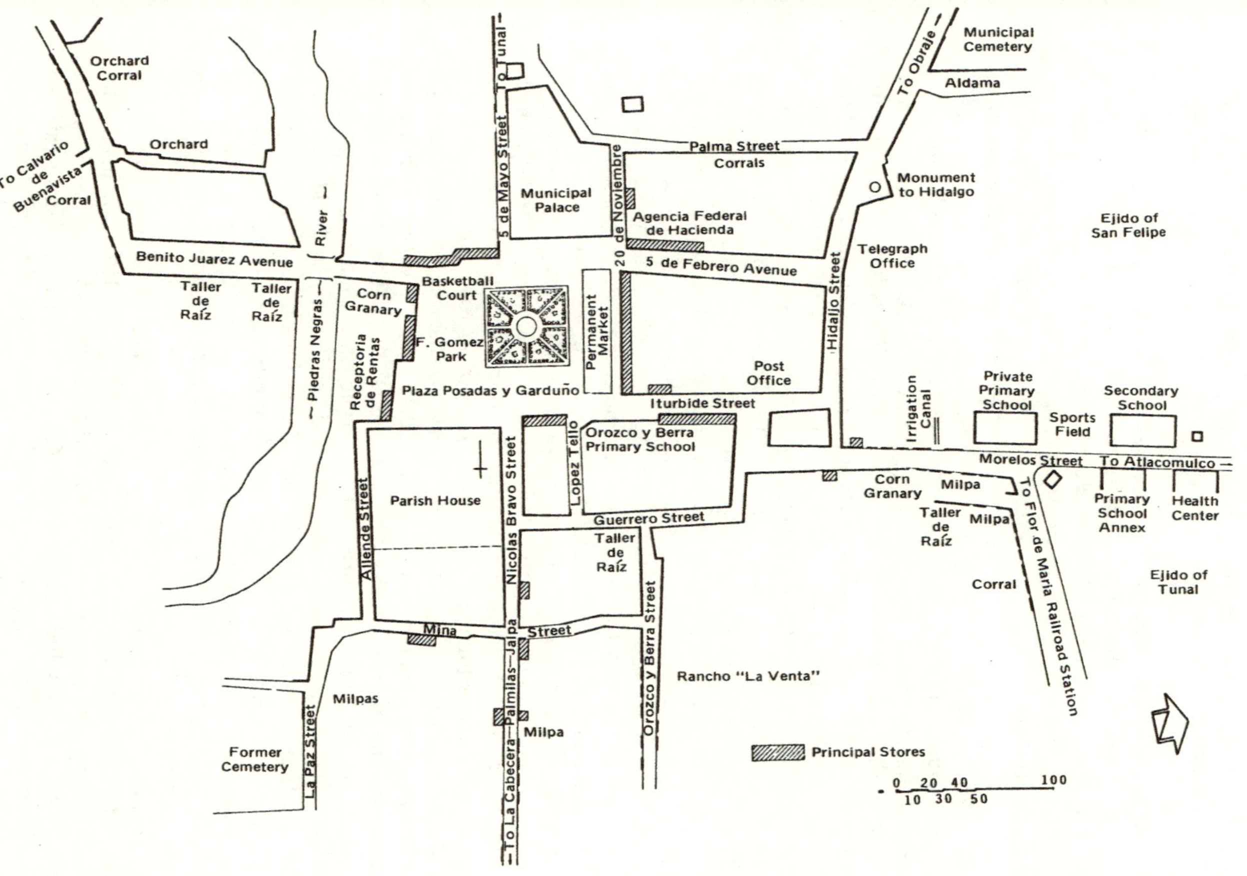

Town of San Felipe del Progreso

discriminatory attitudes, motivated by racial, ethnic or class considerations, from which he suffers, one must turn to the complementary part of Mexican society–the non-Indian. The regional community[1] of San Felipe has been a field of social interaction between Indians and non-Indians since the sixteenth century.

This book is thus a response to the skewed portrait of "Indian society," growing out of analyses made in the tradition of "ideological localism" (Lewis 1963:xxi). These studies inevitably equate community with ethnic homogeneity, community and ethnic group with isolation and autonomy, and ethnic group with the preservation of ancient customs and the determination to maintain a unique cultural identity. Despite the "nation-oriented" community analyses of Steward (1956), Lewis (1963), Wolf (1965, 1966), Richardson (1967, 1970), the Hunts (1969) and others, "ideological localism" still has many adherents. Iwanska, for example, recently published a study on a "traditional, self-conscious, corporate, Mazahua Indian village." In the first book-length study of the Mazahuas, she trys to reconcile the almost greedy desire of peasants for more land, more schools and a higher standard of living with the simultaneous contention that they are "deeply rooted in the past" (1971:7). The "village," in fact, is a neighborhood barrio whose residents farm, do business, and attend church and school in town; yet the barrio is conceptualized as a "village" because of the presumed persistence of "traditional institutions" (28) and the "mazahua-ization" within it of national institutions (1971:30). "Isolation" is a convenient concept, adroitly used in claiming that the Indians are committed to the past; but it is neither explicatory nor accurate. Neither Indians nor the Indian communities were or are "isolated."

In the regional community of San Felipe it was precisely the avenues of articulation with the "wider society" that acted as a catalyst in the differentiation of ethnic groups. Indians were taught the Christian doctrine in their own language, they were tributaries of Spanish *encomenderos*[2] who invaded the fertile Valley of Ixtlahuaca, and by the early eighteenth century when the *Criollo*[3] town of San Felipe was founded, Indians were involved in litigation over the despoiling of communal lands by sheep ranchers. The consolidation of the haciendas in the late nineteenth century was accomplished at the expense of free Indian villages; as the haciendas expanded territorially and widened their markets, the Indians were progressively sucked into their orbit as landless peons. Indians were not isolated, but deliberately quarantined and detained through various mechanisms. This quarantine was so successful that it was not lifted until the 1930s, twenty years after the beginning of agrarian unrest, when it was politically expedient to do so.

The concepts of "national culture" and "incorporation" are post-revolutionary ideas which have served to exculpate the Mestizo from his former mediocre status position and biological inferiority. Indian America was displaced by Mestizo America; for Indians and rural Mestizos of recent Indian ancestry to be incorporated into the "national culture" or the "national life" they must superficially look and behave like proper Mestizos. Many Indian groups have undergone this process, generally known as acculturation, yet they have not been assimilated and continue to be the most marginal citizens of Mexican society. Why are they not changing at what policy makers, politicians and social scientists consider a decent rate? The most general explanation has been a citation of the peasant's "traditional social structure" which has persisted as a result of his conservative and fatalistic world view. Brief references are made to historical circumstances, yet analysis is couched in terms of cultural peculiarities. An example of this approach is *The Waiting Village* (Nelson 1971), in which villagers' perceptions of the world are treated as causal in impeding change:

> Although many patterns of interaction may have a historical rather than a functional basis, the study of change has been approached through a description and analysis of the existing social world and value system under the assumption that one cannot talk of change until one understands what exists. For this reason the focus has been on how villagers pattern and perceive their world, and the implications of this perception to social change [1971:128].

My argument in this book is based on the notion of "institutionalized exclusion." Why is the peasant a marginal sector of national society? Cultural peculiarities? A prestige economy? Habitation in hostile regions? Or the indifference and equivocations of a polity which loses sight of its revolutionary objective of Incorporation during the rhetorical game of politicking? The Revolution continues to be palpable because it is cyclically revitalized:

> We consciously continue to employ it (the Revolution) as long as the expression signifies the execution, little by little, of the original principles and political and economic objectives which have obviously been only partially fulfilled [Excelsior 1970:18a].

The Revolution succeeded in raising the expectations of the peasants, whether Indian or Mestizo, and revolutionary ideology has effectively assuaged them, yet the peasant is still excluded because he is forgotten by national development programs, while consistently remembered in electoral programs. The peasant is a victim of a revolutionary doctrine which disciplines his loyalties, not the captive of a cultural system which anachronistically perpetuates itself.

2

THE HACIENDA: CYNOSURE OF THE DISPOSSESSED

> *Vino la ley a despoblar tu cielo a arrancarte terrones adorados, a discutir el agua de los ríos, a robarte el reinado de los árboles. Te sepultaron en edictos fríos, y cuando despertaste en la frontera de la más despeñada desventura, desposeído, solitario, errante, te dieron calabozo, te amarraron, te maniataron para que nadando no salieras del agua de los pobres, sino que te ahogaras pataleando.*
>
> –Pablo Neruda

The hacienda as an agrarian system has been distinguished on the basis of its self-containment, its voracity for land, its immobilization of labor and its small-scale operations, restricted by a lack of capital and an extensive market. In Mexico, it has repeatedly been emphasized that: the family-owned hacienda was a source of prestige, and the satisfaction of immediate, personal status needs received priority over capital reinvestment; gratification resulted from land ownership and stable, secure returns rather than from technical innovations and the improvement of the estate; primitive techniques were moderately successful because the hacienda was labor-intensive, with the burden of production borne by peons, renters and croppers; labor was captured by means of various devices, ranging from encroachment on village lands and the incorporation of the indigenous population to bondage by debt-peonage.

The attribute consistently singled out has been the hacienda's low productivity in relation to its total area:

> a hacienda would farm only a small portion of its total land resources–its best land–but would do so with an unchanging and antiquated sixteenth century technology . . . [Wolf 1959:205].

> The hacienda, with its scarcity of capital and its need to bind labour, retains a labour-intensive technology often based on the tools and techniques traditional in the culture from which the labour force is drawn [Wolf and Mintz 1957:405].

> even those with magnificent extensions of arable land, left a large portion of the soil to lie fallow year after year . . . . As a general rule the haciendas, with some notable exceptions to be sure, continued the same primitive agricultural technology which their owners had inherited from their forebears [Cumberland 1968:203].

> the hacienda lacked the enterprise, the capital equipment, and the access to the markets to cultivate more than a fraction of the tillable soil [Tannenbaum 1929:106].

> Reinvestment or changes in ageless patterns of cultivation were seldom considered–raising corn year after year for centuries on the same land was good enough! [Brandenburg 1964:39].

The hacienda was commonly the product of a seventeenth-century economic depression and owed its long continuity to the absence of risk-oriented strategies. During most of its history, the hacienda did not slough off its colonial heritage. But during the last decades of its existence, it underwent a series of internal transformations in response to changes in the wider society. These have generally been neglected in favor of emphasis on earlier, more classic characteristics.

Not all haciendas developed in the seventeenth century, passed through the golden eighteenth century, and survived unscathed until the Revolution. Haciendas also had unspectacular and humble origins during the Independence period and failed to exhibit many of the typical attributes. The latifundium that evolved during the colonial depression and was controlled for successive generations by families obsessed with "their ancestry" was often quite different from the same institution that developed under other circumstances.

The large landed estate did not become the dominant form of land tenure in the region of San Felipe until the nineteenth century and it diverged from the "classic" hacienda in vital respects. Although it conformed closely to the model in its exploitation of an Indian group, the late nineteenth- and early twentieth-century hacienda was a highly successful commercial venture, specialized in a variety of cash crops which supplied a supra-local market, and farmed by the most innovative, scientific techniques then available.

Colonial San Felipe had long been an area of yeomanry in which the typical settlement pattern among the Criollos and Mestizos consisted of small family ranches. With the exception of two estates that date from the 1600s, the formation of the hacienda was a steady process involving the accumulation of land under a single proprietorship throughout the nineteenth century. Properties frequently changed hands and were inevitably enlarged in the transfer. These purchases were facilitated during the latter half of the century as a result of the distribution of village common lands in 1856, and on later occasions, the sale of "vacant lands." Buyers were repeatedly able to obtain lands for a pittance not only from ranchers but also from the Indian communities. Indians were the special victims of speculators and rapidly lost their properties. Their land was usually taken in one of two ways: parcels were either sold to buy corn during periods of scarcity or offered as collateral against loans. In the latter instance, the parcel was confiscated when the debtor could not repay the loan. Perhaps the most striking example of an estate's expansion through mergers is Providencia, a hacienda sold various times, ultimately in the 1890s. The last owner nearly doubled the size of the estate over a ten-year period by buying neighboring properties.

Toward the end of the century, the haciendas had swelled to their physical limits and were flourishing. This growth corresponded with the opening of new markets, generated by the exploitation of gold and copper mines in Michoacán, and the completion of a national railroad system. Former Indian villages were for the most part engulfed by the hacienda; the few villages which retained their integrity were drastically reduced in land resources and could no longer fulfill subsistence requirements. Tepetitlán, San Onofre and Providencia crosscut municipal and even state lines with vast tracts exceeding 10,000 hectares (1 hectare = 2.471 acres), while thirteen haciendas consisted of approximately

2000 hectares. The seven Indian communities which remained beyond the hacienda's borders averaged eighty-five hectares in area, of which half was marginal, uncultivable land. The population of each village exceeded 500, insuring its dependency on the neighboring estate.

The haciendas were typically divided into annexes or ranches, some directly attached to the estate and others scattered throughout the municipality. The number and size of ranches pertaining to each hacienda varied widely, depending on the quality of land and the total area of the hacienda. Each annex was under the vigilance of a caretaker and contained a minimal set of equipment–threshing floor, oxcarts and tractor. Some ranches were composed entirely of grazing lands, forests or irrigated fields; others duplicated on a smaller scale the organization of the main hacienda and included in addition to a variety of land types, various households of *peones acasillados* (resident laborers) supervised by a major-domo. These *cuadrillas* often corresponded with the former core of the Indian village. As Don Fidel, the former administrator of Tepetitlán explained:

> Tepetitlán, itself, had two cuadrillas. Peons were sent from the first to work in San Isidro and from the second to work in Tungareo and Torecillas (wheat fields). San Pedro and Estutempa each had one cuadrilla of peons who worked there. Espigueo, Cotepeque and Santa Cruz were purely pastoral lands and in these ranches we had only a caretaker.

Many ranches had been purchased in their entirety from small independent farmers and the hacendado was assured not only of a variety of land resources, but also a cuadrilla or two of ready labor.

For both hacendado and acasillado, the nerve center of the hacienda was the *casco*, which contained the principal buildings, service facilities, and the residence of the owner. Since the breakup of the hacienda, almost all the cascos have fallen into ruin, but it is still possible to recall the past through a visit to San Onofre. San Onofre is one of the few haciendas in Mexico that has been maintained with complete fidelity; by passing through its main gates, one effectively closes the door to the present. The casco of the hacienda was built like a fortress and protected from the surrounding fields and cuadrillas by a massive stone wall. Each exposure provided entry, however, through thick wooden doors, the main entrance distinguished by an iron crest inscribed with the name of the hacienda and the date of its foundation. One enters a broad avenue lined with fir trees which shield from view the former houses of the clerks, the schoolteacher, craftsmen and various caretakers. The avenue abruptly terminates in a wide plaza, bounded on the east by an inner walled compound, the private grounds of the hacendado.

The inner compound was immaculately groomed and imaginatively landscaped, its buildings set against soaring pines. The most impressive buildings–the gatehouse, the playhouse, and the "big house"–faithfully complied with late nineteenth-century French neoclassical design, attaining an illusory elegance through false stone façades and elaborate scrollwork cut from plaster. Although unique in the countryside, this style had been highly popular among the well-to-do since the time of Maximilian's monarchy in the 1860s and was copied by the family when the site of the casco was changed. The main house was provided with all the necessary comforts ranging from gas and electricity to English plumbing and furnished with heavy European pieces. Dominating the entry hall

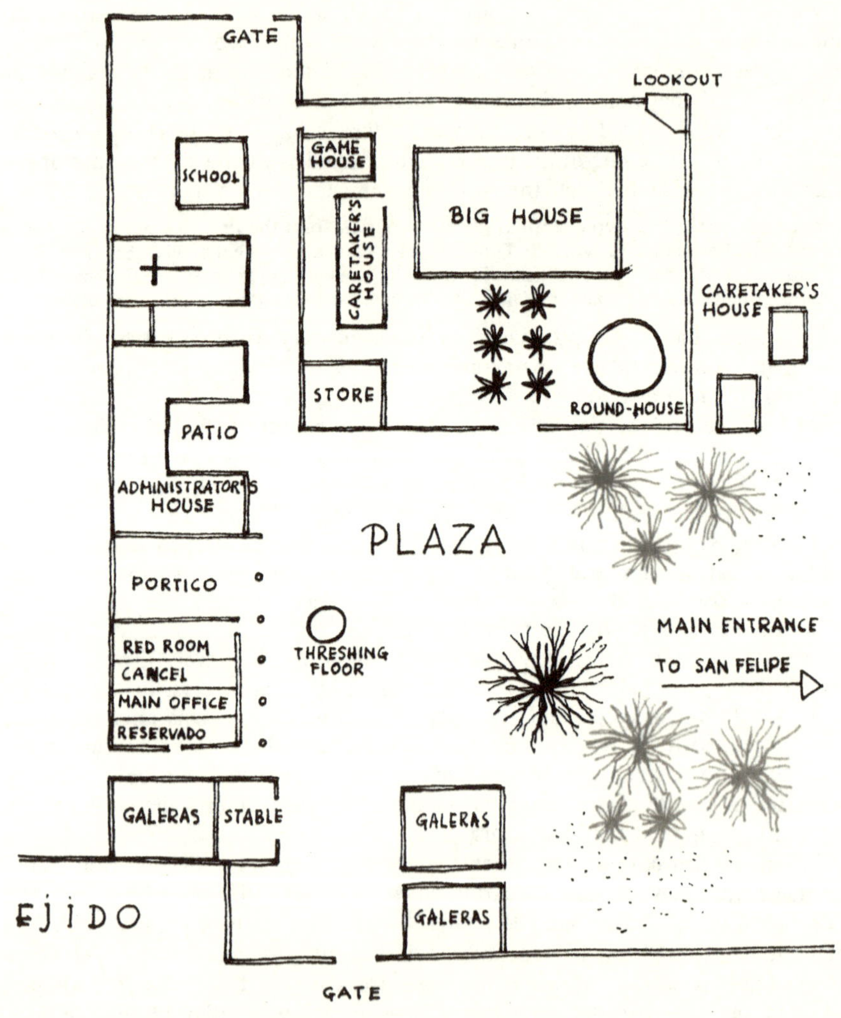
SAN ONOFRE - 1970
CASCO
GATE
LOOKOUT
GAME HOUSE
SCHOOL
BIG HOUSE
CARETAKER'S HOUSE
CARETAKER'S HOUSE
STORE
ROUND-HOUSE
PATIO
ADMINISTRATOR'S HOUSE
PLAZA
PORTICO
THRESHING FLOOR
MAIN ENTRANCE
TO SAN FELIPE
RED ROOM
CANCEL
MAIN OFFICE
RESERVADO
GALERAS
STABLE
GALERAS
GALERAS
EJIDO
GATE

and visible from all angles of the drawing room were the ancestral oil paintings of the Legueys, greatgrandparents of the present owner. Contrasting with the formality of the residence was the playhouse, a cornucopia of amusement, containing a ballroom with its piano and phonograph and a more intimate room with a table tennis set, an English dolls' house, a chess table and musical instruments. Along the eastern wall a large lookout, La Romita, commanded a panoramic view of the estate and the town of San Felipe along the horizon. La Romita was the guests' favorite spot for relaxation and summer drinks. Descending from the lookout and crossing under a series of arches formed by rows of shrubs, one arrives at the garden house, a round wooden structure with a railed porch. Amply furnished, it was treated basically as a pleasure spot and used for picnics, although it occasionally doubled as a guesthouse.

On leaving the compound, one enters the general store, centrally located on the plaza, but at the same time accessible by means of secondary entrances from the grounds of the "casa grande," and diagonally opposite, a one-room schoolhouse and the chapel. Continuing along the northern edge of the plaza lies another complex, the administrator's house and the offices, connected by a number of inner corridors. The administrator's house, the oldest building on the hacienda, is a typical colonial structure with galleries surrounding a central patio and numerous high-ceilinged rooms leading off the galleries. The office was originally located in the entryway of the house, but with the expansion of the hacienda an addition was constructed and attached to the administrator's house by means of a portico. The annex contained three spacious rooms, the most pretentious of which was the "Red Room." Whereas the "big house" comprised

—photo by B. L. Margolies

the gatehouse, San Onofre

the personal quarters for family and friends, the "Red Room" was the official reception hall and the stranger's first impression of the estate. It was ostentatiously decorated with walls papered in red stenciled velvet and windows draped in burgundy velvet; damask upholstered chairs and loveseats in Louis XV style repeated this color scheme and even the crystal chandelier shimmered a florid reflection. The "Red Room" adjoined the *cancel*, a depository for the hacienda's archives and the location of a commodious telephone booth imported from Sweden. Off the cancel was the main office, where working files as well as the large leather inventory and account books were stored in tall wooden cabinets. The office contained a full complement of necessary equipment—roll-top desks, several Oliver typewriters, a Mosler safe, various small strongboxes imported from France and a calculator of American design. A large grilled window opened onto the plaza and it was here the work chits were passed to the peons. A small private office completed the office complex; appropriately known as the *reservado*, this room was for the exclusive use of the patron and was intimately decorated with family photographs and picture postcards collected on trips to Europe and Africa.

The last major complex of the casco, located on the western side of the plaza, consisted of a series of courtyards lined with distinctive *galeras*—the granaries, stables, chicken coops, carriage room, machinery repositories, butchery, creamery, carpenters' shop and broom factory. All patios were finished in brick and used for drying corn ears, drying *zacatón* fibers which would later be made into brooms, and threshing wheat.

The families that belonged to the landowning class were often of humble origins. Yet after a time span of two or three generations, they had adopted the cultural forms of a pseudo nobility. The trajectory of the Venegas[4] hacendados clearly illustrates this process. The history of this family begins with the appearance of Colonel Leguey, a deserter from the French brigade sent to Mexico during a brief skirmish in the 1830s, who eventually made his way to the municipality and married the daughter of a criollo rancher. Although the estate was still considered only a prosperous ranch at the time of his death, he had definitely moved up the social ladder; his daughter's legacy included both a thriving property and a townhouse on the main plaza of San Felipe. As an only child, María had apparently married down; her husband, Jesús Carmona, was known as "a poor boy." But the time was right and from the 1880s on, San Onofre became one of the principal suppliers of cross-ties to the Mexican National Railroad Company. Jesús Carmona was the driving force behind the hacienda. He incorporated numerous ranches into the estate, he built a railroad station which bears his name, he initiated contacts with foreign mining companies and he bought properties in the mining cities and there established social relationships. He diversified production and cooperated with other hacendados toward this end. Finally, he extended his network of activities to Mexico City. He bought a home in an elegant section and increasingly divided his time between the hacienda and the city. A man about town, he was known in the capital as the "millionaire farmer" by his cronies at the American Club. He also found time for cultural activities and made extensive and extended trips to Europe. His daughter Dolores continued this tradition by investing in real estate both in the capital and the resort city of Cuernavaca. Each house was staffed with servants from the hacienda and always ready for unexpected arrivals, but by now, San Felipe was considered provincial and to be avoided if possible. With improved transportation between the hacienda and Mexico City, it was no longer necessary to spend the night in San Felipe before proceeding to one's destination. Dolores' husband, Adolfo Venegas, had little opportunity to manipulate the estate; he died in 1912, shortly after his father-in-law. A lover of car-racing, he was killed during a national meet. Alfonso Venegas was born the same day. Dolores' second husband was a prominent lawyer from an affluent family of Toluca (the state capital) and he not only managed the hacienda with an iron hand, but later put up a valiant fight to prevent the property from being broken up. Despite the professional activities of his step-father, Alfonso was raised in true landowning tradition; he resided in Mexico City and spent his summer vacations and holidays at the hacienda. From childhood, Alfonso was served by a personal valet and educated to be a gentleman. He entered law school, then medical school, but never completed his studies. Unlike his father, his great loves were weight lifting and *charreada*, feats of horsemanship which he perfected at the hacienda. The family's relationship with important mining concerns was solidified through Alfonso's marriage to the daughter of an English mining director. Their monopoly of the lumber business was now assured.

Not all families were as fortunate in amassing and retaining their properties as the descendants of the Legueys. The original founder of Tepetitlán, Don Luis Monteverde, was a member of the exclusive military order of Calatrava, on whom the title of "Count of Toledo" was conferred in the late seventeenth century, yet the family line quickly disappeared from the local scene. The hacienda passed through a succession of hands and by the mid-nineteenth century was owned by a branch of the Pliegos. Tepetitlán was only one of a series of annexes controlled by this family. Pliego y Carmona owned Cote, a small hacienda in the municipality, as well as other properties in the state of Mexico, while Pliego y Pastraña had a continuous latifundium of 100,000 hectares divided between Tepetitlán and Enyejé, and extending into the temperate Valley of Toluca. The family also invested in jewelry, petroleum and mining, and were true absentee landlords, leaving the estate completely to the management of Fidel Garduño. During Don Fidel's administration, the family came to Tepetitlán every four years and "sometimes passed eight or ten years without a visit." After the death of the patron, his widow never appeared at the hacienda.

Don Fidel, himself, was descended from a line of wealthy ranchers; his grandfather owned several hundred hectares in the municipality and had inherited the magnificent "House of the Portals," the first townhouse constructed in San Felipe. Although the Garduños attained a certain prominence and were respected townsmen, they never obtained the status of "hacendados." Their family history is one of constant property sales and Fidel, in the tradition of his father, brother and cousin, worked his way up the personnel hierarchy of Tepetitlán until reaching the plum post of administrator. Manuel Soriano is another example of arrested landownership. During the 1870s he was one of the illustrious citizens of San Felipe. He owned the haciendas of Providencia and Flor de María, served as municipal president and is still commemorated for his numerous public works. In the 1890s, he was forced to sell his properties and his son and grandnephew went on to become administrators.

Several hacendados were relative latecomers to the municipality and to large-scale landownership. They brought with them outside experiences which were indisputably advantageous in running an estate. The new patron of Providencia, a gachupín,[5] glimpsed the economic potential of the municipality, an assessment which had escaped previous hacendados. He was to initiate an industry, the manufacture of brooms and brushes, which pushed the municipality into an international market. He was considered an extraordinary man:

> Don Juan de la Fuente Parres came to Mexico as a middle-aged man. A man of great dynamism, he was primarily a publisher and was best known for his editions of "México a través de los siglos" and "Los bandidos de río Frío." He first came here in the company of the Frenchman Valduront and they discussed the question of the zacatón plant and the possibility of processing the fibers in Providencia . . . Don Juan traveled extensively throughout the republic–he was no *patan* (yokel)–he was a cultivated man. To give you some idea of what this man thought of making Providencia–Providencia had cattle, sheep, horses, and consistently won first prize in the exhibitions of Coyoacán and Mixcoac during the epoch of General Porfirio. Providencia was much smaller in the days of Manual Soriano and Don Juan enlarged it through cumulative purchases–Purísima, San Nicolás, Agua Bendita . . . . Providencia was one of the first fincas [haciendas] to have telephone and telegraph services; by 1906, electricity had been generated in many villages with his construction of the dam in El Salto. He constantly tried to improve the conditions of the finca and the region.

After 1922, his progeny continued an active interest in the hacienda:

> Although they resided in Mexico City, they came here with frequency–for many motives; primarily they enjoyed being at the finca, and then, too, they enjoyed seeing the work. They were always preoccupied with making Providencia a truly industrial finca.

Don Juan not only expanded his operations to include the town of San Felipe, but wrote home with great enthusiasm of fertile opportunities. The first arrival from his natal village was his brother who acted as right-hand man in all business affairs. A later contingent included his nephews, the brothers Díaz de la Fuente; by 1900, they owned Yondesé and Mayorazgo and were actively engaged in the zacatón industry. The Fuentes were the last family in the municipality to manipulate frequent property transfers. Family ownership and family fortune were to remain stabilized until the Revolution.

While the eighteenth century might have been the golden age for the colonial hacienda, the Porfirian era may be considered its renaissance culminating in an unparalleled fall. Many extravagant claims have been made regarding the haciendas of this period: San Onofre had the largest lumbermill in the republic and Tepetitlán the finest bulls, Purísima had more than a million *magueys* and fermented 10,000 liters of *pulque*[6] daily, Providencia could never satisfy world demand despite its runaway production of zacatón; exaggerations symptomatic of a changing institution that had shed its localistic tendencies. The haciendas of San Felipe were adjunct beneficiaries of policies introduced during the Díaz regime and aimed at the incipient industrial sector. San Felipe was centrally located between the state and national capitals to the south and the mining centers to the north. The gold and silver deposits of Michoacán had been relatively neglected during the colonial period, but with the influx of foreign capital under the encouragement of Díaz, previously unimportant regions took on boom characteristics. El Oro, Tlalpujahua, and Angangueo, the mining towns most accessible to the municipality, became desirable localities as foreign residents and foreign goods flowed in.

The hacendados of San Felipe moved with the tide. Not only did they take advantage of the abolition of the interior customs dues, but they quickly underwrote the construction of railroad stations along the newly completed Morelia-Mexico City line. By 1890, the haciendas were in close communication with markets to the north and south. Indeed, some of the hacendados had added extension lines which intersected their properties and facilitated bulk transport. Those who lacked the means for this additional step simply moved their produce to the station by oxcart, and from there, on to the various markets. The hacendados also restricted production of the traditional trilogy of corn, beans and squash, and were now relying heavily on commercial crops. Land formerly considered marginal was brought under cultivation. Many hacendados had left large tracts uncultivated, believing that they were uncultivable. This was rarely the case. "Waste" lands were either regenerated through the application of new techniques or put to work upon recognition of their intrinsic value. In actuality, the majority of unused lands extended along the western portion of the municipality where wild growths of the zacatón plant could be found. Zacatón was considered a nuisance; it was customary to burn these lands in preparation for grain planting, but the soils were unsuitable and yields proved disappointing. Allowed to revert to its former state, *Tierra Quemada* remained unused until the plant took on significance as an export item.

The haciendas fell into three categories: grain and animal raising, zacatón, or lumber. All haciendas possessed heterogeneous land resources (crop land, pasturage and forests) and continued multi-crop production, but the principal cash commodity varied with the ecological zone in which the hacienda was located. San Felipe has significant differences in altitude, temperature and soils and may be divided into three primary areas—the fertile lowlands to the south and east touched by the tributaries of the Lerma River, a western semi-cold zone lacking drainage channels, and a northwestern mountainous region bordering on the state of Michoacán. Before the construction of the railroad, the haciendas had been devoted almost exclusively to agricultural produce with a secondary interest in animal husbandry. But by the end of the nineteenth century, the haciendas had diversified in relation to their prime land resources.

The important agricultural estates were now situated completely within the lowland area near the town of San Felipe and were distinguished by their vast pastoral lands and emphasis on irrigation works. They continued to produce corn, carbon and pulque for local markets, but major economic activity revolved about wheat production and cattle-raising. Tepetitlán was the most prominent example of this type of hacienda. Tepetitlán had approximately 9000 head of bovine and 10,000 head of sheep which were shipped to the stockyards of Mexico City. Its wheat harvest amounted to 11,000 cargas (1 carga = 161 kilos) annually, and was sold through a business agent to numerous mills in Toluca and Mexico City. Of the estate's 100,000 hectares, 80,000 were utilized for pasturage and 6000 benefited from irrigation. A successful wheat yield requires extensive irrigation and the hacienda had impressive irrigation works. Several dozen dams had been constructed by diverting water from the nearby confluence of the Lerma River, and twenty-three kilometers of canals crisscrossed the fields, their water flow controlled by floodgates. Another 5000 hectares were composed of woodlands, while the remaining lands were uncultivated or uncultivable and reserved, in part, for the cuadrillas of resident workers. Only in those years when corn was rotated with wheat, did corn enter the national market, and during these periods the harvest averaged 9500 cargas (1 carga = 150 kilos). Barley was another strong crop, but an annual yield of 450 cargas (1 carga = 100 kilos) was utilized entirely for animal consumption.[7]

The zacatón haciendas evolved during the 1890s as a result of the large-scale exploitation of *raíz de zacatón*. (zacatón root). It was in San Felipe, or more precisely in Providencia, that zacatón was first planted and adapted for a European market. Before this time, the estates situated in the western ecological belt were characterized by the inefficient use of their lands and small-scale production of traditional crops. La Labor, for example, contained 1877 hectares, but only 227 hectares were tilled; 250 hectares of forest lands provided wood for carbon production and 1400 hectares were left fallow. Of the 2300 hectares which composed the hacienda of Mayorazgo, 60 hectares were cultivated, while 900 hectares served as pasturage and 40 hectares for forest exploitation. The remaining 1300 hectares were classified as marginal. In both haciendas, these uncultivated lands were magnificient tracts of zacatón (Municipal Archives 1903).

Zacatón is a wild plant indigenous to central Mexico. The finest quality grows most profusely, however, in a core region fanning out from San Felipe, south through Toluca and Zinacantepec to Xochimilco. The plant grows best at high altitudes of *tierra fria* (cold country) and in open unforested areas. It is extremely hardy and resistant to both drought and frost.

The Indians had long been aware of the uses of zacatón and had exploited it in a desultory fashion during the nineteenth century, selling their products in the weekly market. The first attempt to organize production was made in 1876 when a Spaniard, Miguel de Labra, opened a *taller* (workshop) on his ranch, La Venta. He extracted the wild plant from the vicinity of Mayorazgo and processed the fibers of the root to make besoms and small brushes which he sold in Mexico City and Toluca. He was followed by a succession of itinerant buyers who bought raíz in San Felipe and either sold it to processors in Toluca or processed it themselves in their own small workshops. The first successful entrepreneur, however, was Juan de la Fuente Parres.

Don Juan was the only person who thought of systematically cultivating zacatón and he possessed the resources to do so. Zacatón is a perennial that requires large capital investments and a growing period of four to five years. Once the plant is artifically seeded, it will not tolerate either burning or trampling by animals. Don Juan realized that the hacienda was the ideal institution for exploiting zacatón; he needed both contiguous extensions of enclosed land and a large accessible work force. By 1906, he and his relatives owned several haciendas in the municipality, had opened workshops in town, and employed several thousand laborers. They ignored the domestic market completely and produced a fine quality brush used to groom horses; packs of fifty-two kilos were shipped to Veracruz by rail and from there to distributors in Le Havre and Hamburg. These transactions were originally handled by the family's business representative through shipping agencies, but as production expanded, the product was sold directly to the maritime companies. By 1930, Don Juan had eliminated his competitors and totally dominated the industry. He provided free seed to the other haciendas in the zacatón zone–Trinidad, La Luz, San Onofre–and even to small ranches, on condition that the only processing they carried out would be the first step of washing the raíz. All clean fibers would be sold to him. Only Don Juan's nephews were allowed to process the plant completely and they, too, bought raíz from the other hacendados. Between 1900 and 1934, when production was curtailed as a result of land distribution, Providencia has extracted approximately 2,000,000 kilos of crude raíz from its own fields and exported more than 20,000 packs. Preference was always given to zacatón in Providencia; of the 11,500 hectares that comprised the estate, 5500 hectares, alone, were planted with zacatón. Providencia contained 3000 hectares of forest lands and supplied lumber to the mining companies as a secondary interest. The hacienda also had approximately 3000 to 4000 head of cattle and continued maguey, carbon and grain (corn, wheat and barley) production on a minor scale.

The lumber haciendas, too, perceptibly reduced their dependence on traditional grain crops once a demand had been created to warrant production expansion in favor of a single economic activity. Before national railroad construction, the haciendas of the mountainous zone had exploited their forest resources in three ways–through the sale of dead wood, through the sale of green wood, used in housing construction, and through the production of carbon. San Onofre, Providencia, and La Trinidad first supplied lumber to the railroad companies, and with the completion of the Mexico-Acámbaro line, they shortly became the principal suppliers of the mining enterprises. With the exception of the post-revolutionary slump, the haciendas continued full and uninterrupted production until the 1930s. The roster of mining companies was impressive; Dos Estrellas, Tlalpujahua, Esperanza Mining Company, Mexico Mines of El Oro, and El Oro Mining & Railroad Company were the major customers of the hacendados. Most of these companies were subsidiaries of the Suchi Mining Company which had constructed a feeder diverging from the Mexico-Acámbaro line at Tultenango and running north from there to Palizada, the site of its sawmill, and El Oro. By 1904, the largest estates were connected to the feeder and sold trunks and planks directly to Suchi, while the smaller haciendas and ranches conducted business with San Onofre which had its own lumber cars and sawmills.

In many parts of Mexico, sharp antagonisms characterized the relationship between hacienda and mining company (Vernon 1965:51), but in San Felipe, the fortune of the hacienda was inextricably tied to that of the mining companies. What was a spectacular brief economic boom later contributed to the final collapse of these haciendas as the twenty-three gold mines in the vicinity of San Felipe closed one by one.

San Onofre, the most successful lumber hacienda, had been characteristically committed to diversified agricultural production. Until the late nineteenth century, its 10,000 hectares of forest land, rich in pine, pitch-pine, evergreen oak, and fir remained relatively unexploited. The family made the first move away from staple production by planting the estate's unirrigated fields with zacatón. In the early 1900s, they further committed themselves to commercial production when the Suchi Mining Company offered to subsidize the construction of a private railroad. By 1914, the hacienda had stations at its sawmills and the casco, as well as its own locomotives. The hacienda was guaranteed a minimum of 25,000 pesos annually through its concession with Dos Estrellas and also averaged a monthly income of several thousand pesos through business with smaller companies. By 1930, Doña Dolores had invested heavily in her lumber interests; the railroad line, alone, was worth 53,000 pesos, the trains, 42,000 pesos, the stations, nearly 20,000 pesos, and the sawmills were valued at 38,000 pesos.

SECONDARY ECONOMIC SPECIALIZATION: SAN ONOFRE, 1932

Product	*Quantity*	*Unit Cost*	*Value (pesos)*
Corn	835,900 liters	.04	33,436.00
Maguey	–	–	5,500.00
Barley	120,347 liters	.02	2,406.94
Black Beans	12,966 liters	.06	777.96
Wheat	10,918 liters	.06	655.08
Hay	120,000 kilos	.01	1,200.00
Kidney Beans	4,000 liters	.04	160.00
Zacatón	48,000 kilos	.35	16,800.00
Cattle	1,300		33,881.00
Horses, mules	108		4,660.00
Sheep	881		2,743.00
Hogs	47		520.00
Fowl	–		570.50

The cultivation of basic agricultural crops and cattle-raising continued to provide a steady income through both bulk sales in Mexico City and constant petty sales in El Oro, a hamlet which had swelling to a bustling mining city of 90,000 inhabitants. Investment in these sectors was limited to maintenance; the extensive irrigation systems and the duplication of modern farm implements that were commonplace in Tepetitlán and Providencia were not found in San Onofre. Yet, the sale of both staple crops at almost double their harvest value and animal products (milk, cheese, suet, wool, and skins) adequately covered normal expenditures. By the thirties, the proprietor had cached approximately 350,000 pesos in liquid assets in his city office and owned an estate valued at one million pesos.

One might expect that the brief florescence of the hacienda, typified by the production of commercial crops, the marketing of a new export crop, spurts of capital input and incipient mechanization would have positive repercussions in the peasant sector. On the contrary, the development of the internal complexity of the hacienda reinforced the previous situation of the indigenous population. Not only did the hacienda continue to be labor-intensive, but the additional requirements of a changing market resulted in a further depression of the Indian group, that left its dependence on the landlords absolute. Still, although exacerbated, the situation of the Indians was not wholly intolerable because of the granting of nonmonetary perquisites by the landowner. It was the deceptive flexibility of the patron-peon relationship which prevented the estate system from disintegrating at this point; as the peon was pressured to the extent of becoming incapable of maintaining a minimum level of subsistence, he was increasingly subsidized by the patron at the expense of his liberty.

The hacienda system, based upon asymmetrical social and economic relations, appeared to have a momentum and an independent existence of its own, yet it had its origins in the quasi-racial stratificational system which legally endured until Independence. During the greater part of the nineteenth century, when the characteristic attributes of the local agrarian estate were solidified, the *castas* continued to receive formal recognition. With the late abandonment of legal stratification at the provincial level, the Indian wards were merely transferred from state control to undisputed estate control. The hierarchical nature of social relationships inherent in the twentieth-century hacienda carried as much weight as legal stratification had previously. Each group had its niche in the estate system and was differentiated by a series of obligations, privileges, and perquisites. The system was elastic. One could move from one status position to another in the hierarchy and the particular symbols of status differentiation, sets of perquisites and privileges, often responded to external factors–drought, a changing market, rumors of unrest, government edicts, etc. Accommodation of different social group forms was accomplished with a minimum of friction through spatial, cultural, and economic segregation. The static quality of the hierarchy derived from the immutable and exclusive nature of the end point groups, "patrons" and "peons."

What has often been referred to as the "table of organization," "the division of labor," or the "personnel hierarchy" in describing the allocation of work on the hacienda may be considered a function of the hierarchical ranking system. There was always a finite number of tasks to be performed which varied from hacienda to hacienda as well as diachronically, in relation to both larger historical changes and the cyclical requirements of the productive processes. The majority of these operations were generalized and easily interchangeable, some were more specific and required a special body of knowledge or period of training, and a few were esoteric. While the hacienda may be analyzed in relation to the organization of work activities and resultant efficiency in achieving certain goals, this perspective would be incomplete without a consideration of structural factors–the relationship of the allocated work task, along with its pertinent status symbols of deprivation or gratification, to the hierarchical social system. Rather than a "hierarchical system based on an intricate division of labor" (Wolf and Mintz 1957:392), the reverse situation prevailed in the haciendas of San Felipe. A continuously mutable division of labor was simply integrated into a preexisting hierarchy of socioeconomic and ethnic divisions so that what one did was of lesser importance than who one was. One's status might vary in accordance with a particular work task that permitted higher cash returns and easier access to special services; one's ultimate position in the hierarchy irrevocably depended on group identity.

The apparent contradiction in the statements of two former administrators concerning the organization of labor on the hacienda is resolved by considering

PERSONNEL HIERARCHY: TEPETITLAN

	Patron	
Mestizo		
	General Administrator	Business Agent (Mexico City)
Store-merchant	Pagador (paymaster)	Accountant (Mexico City)
Teacher	Escribiente (clerk)	Priest (San Felipe)
Veterinarian		Doctor (Ixtlahuaca)
	Carpenters	
	Herreros (smiths)	
	Albañiles (masons)	
Indigena		
	Major-domos (ranch stewards)	
	Captains (overseers of work parties)	
	Caporales (foremen)	
	caporal of cattle	
	caporal of sheep	
	caporal of saddle horses	
	caporal of planting	
	caporal of corn rations	
	Contracaporales (assistants to caporales)	
	Vaqueros (cowhands)	
	Ordeñadores (milkers)	
	Pastores (shepherds)	
	Çoleros (assistants to pastores)	
	Canaleros (caretakers of sluices)	
Medieros (sharecroppers)	Acasillados (resident laborers)	Gente de sobra (nonresident laborers)

the structural factors. Don Fidel was born and raised in Tepetitlán and entered into formal employment in early adolescence. He was intimately associated with the hacienda for more than forty years and was able to recall several dozen distinct work patterns as well as the number of persons performing each one. Don Ernesto, however, whose activities focused primarily on the taller, insisted that there were "no divisions" in Providencia:

> There was no hierarchy except for the general administrator, the accountant, and the cashier . . .,the rest were employees who reported directly to the general administrator and were in charge of the various activities . . . to manage 5,000 men, a quantity of employees was necessary.

While Don Fidel conveyed the nuances of a personnel hierarchy that had burgeoned during the last decade of the hacienda's existence, Don Ernesto trenchantly clarified the dualistic nature of the hierarchy, the hiatus between the "haves" and the "have-nots"–between employees and workers, between *gente de razón*[8] and *indígenas*, between prerogatives and marginality–the salient feature of a labor-intensive estate system.

Despite the partial modernization of the commercial aspects of the hacienda, the hacendado's success continued to depend on his facility in mobilizing large masses of unskilled labor. The hacienda's perpetuation was assured by means of an unquestioned contract between the landlord and his labor force. Euphemistically called "workers" and vernacularly known as "peons" or "acasillados," the indigenous labor force lived on the hacienda, worked on the hacienda, and owed strict allegiance to the patron. In the words of Don Fidel, "the patron had the necessity to provide work for the peon, and the peon, in turn, was obligated to work for his patron." The acasillado was available not only during the most important periods of the productive cycle, but also for the most trivial task that might arise. Although the actual allocation of work tasks was left to the discretion of the administrator, the hacendado was the ultimate authority in determining the organization of work patterns. It was his responsibility to draw up a weekly skeletal plan which was then circulated to the various ranches and annexes of the hacienda.

Peons were rarely specialized in the jobs they performed; the major limiting factors were age and sex. By the age of seven, children of both sexes entered the labor force as shepherds. Puberty marked the assumption of adult work responsibilities; male peons could perform a wide variety of different tasks and would often be transferred from annex to annex, while women were expected to perform agricultural duties during the busy season. According to the customary law of the hacienda, they were obligated to do "whatever work" the major-domo ordered.

By 1910, the resident population of the hacienda had reached its optimum level in relation to the requirements of the different production cycles, and ranged from an average of 350 acasillados in the grain and cattle estates to 800 in the timber region, exceeding 1000 in the zacatón zone. Nearly three-quarters of the population of the municipality now resided on the hacienda or on hacienda controlled ranches. The majority of this populace was indigenous and had been subjected to the typical land-grab, labor capture process. The peons of San Felipe were not victims of the more highly popularized aspects of the hacienda system; neither the hacienda-owned store, nor contract labor, nor a private police force was the principal instrument of control. The peons were attached to the estate by a more fundamental phenomenon:

> Thus did the villagers pass through a classic sequence. They had been forced out of the subsistence economy of their village and away from a world-view built of sacred connotations and age-old indigenous traditions. They were cast into a large, impersonal labor market, not of rising industrialization, but of the efficient large-scale maize haciendas and sugar plantations, producing for the national and international markets. After 1900, most Naranjeños lived by selling their agricultural labor to landlords. Naranja had become a village of hired men and migrant plantation hands, a sort of rural semi-migrant proletariat [Friedrich 1970:46].

At first, the hacienda had grafted itself upon the indigenous economy, utilizing the same technology and producing the same staples. The fundamental structure of family-oriented subsistence agriculture remained unchanged. But as the hacienda expanded and diversified, consumption requirements in the indigenous sector became increasingly difficult to fulfill. By 1866, it was recognized that the Indians were approaching a state of "destitution" because of the absence of "work sources" other than agriculture (Municipal Archives). It was at this time, however, that the scramble for land became intensified and new population clusters were stabilized in the formation of the cuadrilla pattern of residential segregation. By 1900, the Indian sector had been compressed to the degree that there were no alternative work sources outside the hacienda structure and scanty chance of fulfilling domestic requirements within it. The response of the hacendados to a commerical and export market during the Díaz regime further aggravated the peasant sector and exaggerated the so-called dualistic nature of the economy. Irrigation works, experimentation with fertilizers and new plant varieties, importation of farm machinery, and private rail construction committed the hacendado to a unilateral emphasis on cash crops (and diminished his ability to sustain the estate during a market crisis). The peasant did not participate even passively in this wider economy. Not only did he owe his time to the hacienda, but he was also primarily responsible for the production of comestibles. The type of neat ecological link between staple and commercial production that existed in other "dualistic" situations, where growth in one sector led to growth in the other (Geertz 1963) was absent in Mexico. The investments made in the commercial sector did not extend to the peasant economy. Production of staple crops suffered because the hacendado devoted more and more of his land resources to cash crops, while the peasant continued to till an exhuasted miniparcel in the traditional manner.

Although acasillados and their families were subject to some extremely subtle forms of control—socialization by Mestizo teachers and priests, and other less subtle forms—residential segregation from other groups, division into dispersed working parties under the vigilance of a major-domo, and the omnipresence of a municipal deputy empowered to deliver intransigents to the proper governmental authorities, their attachment to the hacienda was sanctioned by "custom." Almost all relationships that tied peon to patron were couched in terms of "traditional obligations." The primary obligation of the peon was to fulfill his work tasks; it was his duty to labor from sunrise to sunset, six days a week, without questioning his assignment. Equally pertinent were his moral obligations to the patron; he was expected to offer his unswerving fidelity, behave in accordance with respect relationships, and demonstrate his gratitude for the hacendado's protection. The hacendado, on the other hand, was obligated to provide work for his resident force and offer remuneration in the form of cash wages and a series of nonpecuniary rewards and services. He also felt a responsibility to subsidize his peons heavily during crises. Such were the basic obligations in all haciendas whether the hacendado ran a personally oriented enterprise as in San Onofre or attempted to impersonalize work relationships as in Yondesé and Providencia. Yet despite the reciprocal quality of these obligations, the hacendado felt at all times that he was doing his workers a favor—"favors" that were exchanged for a work performance consistently and proportionately exceeding cash remuneration:

> The acasillado lived on a parcel large enough to keep him alive and support six to ten children. It was held with the permission of Doña Dolores and was for his own use and benefit.
>
> The hacendado gave them a piece of land to help them. Whatever the acasillado produced on his plot was for him. He didn't pay any rent—either for the parcel or the house.
>
> The acasillados of Providencia didn't have a fixed amount of land. Whatever they held was exploited by them and for them, without the hacienda charging them a single cent.
>
> They ate well before because Señora V. gave a dinner . . . . She bought them material, presents for them—to make clothing.
>
> When there was a drought, we did everything possible so the people wouldn't suffer so.
>
> They ate the corn which they, themselves, produced. When they ran out—because some families were very large—then they came to the hacienda. The little corn that was produced in Providencia was used exclusively for rations and it was sold to them at a very low price. The finca provided corn at cost. Never, never, did it charge more than the market price at that time.

During the 1880s, the capital scarcity on the hacienda necessitated the development of non-monetary forms of remuneration to hold onto labor. Later on, however, the hacendado was quite capable of providing greater cash outlays for the workers, and in the zacatón haciendas where heavy labor requirements would have made more permanent forms of subsidy an impracticality he did. The others were shrewd enough to realize that non-monetary rewards were the prime attraction for the resident peons and the instrumental means for immobilizing them. Wages were nominal and rarely commensurate with labor performed, but money was only one of numerous forms of payment. Cash rewards formed an insignificant proportion of total payment. The injustice of this system does not lie in the paucity of the cash reward, itself; it was derived from the coercion of the peon to return his salary to the hacendado in exchange for basic necessities.

The peon did not fare badly in comparison with his contemporaries outside the hacienda. At the urban textile mills, wages ranged from 11 to 75 cents for a twelve- to fifteen-hour day and were frequently reduced by discounts for a plethora of inconsequential reasons. Unskilled miners averaged between 50 and 75 cents daily, while skilled miners earned a daily salary of 3 pesos (Cumberland 1968:225,251; Vernon 1965:51). Cash wages diverged widely in San Felipe. The grain haciendas were notorious for their low wages; peons earned a fixed daily sum which varied according to the particular task but rarely exceeded 75 cents.

Those with a special position–major-domo or captain–were guaranteed a minimum wage of one peso. According to a complaint presented to the governor by a state deputy:

> In the haciendas of Enyejé and Tepetitlán, property of José de Jesus Pliego, a millionaire several times over, men, women, and minors are obligated to work like beasts of burden from 6:00 in the morning to 6:00 at night, with only two half-hour rest periods to eat a meager meal. The poor women are paid day-wages of 7 cents, equivalent to less than 1 cent per hour, and the men receive day-wages of 18 cents. Women are rationed twelve double-liters of corn and men, twenty-four double-liters, for which wages are reduced by 25 and 50 cents weekly. The woman who is paid 42 cents and docked 25 cents for corn and 10 cents for Mass receives in hand only 7 cents. The man who earns a weekly wage of 1.08 pesos is docked 50 cents for corn and 10 cents for Mass, receiving only 48 cents [Municipal Archives, Fomentation Section 1922].

Peons employed in lumber and zacatón production worked by *destajo* (piecework) and were paid according to both the type of task and the amount of work completed. In San Onofre, for example, normal timber operations involved nearly 70 peons whose wages totaled 305 pesos weekly (averaging 4.5 pesos). Yet individual salaries varied from 56 cents to 25 pesos, depending on the number of planks cut, the feet of wood freighted, the weight of carbon burned, the quantity of fagots gathered, and so on. Piecework was also the preferred system of payment in Providencia and Yondesé, and salaries were considerably higher than in the other estates. Approximately 20,000 pesos were expended weekly to support a predominantly migrant labor force. Neither contracts were made nor hours set. Migrant workers were free to return to their villages for planting and harvesting and were frequently shifted to other workshops of the family. When they were at the hacienda they knew that the taller opened at 7:00 am and closed late in the afternoon, six days a week. Predetermined amounts of work were never assigned and wages were in proportion to the number of kilos of raíz processed. This system was later extended to the field workers who extracted the plant and centers were set up in each annex to facilitate reception, weighing, and immediate payment.

More significant than cash wages were the special perquisites offered the acsasillados. Not only did these perquisites tend to reinforce many aspects of indigenous culture, but they were far more effective instruments than debt-peonage and indenture in holding the Indian workers. As with money wages, the range of perquisites varied from hacienda to hacienda; all resident workers, however, were provided with an allotment of corn and a piece of land. The *pegujal*, as it was locally known, was both the residential and occupational site for the peon. It was here that he built his "hut" and planted his *milpa* (maize field). Traditionally the pegujal consisted of two *cuartillos* of land, but some encompassed twelve cuartillos–one hectare–as the result of receiving extra prerogatives. On two cuartillos of land, the peon could plant 2.76 liters of seed, which yielded a quantity insufficient to feed a family as well as a few livestock.

The acasillado could fulfill some, but not all of his consumption requirements. Yet even this was accomplished through the good graces of the patron; it was the rare peon who owned his own oxen, so he depended on his patron for leasing work animals. He was also forced to rely on the hacendado for the completion of his grain supply. It was this aspect of the patron-peon relationship where the dominance of the hacendado was indisputably and extravagantly displayed. First, he had the ability to regulate the acasillado's grain supply through the allocation of subsistence parcels; the size of the plot invariably fell short of minimal requirements. Second, he controlled the distribution of grain and had the power to withhold grain. For the Indian peon, grain was wealth and grain was prestige, but above all, grain was food and grain was life. Land was cherished solely for its yield and money was valued because it could be exchanged for grain. By deliberately depriving the acasillado of sufficient land resources, the hacendado encountered his most effective mechanism for holding his peons. He was their source of the necessary grain ration, the avenue toward a marginal security, and the manipulator of life itself.

The hacendado had a vested interest in his peons' welfare, and they knew they would never starve. This fact was made clear to them under extraordinary circumstances, when the patron willingly used all of his faculties to maintain his "household." The tragic influenza epidemic of 1918 is still remembered as the year when family heads succumbed and the milpas remained unsowed. The patron not only supplied free corn grain, but also distributed rice and beans and slaughtered cattle for the ailing peons. During periods of scarcity when the price of corn was prohibitive, the peon was witness to the patron's feat in insuring the daily arrival of cargas of corn for sale at discount prices. During the normal course of the year, the patron's munificence was reiterated by the lavish offerings of the post-harvest thanksgiving feast, the *combate*. Corn was prepared in all of its ritual forms and accompanied by festive plates of *mole*[9] and roasted mutton. Pulque and tequila were generously dispensed while children were treated as children with gifts of candy and cookies.

In addition to the system of distribution, the hacendado provided a number of services for his labor force. Those who owned draft teams were granted grazing rights on hacienda land. All peons were allowed to forage in the hacienda's woodlands. If a peon were ill or had been injured, it was customary to send him to the town doctor with a note signed by the administrator saying that the carrier had "no means." If the peon had excessive expenses from a baptism, marriage or funeral, he had recourse to the hacendado who readily lent him money. All that he received was entered on his account and it was possible to accumulate debts of several hundred pesos before being reprimanded for nonpayment. The hacendado never expected to be paid back in full—"they still owe me money," was a recent lament—and rarely applied sanctions to those who were behind; he knew that he both obligated his peons and kept them coming back for more. Many peons tried to avoid these debts by forming *compadrazgo* (godparent) relationships with the patron or administrator. In this way they could avoid much of the onerous expense of a particular ceremony, but they were liable to a spiritual fetter which implied a promise of lifelong respect.

The incurring of debts at the company store has been cited as one of the hacendado's principal mechanisms for retaining the acasillados (Cumberland 1968; Tannenbaum 1929; Wolf and Mintz 1957). Indebtedness, however, was merely symptomatic of the perpetual state of want lived by the peon on the estate. The classic *tienda de raya*, the store owned and operated by the hacendado, did not exist in San Felipe. Stores were located in each hacienda, but they were private enterprises that functioned in a situation of free commerce. Resident workers were not compelled to buy there. In Providencia the store was run by a professional merchant from Toluca, and in Tepetitlán it was owned by the administrator; in the smaller haciendas, town merchants often opened branch stores. Only in San Onofre did the situation approach the classic example, but even here the hacendado did not want full responsibility. The same system practiced in agriculture, "a medias," was practiced in the store. Both capital input and profits were shared equally between the hacendado and a local Mestizo merchant. These stores operated in competition with the commercial establishments of the town as well as various rotating markets in the municipality. Peons were encouraged to buy locally, however, through the ready granting of credit. In San Onofre, credit was further facilitated through the circulation of colored vouchers in place of money. This innovation was highly successful in securing clients, but fatal to the solvency of the business. In a typical store inventory, for example, liquid assets were valued at 1067 pesos; the cash register held 13 pesos, the merchandise was assessed at 445 pesos, and the remainder consisted of pending debts. Most of these debts were a consequence of the peon's attempts to fulfill his corn requirements. The peon received his grain ration on Monday, the minimum quantity consisting of 12 cuartillos (in excess of 16 liters). On Saturday he received his "work chit," generally reduced by more than half as a result of the previous grain purchase at 9 cents a liter. Before the week had completed its cycle, he had spent his residual reserve on other dietary requirements–pulque, salt, rice, chiles and minor staples. For such basic items as matches, candles, soap, cooking containers, cloth, and agricultural tools, he had to rely on credit.

Not all hacendados granted perquisites to obligate labor. In Yondesé and Providencia, the greater part of the work force consisted of migrant laborers, attracted from as far away as Toluca and Zinacantepec by a reputation for high wages and fair treatment. These seasonal workers were employed in the zacatón factories and housed in tenement blocks located near the "big house." This situation was unique in the municipality. During the busy periods of the agricultural cycle most hacendados depended either on permanent sharecroppers who owed them work days or the sporadic hiring of day laborers. The *gente de sobra*, (extras) as this group was known commuted between the hacienda and local free villages; their numbers rarely exceeded by a third the size of the resident work force. Providencia, too, had a permanent force of acasillados, but as zacatón production increased, concerted efforts were made to attract migrants through strictly monetary rewards; by 1930, Providencia's migrant force was the chief source of labor. Don Juan had envisioned the creation of a truly industrial enterprise within the framework of the hacienda. He never quite succeeded because of his failure in technological applications to the raíz process, but he was single-minded about putting work relationships on an impersonal business level:

> The owner always avoided direct contact with the people. The only thing that interested him was work, among both the laborers and the employees. In Providencia, there were no predilections for particular individuals. One's salary depended on one's efforts and anybody who worked harder had the right to receive higher wages. Don Juan wasn't interested in the workers' religion, their customs, or their families. He wanted to operate the finca as efficiently as possible, he looked for this, and yes, he obtained it. Where this freedom of action existed, it was best to avoid all obligations.

Accordingly, the Fuente family eliminated many of the perquisites considered essential by the other hacendados. Formal personalized relationships between employees and free or resident laborers were prohibited, requests for loans were denied, cash payment rather than credit was the rule in the stores, and the annual harvest festivities were banished. The only service permitted the free laborer in addition to housing accommodations was the proportioning of a grain ration which had to be paid for in full before receipt of further rations.

Perquisites were always evaluated from the point of view of practicality. Originally given precedence by the hacendado as the most efficient device for controlling the acasillados, they were later replaced by money wages with the intention of drawing freely on a transient labor market. But even where the attempt was made to streamline operations, these efforts did not extend to the group of employees.

Perquisites were synonymous with privileges for "trusted employees"[10] and were lavishly offered. Beyond salaries, such employees were given houses and servants, were granted bonuses in the form of land, and systematically received meat, milk, cheese, eggs, vegetables, and fuel—all free of charge. These privileges not only effectively isolated them from the peons, but by partaking of some of the same privileges enjoyed by the hacendado, their identification with and loyalty to the estate were guaranteed.

Whereas the fidelity of the acasillado was extracted by and exchanged for the hacendado's subsidizing his basic necessities, the employee warmly and wholeheartedly offered his allegiance. Employees were economically secure and did not depend on the hacienda for sustenance. They came from large families which counted among their members ranchers, merchants, and an occasional ex-hacendado. They were prominent townsmen and intimately involved in regional politics. Highly predisposed to the type of life that the hacienda offered, their values coincided with those of the hacendado. Many had served a lifelong apprenticeship on the hacienda and had moved up the personnel hierarchy from clerk to administrator; others entered the hacienda as mature men but had come highly recommended by the hacendado's personal contacts. The mood of the employee's life was a pleasant one and he oscillated gracefully between the hacienda and town, the hacendado and his own family. For Don Ernesto, who lived in Providencia for twenty years, the hacienda was the romance of his life:

> My first job was in the store "La Union" and several months later, Don Juan de la Fuente Parres, an old friend of the family whom I always admired, wrote to Fedito (his uncle) telling him that he would like me to enter the taller of raíz de zacatón, a dependency of the hacienda La Providencia—the place of my birth, which I still did not know. My salary was 180 pesos a month, a quantity which seemed like an enormous amount of capital. And when I received these honors for the work I did, I felt like the happiest man in the world . . . . My life slipped by from 1915 to 1916 with the repose of the innocent. My work began at five in the morning and terminated at four in the afternoon; upon returning to the house, our diversion was to chat awhile in the portals of Fedito's house until Rosary, when everyone went off to pray . . . . To see those portals, the plaza, the majesty of the church tower, it all seemed something fantastic. A new atmosphere began for me . . . the trajectory of my life commenced with those days.

The hacendado assiduously cultivated both his employees and other townspeople. First, during his absence the administrator was recognized as the supreme authority and delegated considerable responsibility. Employees were expected to represent the hacendado before laborers, townspeople and municipal functionaries. Secondly, the hacendado maintained a house and owned fields in the town, he was under the civil and juridical authority of the municipality, and he relied on the town for medical, religious and other services. In short, he sought a comfortably mutualistic relationship with townsfolk and a toadyish receptivity which permitted him to do whatever he wanted in any contingency. Such latitude allowed the hacendado to satisfy both insignificant whims–appeasing the appetite with Chinese dishes or hotcakes periodically sent to the hacienda by local restaurateurs–and regulatory demands–virtual control of the town granaries regarding the distribution and price of corn.

Although the hacendado privately believed that the town was provincial, he was thoroughly integrated into local society; he formed solid friendships with his top employees and the most prominent townspeople, and the genealogies indicate that occasional marital unions occurred between the children of hacendados and administrators. Just as the acasillado participated, however marginally, in the all-inclusive *combate*, the landowner opened his hacienda to the town at certain times during the year. When the hacendado celebrated his saint's day, the whole town celebrated with him. When the hacendado celebrated Candlemas, there was no need to issue invitations; "everybody," or more accurately, important townspeople, automatically attended. Much as the hacendado flaunted his generosity before his acasillados, he periodically validated his wealth for the townspeople through a standardized offering of festive activities transpiring between town and estate. *Visperas*, the day preceding the actual celebration, was passed at the hacienda where guests were entertained with cockfights and feats of horsemanship. The festive day itself was spent at the hacendado's townhouse and culminated in a banquet-dance enlivened by the presence of several outside bands. The *tornafiesta* signalled a leisurely return to the hacienda and was dedicated solely to consuming the leftovers of the previous evening's celebration. These occasions regularly reiterated the oneness and spirit of cooperation between the hacendado and the townspeople.

Later, the hacendado began to disdain local society as he moved further from his sometimes questionable origins, grew wealthier, sought an education, and married out. His townhouse was boarded up as he extended his social network beyond the bounds of San Felipe. By 1910, he was firmly assimilated to the beat of the capital and was able to indulge in many of the finer aspects of the "good life." Yet, although he may have been neglectful, he continued to treat the townspeople with due respect and they continued to cater to his needs.

Despite his obvious pleasure in preening prestigiously within the hacienda hierarchy, in local and even national society, the hacendado of San Felipe could not be characterized as the irresponsible gentleman farmer so generally portrayed:

> The typical hacendado put little emphasis on high land productivity; his contentment came from ownership of the land itself, and any income over that necessary to satisfy his immediate–and expensive–needs he looked upon as fortunate but not necessary [Cumberland 1968:58].

Cumberland's description refers to the hacendado of the colonial period, but this depiction has lost none of its popularity for later eras:

> The worst features of the latifundismo were likely to appear in the second and third generations, when the spoiled offspring of the hacendados got into the habit of going off to Mexico City or Paris to live . . . . Succeeding generations became progressively more emancipated, until, if the estate could stand the strain, the family emerged as a useless colony of parasites [Simpson 1967:261].

> Rare indeed was the great landowner who experimented with new varieties of basic crops, or used commercial fertilizers, or invested in the bewildering variety of new farm machines sweeping across the United States [Cumberland 1968:203].

> The landowner and the administrator had little interest in improving agricultural methods. Their interest was in the share of the crop, and the burden of cultivation tended to fall upon the cropper and renter who was least equipped for modern improvement, both financially and technically [Tannenbaum 1929:128].

This situation was usually blamed on the hacendado's chronic absence from the estate, his reliance on indirect administration, and his frantic quest for power through playing the great landowner. These characterizations tend to ignore the last decades of the hacienda by concentrating on the hacienda as a colonial institution, when the hacendado's principal goal was to maximize his security at the expense of innovation, capital investment, and profit considerations.

The twentieth-century haciendas of San Felipe were owned by individuals who had other business or professional interests. The hacienda may have been the principal source of wealth, but the owner did not seek his material and nonmaterial satisfactions through the estate alone. Apart from the attitude which allowed the majority of the hacendados to exploit an indigenous populace with impunity, they were actively concerned with managing a viable business. Rather than succumbing to a life of ease, the hacendado was involved in all aspects of the hacienda's operations. He was motivated by the unwritten rule of maintaining absolute control of the hacienda; he made decisions, he initated orders, and he meddled and prodded. His partial absence was rarely detrimental to his goals. Partial absenteeism signified constant shuttling between Mexico City and the hacienda. The hacendado was always present during the seasonal agricultural peaks and for important business transactions; between these periods he made regularly paced visits. In the course of his absence he engaged in a voluminous and detailed correspondence with his administrator. He was not above the most picayune instructions—from doctoring the trampled garden hedge to sending gifts of cheese and liquor, to ordering that an extra peon was needed in sweeping the terrace. He tediously reminded the administrator of matters which any competent farmer had learned during his apprenticeship—crops should be rotated in said manner or harvesting and sowing would proceed according to an enclosed scheduled. All business transactions were personally conducted by the owner at the hacienda or at his city office; he negotiated quantity and price, and informed the administrator how and when to carry out the actual transfer of goods or property.

Seemingly, the administrator had a good deal of authority, yet he held a dependent position as representative and right-hand man. It was the hacendado's practice to delegate responsibility without sacrificing his supremacy. He withheld certain types of information from his administrative staff so that he, alone, had an accurate global view of the value of the estate and the annual movement of capital. Employees involved in cattle, grains or raíz, while knowledgeable about their particular fields, were unable to formulate precise patterns of activity in other specialties. The administrator of the hacienda's taller, for example, would have, at most, a generalized and secondary view of other operations. Even the general administrator was limited to making astute estimates because final accounting was done in Mexico City; all money was received there and all valuations were determined by the hacendado and his legal staff.

A favorite device of the hacendado's for delegating responsibility without prejudicing his control was the sharecrop contract. Here I am referring not to the share-cropping arrangements made between peon and patron and employed as a convenient device for capturing seasonal labor, but to the carefully stipulated "half and half" agreement between hacendado and rancher concerning extensive land areas of the estate. This system was preferred to renting; not only did the hacendado transfer the burden of the risk to the sharecropper, but he also felt that he had the right to interfere in any contingency. Furthermore, he could legally terminate the arrangement if, in his judgment, the sharecropper was not fulfilling his obligations. The sharecropper was held accountable for both crop lands and animals, and was also expected to improve the hacendado's properties.

To make sure that all went according to the stipulations of the contract, the hacendado depended on the administrator to oversee all crop and calf divisions personally. At other times, the administrator kept a watchful eye on the sharecropper's progress and sent the hacendado periodic accounts of his impressions. The system was known as "half and half," but the hacendado reaped the benefits.

The hacendado also made it his duty to keep abreast of the latest developments in agriculture. By gearing production toward commercial ends, he was committed to a system of farming which could not simply imitate previous methods. The hacendado participated in shows and attended exhibitions, consulted the Secretary of Agriculture, bought the latest manuals, subscribed to journals, and received quantities of commercial literature. He was in constant communication with his colleagues and exchanged experiences and information. He was knowledgeable about seed varieties, cattle strains, the various classes of fertilizer, and innovations in mechanization.

By 1920, the hacendado had invested in interior transportation systems which communicated with national railways, irrigation works consisting of dams and sluiceways that affected several thousand hectares and the necessary implements. His equipment resources generally included tractors (both owned and rented), seeders, cultivators, reapers, threshers, gleaners, huskers, and packers, in addition to the wooden plow, oxen and workhorses formerly relied upon. He increasingly favored chemical over organic fertilizer in his irrigated fields, and he applied various methods of crop rotation in relation to the quality of the soil. He preferred a five-year planting cycle for his irrigated fields—two years of corn followed by three years of wheat, allowing a two-year regeneration period before replanting, while on unirrigated fields, he followed the practice known as *año y vez*, rotating one year of wheat with one year of corn, and allowing a two-year fallow period.

A few hacendados might have succeeded in transforming their estates into qualitatively different institutions if the normal course of events had not been interrupted. The zacatón haciendas, in particular, were noted for their adaptability and high capital investments. Manual methods had been completely eliminated in the planting process, and the hacendados had also tested a number of mechanical extractors. Despite increasing mechanization, the hacendados still required a large labor force in the workshops. Yet they tended to reject the wielding of labor through the promise of perquisites. They perceived the advantages of both mobile labor and cash wages, and they were able to expand and contract the size of the work force, and manipulate the wage scale in relation to supply and demand in the world market. When commodity prices unexpectedly escalated, the hacendado was quick to react, deploying his resources in rushing the raíz to the taller. Later, of course, when the market collapsed, he was no longer able to retreat into isolationism.

But generally, the changing hacienda conformed to the "flexibility within fixity" pattern discussed by Geertz (1968:98). The early stages of the hacienda were marked by disruptive alterations in land tenure systems–destruction of the independent Indian village and impingement on communal lands for the large-scale cultivation of native crops. Later, the hacienda underwent an impressive internal diversification as a result of innovations in cropping, mechanization, more efficient organization of labor, investment in irrigation works, and experimentation with new techniques. In addition to being an agrarian system, however, the hacienda was also a cultural and social system that served to stabilize the hierarchical ordering of the participating aggregates. The hacienda used more and more Indian land and labor and, in the process, squeezed the Indian society into sterility, much like trying to remove blood from a turnip.

The local history of the hacienda is a history of increasing economic impoverishment and social malaise among the Indians. These inequities were officially acknowledged well before the twentieth century, but the complaints remained buried among the sundry archives of the town hall. National demands for social justice had lost their novelty by 1910, but had not yet disturbed local complacency. In 1912, armed Zapatistas rampaged through Providencia, forcibly entered several pegujales, and assaulted a peon who tried to obstruct them. The incident was hushed up and later denied. Providencia returned briefly to an uneasy tranquility, yet agrarian unrest had begun its insidious spread. It was the signal for the gradual extinction of the hacienda.

3

"DEATH TO THE HACENDADOS"

The infamous usurpation of the land,
the property of all like the water
and the air,
has been monopolized by a few
powermongers,
supported by the force of the army
and the iniquity of the laws.

–Emiliano Zapata [1918]

Although the revolutionary cry had been for "Land and Liberty," the actual fulfillment of these demands was in sharp contrast to the upheavals of the last days of the Porfirian era. The thirty-year process of agrarian reform initiated by Madero's pronouncement of 1910 was inevitable, but it often proceeded at a halting rate. Indeed, "Liberty" was an elastic concept to be interpreted by the whims of the prevailing power. The restoration of lands promised by Madero in the "Plan of San Luis Potosi" never materialized, while his successor Huerta passed an uncertain period of nearly two years attempting to defend the presidency. Rumors of the sacking and burning of haciendas spread, and outside the mainstream of action, rumblings and undercurrents of an impending rebellion quickened. The haciendas of San Felipe were intermittently molested by groups of "bandits" and "marauders."

Under the slogan "Independence and Liberty," Huerta assured the hacendados of his support and convened meetings at both state and district levels. The hacendados were reminded of their duties as citizens and ordered to protect their properties by means of arms and men. In September 1913, the district chief of Ixtlahuaca dispatched a circular to the municipal president of San Felipe describing the meeting held in Toluca:

> The Governor was very satisfied with the success of the meeting he had with various hacendados who live in the capital. With obvious good will and patriotism, they agreed to the idea of arming and supplying munitions to ten men in their fincas–at their own expense and for the common defense against thieves. This agrees with the directives of the President of the Republic. They have also appointed a committee which will be in charge of listing all proprietors of rural fincas in the district who can contribute in the form stated. This circular is sent to you through the channels of the Secretaría de Gobernación. As a representative of the government, your duty is to arouse the patriotic sentiment of the hacendados so they will be favorably disposed to a reunion in the district seat. If they cannot attend personally, they may send a representative. The object of this meeting will be the selection of a local commission responsible for noting the names of each proprietor and the quantity of arms and munitions they want. The arms will be Mausers 7 mm which have a simple mechanism and are easy to manipulate. The hacendado will receive a supply of at least 500 cartridges with the purchase of each

weapon. The state government will solicit the federation to eliminate the customs duties so the cost will be more economical. The President, himself, recommends that as soon as the meeting is held and the total number of arms and munitions are known, this information be sent to the general secretary immediately to determine the necessities of the entire state.

. . . YOU WILL INFORM THE HACENDADOS OF THE MUNICIPALITY OF THIS RESOLUTION AND YOU WILL RECOMMEND THAT THEY PRESENT THEMSELVES IN THIS DISTRICT SEAT PERSONALLY OR BY MEANS OF A REPRESENTATIVE, THE 25th OF THIS MONTH, WITHOUT FAIL, SINCE ANY ABSENCE WILL THREATEN THE EFFECTIVENESS OF THIS MEETING.

"INDEPENDENCE AND LIBERTY"

[Municipal Archives 1914:Defense Section]

During the worst years of civil war that followed, the hacendados were increasingly threatened as bands of Carranzistas thrust through the municipality on their way to the mining centers in the north. These incursions were invariably accompanied by looting. As the loss of cattle and grain continued, it became difficult to determine which group of acolytes was harassing the hacendados. Hacendados, townspeople, and ranchers now met voluntarily for the purpose of requesting more arms. Even spiritual aid was not forgotten; the Catholic community of the parish of San Felipe and Santiago del Progreso expressed its sentiments by elevating the *Santísima María de Guadalupe*, famous for her protective powers, to the position of patroness alongside the apostle saints Felipe and Santiago (Parochial Archives 1920). Despite the promulgation of Article 27 calling for the restitution of alienated lands and the formation of the National Agrarian Commission during Carranza's regime, he quietly condoned the armed defense of the haciendas. At the same time that he bent with the conservative elements, he made token land grants and circulated innocuous edicts dealing with sharecropping contracts. He managed, however, to evade the land issue.

By 1920 Carranza had been ousted and conservative concerns deepened. Obregón was the first president to demonstrate a genuine interest in land distribution; yet it soon became evident that drastic expropriations would not occur. Only the rural population living in stipulated communities–*pueblos, rancherías, congregaciones* and abandoned lands of haciendas–were eligible for restitution or donation. The acasillados–resident peons of the hacienda–were denied the right to ask for land. Approximately 40% of the Mexican rural populace lived on the hacienda and was automatically excluded from the agrarian reform program; the hacienda had also engulfed more than 75% of the rural communities in the country (Tannenbaum 1929:321). None of these communities was entitled to apply for land.

These conditions were accurately reflected at the municipal level. By 1921, San Felipe was neatly divided between eighteen haciendas and thirty-nine ranches. The seven free villages, despoiled of all but their most marginal lands, had been almost totally absorbed by their neighbors.[11] Twenty-five percent of the local population resided in these villages and was eligible for restitution.

Although there were rumors and speculations, the immediate concern of the hacendado was not the loss of his lands; his first troubles were more in the line of "labor problems." The acasillados of Tepetitlán were restive. They disliked the work tasks and complained to Don Fidel that the assignments were excessive. Don Fidel explained, "there were various discussions with them; it was a question of words and smoothing things over and after that they continued working." In San Onofre, various major-domos incited unrest by warning the acasillados not to trust the patroness; in neighboring Providencia, Mateo Sánchez, an acasillado, began a ten-year reign of terror by sniping at passing travelers. But the majority remained sufficiently intimidated to continue an existence of passive equilibrium. According to Don Ernesto, "their loyalties remained with the hacendado and they sided with the hacendado." Since their only source of information was the hacendado and his trusted employees, the peons were not in the position to make massive demands at this time.

By 1921, speculations were converted into an inescapable reality with the publication of the first presidential resolution affecting San Felipe. The free village of San Antonio Mextepec received a donation of 286 hectares expropriated from the haciendas of Tepetitlán and Bonchetè (Municipal Archives, Lands and Waters Section 1921). Tepetitlán was a logical target; it was famous, it was the largest estate in the municipality, and it had been in financial straits for several years. In 1900, Don Luis, the owner of Tepetitlán, was forced to sell the annex of Yondesé–prime forest land–to the American Mining Company. With this capital, his son José was able to make limited improvements which included the purchase of adjoining ranch land needed for the enlargement of the reservoir. After José's death in 1912, his widow lost interest in visiting the hacienda and left the administration completely to the control of Don Fidel. As Don Fidel recalled, the hacienda was already stagnant by 1912 because of steadily declining production, but under the widow's ownership it was insolvent. The widow had borrowed money against her land from the Bank of Mexico. After the first expropriation she negotiated with Mennonite colonists for a quick sale, but failed to agree on terms. With increasing expropriations she was unable to discharge her debts. Don Fidel noted with sadness, "now you could say the hacienda was in decadence, because the agrarian movement was on top of us; the hacienda wasn't functioning as in the old days." In 1929, the bank put an embargo on the property and Don Fidel was required to send weekly accountings to Mexico City. The level of production continued to suffer as fractions of land were expropriated from the hacienda:

> These fractions entered the ejido and since the land was redistributed to more than 100 villages, she was left with nothing. She did everything possible to save her property–the bank had the power of attorney–but it was useless because they (the bank) never did anything to prevent them from taking away her lands. In '38 it was all over when the bank foreclosed. Her only child died, but if he had lived, he would have been an inheritor without an inheritance.

The bank sold the casco of the hacienda to a neighboring rancher; control of the dams passed to the Secretary of Hydraulic Resources. The vast tracts of Tepetitlán, however, were now under the domain of the newly formed ejido communities.[12]

Despite the break-up of Tepetitlán, the other haciendas maintained their integrity until the 1930s. Providencia remained undisturbed until 1934 and San Onofre sustained normal levels of production until the end of 1935. This is not to say life attained its former level of tranquility for the landowners; at this stage of the agrarian reform program, government policy was still sufficiently lax to enable the hacendado to impede the process.

While the hacendados took various measures to preserve the estates, the number of incidents continued to escalate. There was little peace in the municipality during the thirties and fear became a way of life. Mateo Sánchez had attracted a clique of followers. He was now a folk hero. Although he was hated by the gente de razón, he was considered "very manly," "virile" and "brave," traits considered alien to the Indian character. As Mateo's aggressions multiplied, it was inadvisable to leave the casco without protection. When Don Ernesto made his rounds, he was armed and accompanied by a trusted employee. This buddy system extended to occasions when it became necessary to leave the grounds of the estate. Doors were locked with iron bars and the wives of employees habitually congregated in the main house when their men were out working. The peons of San Onofre no longer were content with cutting telephone lines; Doña Martha remembers a confrontation which took place in front of the main house shortly after her marriage to the young hacendado of San Onofre:

> It happened on a Monday morning when Alfonso was making his rounds. The Indians approached the house, grouping together like mad dogs. Alfonso went forward to meet them. They had an order for him–they wanted their lands. They said, "our grandfathers had the land and it's our land." But when they saw the figure of their patron on horseback–he cut a fine figure–they hesitated. They still had *respect*. After all, Alfonso had always been fair. Alfonso was by himself; his employees ran and hid under their beds. Alfonso kept his head and told the spokesman of the group, "show me your documents and we can work this out. Bring your documents with you and show me your legal right to this land." Of course, they couldn't and they eventually dispersed without further incident.

Later occurrences did not end peacefully. Once land distribution had taken on a certain momentum and various peasant sectors realized it was possible to detach themselves from their patrons, the confrontations became increasingly violent. At the heart of these encounters was the peasant's attempt to regain his lands before he was legally authorized. During one attempt of forced seizure, a skirmish between the administrative staff and Indian major-domos resulted in the death of a dozen persons and ended with the occupation of San Onofre by federal troops.

Violence was not the only weapon of the peons. Both the patron and the municipal court were by-passed as the peons learned to take their grievances directly to the national authorities. In 1928, for example, the peons of Tres Estrellas sent a written complaint to Gobernación denouncing the hacendado and demanding:

(1) The peasants should receive free wood, water, and feed for their animals, as in San Nicolás, an annex of Providencia;
(2) Each family head should receive 16 liters of seed and daily wages of 41 cents. The corn should be rationed at the rate of 8 pesos per carga or 8 cents per double-liter;
(3) Muleteers should be paid 62 cents daily and receive 6 double-liters of free corn per week;
(4) Shepherds should receive a salary of 8 pesos per month and be charged 8 pesos per carga of corn;
(5) The peasants should have the liberty to continue petitioning for ejido donations [Municipal Archives, Gobernación Section 1928].

Peasant demands went unanswered and it wasn't until the Cárdenas regime in 1934 that the government became actively committed to land distribution. From 1936 to 1938, fifty-two ejido petitions were approved compared to the few donations granted earlier. With the exception of Tepetitlán, most losses before 1936 were more apparent than real. These "losses" were maneuvers by the landlords to remove various fractions from the hacienda's inventory. Repeated land divisions, through semi-legal "sales" or "gifts," would then be categorized as "small properties" with immunity against expropriation. Through his contacts and position, the hacendado was successful in partitioning a good part of his estate, but with the advent of Cárdenas, the "legality" of these acts was disputed.

This process can be illustrated with documentation from San Onofre. Until 1932, the size of the hacienda remained virtually the same although land values fluctuated from year to year. In 1914, the hacienda encompassed 8873 hectares values at $287,816 (pesos). Included in the 8873 hectares were the properties of the hacienda proper, two small annexes situated in other parts of the municipality, and the ranch of Rioyos which was rented and administered independently. Scattered properties of negligible size in and near the town were excluded. An additional 10,000 hectares of forest lands were assessed at $195,000.[13] By 1931, the value of the lands had depreciated to $265,822 and the forests to $105,780, although the area of the estate had not changed.

The first expropriations occurred in 1932 with the donation of 962 hectares to the village of Tlalpujahuilla in Michoacán and the provisional donation of 454 hectares to Santiago Oxtempan in the municipality of San Felipe. Another 1406 hectares were removed from the hacienda's accounts through sales and gifts:

(1) 313 hectares were freely ceded to the acasillados of the cuadrillas El Centro and San Miguel;

(2) 486 hectares were "sold" to the hacendado's daughter, a minor;

(3) 365 hectares were "sold" to the hacendado's son, also a minor;

(4) 242 hectares were "sold" to the acasillados of the cuadrilla El Pedregal in 62 lots *according to contract*. In this manner, a total of 2822 hectares valued at $69,840 were removed from official inventories in 1932 although only 1416 hectares had been expropriated.

Other loopholes in the laws enabled the hacendado to devaluate his lands drastically. According to state policy, the fiscal value of land was set at approximately $25 per hectare. This amount was loosely interpreted by the hacendado and fluctuated wildly depending on the quality and class of land. The hacendado was also allowed a generous discount for depreciation of exploited lands. When the occasion arose, the hacendado adroitly manipulated statistics and discounted lands which had not been exploited.[14]

Upon superficial scrutiny, the free cession and sale of fractions conformed to the necessary legalities; deeds were duly drawn, notarized and registered with the proper authorities. The sale of lots to the acasillados, however, according to the contract stipulated by the hacendado, was neither notarized nor registered. The acasillados were "charged" nominal sums for these lots which left them only further in arrears. This move was motivated by the hacendado's intention to placate the peons while they were still tractable. The hacendado counted on their continued fidelity and respect for his judgment despite growing evidence to the contrary. The hacendado's closest compromise with reality was to blame isolated instigators for his troubles; he was afraid, but tried to contain his panic. This attitude is sharply elucidated in a letter sent to the administrator of Rioyos by the administrator of San Onofre in 1933:

> I have your letters of the 25th and 28th of this month, in which you describe the goings-on of the people of San Juan (a cuadrilla of the ranch), or better said, *your peons*. You say your people don't want to sign their contracts; you should try to see them one, two, or three at a time and not all at once when they can become unmanageable. Speak to them and convince them they're in error and the only thing you want is to help them secure the pieces of land they already have.
>
> You should also single out those who you feel are most compliant. Tell them there's no need to unite with outsiders, since they already have the fractions the hacienda gave them without charging a single cent. However, if they insist on making constant trips to Toluca, it will cost them money and others will benefit, not them. Therefore, they should remain loyal to their patroness whom they know and not have ambitions for what they do not and cannot have.
>
> For your part, don't become demoralized and don't be afraid–you know the people talk a lot and a small thing can become magnified to cause panic among the people. You shouldn't pay attention to everything said, because as you well know there's a proverb that goes, "*de lo que te cuenten nada y de lo que vees la mitad*" (don't believe anything they tell you and only half of what you see). In my opinion, the peons of Rioyos shouldn't be asking when they've just seen their cuadrillas enlarged, absolutely without a single expense.
>
> Regarding Don Pepe's peons, we know of one who's involved in this affair, but since he's from a different cuadrilla he won't be able to do anything. You have my assurance that my peons, for now, don't have anything to do with this business; nor will they allow themselves to be fooled so easily by whoever sees them and tells them to get involved in this business.
>
> You should find out who this person in San Felipe was so you know whom you have to guard against. Although your peons don't want to tell you, I'm sure you'll find somebody who's indiscrete; and in this manner continue questioning to arrive at the heart of the matter.
>
> We'll keep in touch regarding this business until we know who the culprits are [San Onofre Archives 1933].

Other contracts were not signed by the acasillados of San Onofre, but the patroness continued to deed land to family members and loyal employees through ficticious sales. In 1933, she sold five fractions to the owner of the hacienda store and each of his children, while almost half of Rioyos (639 hectares) was divided between her son and the administrator of the hacienda. This process continued in 1934 with the sale of additional properties to the administrator's children. By the end of the year only 4066 hectares entered the books. A brief respite occurred in 1935 with the return of 454 hectares; after various cash gifts had been sent to the state governor, the petition of Santiago Oxtempan–pending since 1932–was denied and the land was returned to the hacienda. Within six months the number of hectares was nearly halved as a result of the first genuine expropriations since 1932. The earlier grants affected cultivable and grazing lands, but by 1937 large segments of forest lands were expropriated. Total ejido donations were assessed at $186,899 and the few remaining fractions, amounting to approximately 170 hectares were now valued at $8038. These fractions constituted protection zones for the hacienda and consisted primarily of pastoral and cultivable lands; the hacienda was also left with forest lands assessed at $26,240. In a few short years, the total value of the hacienda (real estate and movable property) had decreased from $1,039,308 in 1931 to $132,968 in 1939 although land appraisals had practically doubled as a result of the devaluation of the peso during this period.

By the late thirties, the haciendas had been irrevocably weakened and their demise was imminent. But they still monopolized the prime land and continued production on a greatly reduced scale. Of the 24,797 hectares expropriated to form ejido communities, 11,202 hectares were cultivable, while the remainder was composed of grazing land, woodlands, and barren plots (Municipal Archives, First Ejido Census 1938). Under the stipulations of the agrarian law, the ejido's request for amplification would not be considered until ten years after the first grant had been made. This situation precipitated increasing invasions by the ejidatarios in their clamor for more land and better land.

These invasions consisted of the unauthorized occupation or exploitation of lands not yet expropriated. The invaded tracts were contiguous to the ejido communities; for the ejidatario, their possession would result in a more equitable distribution of pasturage, forests and cultivable lands. Although the hacendados regularly complained to the municipal authorities, the invasions continued. When first-class zacatón lands were invaded, the hacendados were sufficiently ired to send a strong reproach to the Secretaría de Gobernación:

> The municipality of San Felipe has an area of 650 square kilometers; 40 percent–the zone corresponding to the plains–is planted in zacatón. Twenty-eight percent of the municipality's 36,000 inhabitants are dedicated to the exploitation and processing of zacatón fiber. Only a few years ago, the quality of the fiber was splendid, its production constant, and it had a great acceptance in the European market. Each shrub produced a kilo of fiber. When the authorities donated the land to the peasants, the production increased and the quality decreased. The industry is now in decadence due to immoderate exploitation and careless extraction. To date, the shrub has produced only a few grams of fiber. Lately, some have committed the greatest stupidity by breaking up the ground to till corn, wheat, or barley, which because of the composition of the soil and the topography of the land will not grow. Finally, without other prospects, they have reverted to robbery and crimes. The aggression and humiliation in which the Indians lived is the reason for their ignorance and the destructive arm of their interests. They are peasants because they live in the countryside, but not farmers–simply destructors of what is theirs and what is not theirs. Therefore, it is imperative to regulate the exploitation of the zacatón plant and teach these peasants how to care for their plots to accomplish the goals of the President of the Republic [Municipal Archives, Gobernación Section 1938].

The indifference of the municipal authorities was deliberately calculated. The national legitimization of the Mexican Revolutionary Party depended on wide public support, gained by means of a revitalized agrarian program. By the end of the Cárdenas period, local officials were no longer right-hand men of vested interests; they were carefully selected by the party machinery, and their sympathies and interests were opposed to those of the landowners.

On the contrary, both the Church and the landlords were denounced by local authorities as "provocators" and "subverters" whose only aim was to create problems for the national government. These accusations did contain a measure of truth, since the hacendados wielded their dwindling powers to defend their interests. During the year, their dilemma had worsened considerably; aside from the myriad problems precipitated by land distribution, it also became evident that the hacendado could expect no further political support from either local or national authorities. Of course, it had been more and more difficult to obtain satisfaction from the government, but in 1939 with the partisan appointment of the insurgent peasant Mateo Sánchez to the municipal presidency, the course of government policy was never more explicit. The national campaign of 1940 provided the hacendados with a convenient guise to obstruct agrarian justice.

The elections of 1940 were charged with tensions and characterized by accusations; instead of presenting an action program, the Almazán campaign was oriented to exposing the excesses of Cárdenas. Almazán was supported by the reactionary National Action Party (PAN). On the local level, the hacendado aligned himself with the newly formed PAN, dubbed the Organized Catholic Party by municipal officials, and the National Union of Sinarquistas–a political offshoot of the *sinarquista* movement and rabidly anti-revolutionary in its search for a new Christian Mexico. Many peasants remained loyal to their patrons while others were dissatisfied with the goods that had been delivered by the revolutionary government. These groups were particularly susceptible to the propaganda of the landholding class that agrarian reform was a folly. Repeated proselytizing was effective: the landowners and those who cooperated with them managed to create various splinters within the peasant sector, identified as "rojos" (Reds), "almazanistas" and "sinarquistas." Clearly, not all the animosity engendered among the peasants was instigated by the landowners. Nevertheless, in light of the strong political undertones which characterized this period of local history, their part cannot be disavowed. Inevitably, antagonisms and rancors among the diverse splinters ended in violence. Don Ernesto lived the experience and explained dispassionately:

> Naturally there was violence in those days–nobody was in agreement. Each village wanted the advantage of x number of hectares of x locality. The villages were at odds with each other and numerous provocations led to assassinations. It was a matter of each one wanting the same thing–the most productive lands, leaving the neighboring villages with the marginal lands. This caused hatreds, vengeances, and intolerable situations which could only be corrected through time by the passage of a law (the Agrarian Code of 1934). The disturbances and rivalries that existed among the peasant class were a natural outcome of the ejido question. But these were momentary circumstances precipitated by the donation of the land. Many, after receiving the ejido, thought their lands would be affected or that they would lose them. Invariably the conflicts led to many tragedies which occurred because of the ignorance of the people during this period.

Finally, after repeated complaints by the agrarian communities of continuous harassments, the municipal authorities sent a communique to Gobernación stating that the hacendados "have participated in subversive activities against the government, provoking divisions among the ejidatarios of the agrarian communities, under the almazanista flag . . . creating discord among the peasants, with the intention to *sinarquizar* the ejidatarios." The municipal president claimed he had evidence of the existence of the National Union of Sinarquistas, whose membership consisted strictly of "regressive" elements–landlords, merchants, church officials and wealthy ranchers. Their motives were unfathomable, but the municipal officials considered them foes of the government (Municipal Archives, Gobernación Section 1941). Following this letter, martial law was imposed in the ex-hacienda of Tepetitlán and federal troops were later sent to other parts of the municipality with the occurrence of fresh outbreaks.

Despite intimidations by the hacendados, agrarian reform proceeded. Despite shifting alignments of hacendado against ejidatario, and ejidatario against ejidatario, the present system of land tenure was clearly formulated by 1940. San Felipe was now composed predominantly of ejido communities which had been granted communal, inalienable lands by the federal government, and "small properties"–privately owned properties whose legal maximum size was specified by the Agrarian Code. Fifty-seven ejido communities had been created by 1940; three years later, the number increased to eighty-four. With the proliferation of minutely sized plots in the municipality, the stage was set for *minifundia*; a total of 2365 parcels encompassed 79,500 hectares and 2082 consisted of five hectares or less (Municipal Archives, Statistics Section 1943).

What happened to the hacienda? Nominally, the hacienda continued to exist on the books–in census reports, official letters, parish and municipal archives, but as an agrarian estate, it ceased to function. This was by no means an abrupt process, but rather a gradual and continuous diminishment of production as the elements most vital to the life of the hacienda–an accessible market, a cheap labor force, and abundant land–were removed. Dwindling export markets, coupled with the multiple problems generated by land distribution guaranteed the hacienda's demise.

The haciendas in San Felipe were intimately linked to the adjacent mining communities of Michoacán. El Oro, alone, received a good part of its meat and grain supply from San Felipe. With the rupture of mining operations, El Oro and similar cities were deserted, and passed into ghost towns. The lumber utilized by the principal mining companies of Michoacán was also supplied by the haciendas of San Felipe. Although the forest lands were not expropriated until the late thirties, the market collapsed before then as a result of repeated mining crises. This was not a simple one-to-one process, however. The haciendas were never monocultural; they concentrated on one principal crop, but were able to fall back on other resources with the tightening of a particular market. Many haciendas were in some way or other involved in zacatón processing, although the industry was controlled by the Fuente family of Providencia. With the drastic drop in exports during the depression, the Fuentes, almost completely dependent on their European markets, were in trouble. Naturally, the repercussions were felt in the other haciendas.

The first labor losses were felt in the early days of the Reform with the disappearance of migrant workers. Their dependability was always somewhat shaky. Not only were they more oriented to working in the mines where they encountered better working conditions, more diversity and higher wages, but they were also among the first beneficiaries of the ejido. Later, although land distribution often proceeded at an unpredictable rate, the number of acasillados steadily declined. In 1925, nearly 4000 acasillados and approximately 300 sharecroppers and their families resided on the 18 estates. Each ranch also had a minimal resident crew of 15 to 20 peons (Municipal Archives, Statistics Section 1925). By 1938, with the growing momentum of land distribution, the number of acasillados had declined to 900, until in 1942, the acasillado had officially ceased to exist (Municipal Archives, Statistics Section 1936).

As land distribution proceeded the number of small private properties, commonly known as ranches, increased. Several ranches that existed alongside the hacienda were legitimate private properties of 50 to 100 hectares; the others were actually annexes of the haciendas, located at some distance from the principal estate. In exceptional instances the hacendado successfully disposed of the whole annex through "sales" once he realized the seriousness of the agrarian reform movement. If the property had then been in the possession of the new proprietor (almost always a relative) for at least ten years and did not exceed the legal size, it would be left intact. In this manner, it was possible to preserve a block of seasonal cultivable land amounting up to 250 hectares. Occasionally the hacendado saved part of the annex. Fractions were expropriated from the annex until all population nuclei within a seven-mile radius had had their petitions for ejidos approved. The remaining land of the annex would automatically fall into the category of "small property" if it did not exceed the specified size. As a small property, it would then be exempt from further petitions and remain under the jurisdiction of the hacendado. But generally, the hacendado was left only with his casco and a fifty hectare zone of protection. Some hacendados later sold the casco to ranchers who live on and work the property as a unit. Other hacendados or their relatives have left the house with a caretaker and rented the protection zone in the form of cultivable plots. In preference to renting or selling, another solution has been to allow the property to fall into ruin–masses of rubble overgrown by weeds. Only two hacendados have maintained their properties and treat them today as weekend retreats.

The hacienda was also spent when the norms characteristic of the social system at that time ceased to be either acceptable or effective. For the hacendado, his cultural definitions of the social hierarchy did not change: they were no longer sanctioned by the wider society. He was no longer the economic boss, the civil authority, or the proverbial provider, and ingenuously he lamented the peon's loss of respect. The peon, or peasant as he was now known, underwent a process of enlightenment in his realization of the basic contradictions between his former circumstances and his potentialities. He was a member of the new agrarian communities and represented by nationally appointed spokesmen. His dependence on the ex-hacendado was broken, as was his obligation of filial obedience. Where previously the hacendado had manipulated all social relationships with the cooperation and support of the government, by the forties this position had been reversed and the government was now the principal mediator between social groups. Both the former patron and the former peon were required to learn new forms of behavior in the acquisition of ends diametrically at variance with one another. During the forties we enter a phase in which the hacendado has been stripped of his power, although he and other private proprietors were offered legal assurance that small property would be respected. At the same time, the ejidatario was warned that further unauthorized invasions would not be tolerated, but previous illegal occupations were duly regularized. Both the ejidatario and the proprietor began to work through the newly formed legal channels. The ejidatario, as we shall see, had the edge.

Previous invasions had been tolerated under conditions of great fluidity; now they were winked at, despite the guarantees protecting the hacendado as a small private property owner. Even when the hacendado had the law on his side and cleverly used the legal facilities at his disposal, he received no satisfaction whatsoever. Disputes and bureaucratic entanglements were bound to arise in a grandiose distribution program; but the hacendado clung to his interests and fought with a tenacity which was often out of proportion to his cause. The hacendados knew what was coming, knew it was inevitable, and held on as long as they could; most hacendados left the municipality, abandoned the fight, and moved on to more fertile fields. Some landowners refused to accept the often irregular consequences of the new agrarianism and the total inefficiency of the agrarian bureaucracy.

The Venegas family, for example, has been involved in continuous litigations since 1952. The family claimed that Rancho Verde (an annex of San Onofre) had been repeatedly invaded by the ejidatarios of El Rosario, Michoacán. Once the mounted police had intercepted the invaders, the family filed a formal complaint in the state capital. The ensuing legal process would implicate almost every dependency of the agrarian reform bureaucracy.

Doña Dolores was legally within her rights. Rancho Verde had been certified as ineligible for further expropriation by President Alemán in 1951. Yet the ejidatarios were acting under the assumption they were exploiting lands which now belonged to them. Rancho Verde, originally consisting of 1112 hectares of woodlands, had been reduced to an area of 300 hectares by a series of expropriations. With the enlargement of San Felipe del Jesús, a former cuadrilla of the estate, in 1957, the status of Rancho Verde was changed to "small property." The certificate of inalienability was granted by presidential resolution and filed with the National Agrarian Register. It superseded a similar certificate pending since 1944 when Doña Dolores had entered into litigation with the hacendado Jesús Nazareno of Michoacán. Jesús Nazareno claimed that a breccia which intersected Rancho Verde formed the boundary of his hacienda; he would then own considerable acreage in the state of Mexico. Doña Dolores countered that the hacienda of Jesús Nazareno never contained land in the state and her property boundary formed a broken line following the state border. The dispute was resolved by the Supreme Court and the boundary line was adjusted in favor of Doña Dolores. A certified copy of the court's decision and several maps were filed with the agrarian delegate in Morelia, the state capital of Michoacán. Rancho Verde, therefore, had been both adequately mapped and declared inalienable. When the ejidatarios of El Rosario (former peons on the hacienda of Jesús Nazareno) applied for and were granted their expansion, the land was to be expropriated from the ex-hacienda of Jesús Nazareno. The old boundary dispute between the two hacendados entered into the matter because the ejidatarios were now exploiting land that belonged to Doña Dolores, but that would have pertained to Jesús Nazareno had the dispute been settled in his favor. The agrarian delegate in Michoacán refused to recognize the maps filed in his department and insisted that new maps be drawn by the Agrarian Department. What was necessary, then, for the resolution of this dispute, was an official topographic mapping of a boundary decision already made by the Supreme Court.

The Agrarian Department was the proper tribunal in a boundary conflict;

each party was to elect two representatives who would prepare titles, documents and any other material pertinent to the case. The Agrarian Department would next survey the disputed land, allowing the parties an additional two months for the final formulation of their presentations. Within five days of the termination of this period, a presidential resolution would be prepared; it would be considered irrevocable if the parties were in agreement. Any appeals were to be processed by the local representatives; they would then be channeled through the proper administrative levels. In the case of San Onofre versus El Rosario, where we are dealing with a boundary dispute involving two states, it was necessary to initiate the proceedings with the agrarian delegate in Toluca (the state representative of the Agrarian Department). The case would then be passed on to the main office in Mexico City and decisions would be transmitted from there to the agrarian delegate in Morelia. Communication in the opposite direction would follow the same course.

Doña Dolores respected the proper channels and filed her complaint with the Agrarian Department in Toluca. After several months delay, she received a reply directly from the delegate in Morelia. He accused Doña Dolores of invading the ejido and ordered her to stop. In the spring of 1952, she again complained to state officials, enclosing a copy of the "order" from Morelia. Again her complaint traveled the bureaucratic circuit and the agrarian delegate was told to resolve the conflict by mapping the disputed property. In the meantime, Doña Dolores wrote directly to President Alemán, reiterating her case and reminding him he had been responsible for the classification of her ranch as "small property." Not only were her rights as a small private property owner being violated, but also the sovereignty of the state itself because of prohibitions against forest exploitation. She sent copies of this letter to the state governor, the delegates of the Agrarian Department in Toluca and Morelia, the chief of the Department in Mexico City, and the Secretary of Agriculture.

By 1955, the Morelian officials had received several dozen letters from various departments and levels of the bureaucracy as well as repeated warnings from Doña Dolores, herself. Not only did the ejidatarios continue the invasion, but the letters were never acknowledged. By now, the Department of Complaints had entered the scene. Although previous officials had accepted the validity of the accusations, this department insisted it could not adjudicate until the land had been officially mapped. The Morelian officials were told to complete the mapping promptly and warned that sanctions would be applied if instructions were not complied with. The response was utter silence.

Doña Dolores reacted to the insouciance of the Michoacán officials by dispatching a telegram to President Cortines:

> On numerous occasions we have directed complaints to you, the maximum agrarian authority, and agrarian functionaries, asking for the cessation of the invasion of my small property Rancho Verde, municipality of San Felipe del Progreso, state of Mexico, without having obtained the dislodgment of the ejidatarios of El Rosario, municipality of Ocampo, Michoacán. Each complaint has been turned over to the Agrarian Department without an effective resolution. Specifically, the said department has asked for information from the agrarian delegate in Morelia, who never answers. Lately the invasion has intensified–with total destruction of living trees and dead wood–causing me irreparable damages and numerous losses. Attention–the gravity of the case. I beg you to take the urgent necessary measures directly. Honorable President–if this case is

transferred to the Agrarian Department, they will achieve nothing, as they have achieved nothing on past occasions. Specifically, I am putting this request to the highest authority that I may be granted the guarantees I have a right to.

Contrary to her request, the President sent the telegram to Gobernación. From there, it eventually found its way to the state governor several months after he had received this appeal:

> . . . As a result of the situation caused by the arbitrary invasion, I have been making both verbal and written appeals before the President of the Republic and other agrarian authorities without having obtained a single practical result, even though my appeals are in legitimate defense of my interests. Rather than the invasion stopping, lately it has intensified. The invaders are razing the groves, pasturage and the rest; for this reason, I am presenting the situation to you and asking for justice, to which I have a right. Thus, I declare:
>
> . . . after contributions toward various agrarian donations petitioned by neighboring villages, my property was reduced to "small property, inalienable" consisting of 300 hectares of mountainous land.
>
> This property is absolutely inalienable, by express mandate of the law; it is not affected by presidential resolutions dictated in expedients of donation and amplification of lands requested by the ejidatarios of El Rosario because the cited property is untouchable, legally speaking. Under these circumstances, I have the right to ask that what is legitimately my property be respected and my guarantees in accordance with the Constitution of the Republic be assured.
>
> Since the beginning of the year, these unlawful and criminal acts committed on my property have increased. The same ejidatarios are completely destroying the forests by felling trees and sacking the loose wood for fuel, without any consideration that this is my exclusive property. They have converted Rancho Verde into a veritable desert.
>
> As a result of my latest appeal to the Agrarian Department, the Office of Promotion and Complaints sent a decree to the delegate of the Agrarian Department in Morelia, with a copy for the ejido commissary in El Rosario . . . in addition, I sent a telegram to the President of the Republic which states . . . .
>
> In regard to the above statements, I ask you as governor:
>
> (1) This complaint be transmitted to the Proctor of Justice in the state of Mexico to inform him of the necessary facts. He can verify the truth of my complaint and order the apprehension of the ejidatarios and the confiscation of all arms and tools used in the despoliation of property which is not theirs;
> (2) The ejidatarios be brought before the Claims Court of Ixtlahuaca (the district capital) and the corresponding punishment meted out to the responsible parties in accordance with state legislation;
> (3) The necessary authorities declare that my rights to the property be respected so that the ownership of this property is no longer disputed . . . .

Doña Dolores also attempted to intimidate the ejido commissary by warning him she had the backing of the agrarian authorities and would appeal to whatever other authority necessary to exact the respect she deserved. She ordered him to instruct his ejidatarios to stop sacking her property. She reminded him that according to the Agrarian Code, he was ultimately responsible for the unlawful invasion and was in danger of losing his office, was liable for fines up to 500 pesos, and might possibly end up with a prison term of two years.

The ejido commissary, on the contrary, was not the least perturbed and contended:

> I received the letter in which you complain that until this date, the breccia of the place called Rancho Verde has not been respected. You believe the people of my ejido are chopping down green wood and taking dead wood. Well, señora, I don't believe it's the

people of my ejido. Since this place is in litigation, it won't be known definitely what's yours and what's ours until the maps are made.

And for this reason, I implore you, my people don't go around cutting down trees–I, as commissary, insist in this matter–to the point where I don't see what you're complaining about. I think those who are destroying your trees are from Angangueo and other places.

Doña Dolores was incensed and told the commissary to do his homework. She pointed out that the breccia was not under litigation–her property had been perfectly delineated by the pertinent authorities and was also protected from illegal invasion by writ. She told the commissary to consult the maps and the Supreme Court decision. She threatened him with more legal sanctions:

. . . the presidential resolutions dictated to donate the ejido and its amplification to the neighbors of El Rosario whom you represent, never mention land could be taken from my property. The resolutions, published in the Official Diary of the Federation absolutely NEVER MENTION THAT ONE SINGLE INCH OF MY PROPERTY COULD BE TAKEN FOR THE DONATION OF THE EJIDOS. What doubts can you have when my rights are clearly defined and when it is perfectly reasonable to ask that my property be respected . . . .

I have precise information from the forest authorities that the people of El Rosario are invading my property. For this reason I have addressed myself to you, asking that the arbitrary invasions stop . . . you will not continue in the erroneous beliefs that you have the right to a piece of land which by no stretch of the imagination corresponds to you. If you continue in the same vein, I will be forced to insist before the proper authorities that the sanctions which I referred to in my previous letter be vigorously applied.

Having answered every point, I hope you will be convinced I have reason and justice on my side and you will use whatever means at your disposal to stop your people from invading my property and causing the severe damages I have complained about.

By the late spring of 1955, Doña Dolores sent her "hundredth" complaint, this time to the Department of Complaints in Mexico City, criticizing the local officials for their incompetence, alluding to their venality, and hinting at hidden interests:

. . . I would like to think there existed some impediment in the beginning–for lack of personnel or whatever–but given the time, they have more than exceeded a reasonable period for the delineation of boundaries and the filing of the corresponding documents with the Agrarian Department in Mexico City.

. . . How does one explain the fact that a public functionary can ignore the orders sent from a superior officer?

What motive could the delegate have for not answering official letters received from his superiors?

Is it possible to think there are certain interests which are in oppostion?

And her letters to the agrarian delegate in Michoacán continued:

. . . now these ejidatarios have reached the point where they are trying to prevent *my* cattle from grazing on *my* property since they claim it is theirs and an engineer will measure the land and give them possession.

. . . Since 1952, when the Agrarian Department in Mexico City sent me your telegram stating that an engineer had been commissioned to measure the ejido of El Rosario, almost four years have gone by and you either cannot or do not want to terminate this project.

. . . Since I assume the visit of the engineer is related to my petition, I hope–finally–the delineation is made, putting each party in possession of what is legally his.

By the end of 1955, the case had been transferred to the Forestry Department, a branch of the Secretariat of Agriculture and Cattle, and a tentative date for the engineer's visit was set. It seemed likely the dispute would be settled soon. The government indicated it would no longer tolerate unauthorized invasions and notified the auxiliary departments that all complaints made by small private property owners would be accepted and processed according to the letter of the law. It was firmly declared that "ejidatarios who invade fractions of small property will be prosecuted according to federal procedure" (Excelsior, August 17, 1955:1). By 1958 the topographic survey had been completed and the inalienability of Rancho Verde was confirmed by the director of the Agrarian Department. Plans were still pending for the expansion of El Rosario, but it was clear this expansion would consist entirely of land expropriated from the ex-hacienda of Jesús Nazareno. As far as Doña Dolores was concerned, the case was closed and she was satisfied.

Within two years she became involved in another litigation when the former cuadrilla of San Felipe del Jesús again applied for amplification, citing Rancho Verde as a possible source of land. The proceedings have followed the same pattern as in San Onofre versus El Rosario; again discontented ejidatarios repeatedly invaded her property and court litigations have continued to the present day.

For those who have "remained" in the municipality by holding on to their small properties, the experience has been one of continual confrontations and frustrations. The proud landlord has become an anomaly and faded from today's local social schema. San Felipeños like to think the ex-hacendados "were left with nothing," "live poorly" and "are not even well-off." Yet some have married well and some have merged into the white-collar world, while others have hung on to the tailcoats of a family branch, assuring themselves of a respectable social position and occasional appearances in the society pages. Despite local claims to the effect that the ex-hacendados are "doing badly," none lives indigently; they have merged into an amorphous, urban middle class, distinguished from their counterparts by an exaggerated but superficial gentility and a grating resentment over their powerlessness. The generation that grew up on the hacienda is slowly disappearing and younger family members have flocked to the professions.

The ex-hacendados who have continued to fight for their properties live in a different epoch, and have refused or are unable to accept the realities of the present. The Venegas family, for example, resides year-round in a Mexico City neighborhood that was once the most exclusive residential area on the edge of town and is now the haven of recently impoverished families. They run a small but elegant boarding house, euphemistically known as the *posada* (inn) and apologetically described as their son's business. It would be indistinguishable from any other comfortable neocolonial house furnished in a potpourri of pseudocolonial pieces and parental hand-me-downs, except for the prominently displayed oil painting of San Onofre in the living room and the casual draping of Indian belts over the furnishings. Alfonso, as countless other family heads, leaves the house punctually every morning, sporting an attaché case and immaculately dressed. He does not have a job and does not go to an office; he is "looking after the family business." This business consists of the management of various pieces of real estate in Mexico City, Cuernavaca and El Oro, which Doña Dolores had purchased during the heyday of the hacienda. Their rents are plowed back into the maintenance of the casco and the continuing expense of litigation. Only recently with the death of Alfonso's father-in-law and the assurance of a private income, has he been able to contemplate the closing of the boarding house.

The family was required to make an enormous adjustment in lifestyle after the loss of their lands, but their basic habits have not changed. Alfonso is still an independent gentleman and would never consider working for another person. Household servants are still imported from the countryside, and, although well-treated, are not expected to have other ambitions in life. The family still travels from residence to residence, and when they visit the hacienda, they find a deferential staff waiting to serve them. The hacienda itself is the strongest requiem to the past. The Red Room is covered over with sheets, yet the furnishings and draperies have been left intact; the toys in the playhouse are layered with dust, but have not been moved. The office is a living museum, and the musty leather-bound inventory and account books are exactly as they were in 1920. Only on viewing the ejido villages beyond the walls of the casco, does one sense the futility of trying to recapture bygone days.

As for attitudes, the family conforms with what Simpson has called "psychological latifundismo" (1967:263), an anachronistic outlook on the nature of society so strongly formed under the experience of the hacienda that it is impervious to change. According to Simpson, one encounters a sort of ritual among the ex-landowners which has not disappeared and will continue to exist, regardless of the disappearance of the latifundium itself. This ritual may be considered in two aspects–attitudes regarding the agrarian reform per se, and attitudes toward those who benefited most from the reform, the former peons. At times these attitudes merge and it is difficult to determine whom the hacendados resent most, the government for expropriating their land or the peasant for exploiting their land.

In San Felipe, this ritual–"the Indians are an inferior race," and "look how things have been going since the Revolution" (1967:264)–is consistently duplicated. The Venegas family genuinely believes the hacienda was and is the best system for Mexico. For them, the agrarian reform was not only a drastic, hasty step, but also a mistake. Martha Venegas was bitter when she spoke: the forests have been completely destroyed since the reform because they were never replanted. During the years the hacienda exploited the forests, they were always verdant. Reforestation and conservation were ensured through government regulation and inspection. The land was distributed indiscriminately and the ejidatarios were ignorant of its cultivation. The agrarian reform has done nothing to improve the lot of the Indians; if anything, it has worsened it. The family also agreed the Indians were better off under their guardianship for "at least in those days, the peons had something to eat, while now they live like animals." Although the land is now his, the Indian still does not do anything that will make it productive, because "the Indian will always be an Indian." In Señora Venegas' opinion, the Indian has done nothing to change; in fact, he has deteriorated. When asked in what sense the Indian has deteriorated, she contended that previously the Indian had respect, "he always said 'good morning, patron.' "

Now, she lamented, he had no respect toward the family because of "personal deterioration."

Simpson has stated that "psychological latifundismo" is often catching. This has not occurred in San Felipe. Undoubtedly the hacendados have left a heavy legacy. Certain aspects of the patron-peon relationship have not disappeared and have remained as the inheritance of today's social groups. There are prejudices, there are sharply defined hierarchical groupings, and there is exploitation of many by the present Mestizo elite. Yet the special frame of mind that characterized the hacendado could not be duplicated. San Felipeños today speak of social justice and social equities, while the ex-hacendado tends to evaluate the agrarian reform purely from an economic point of view. Some of the hacendados' complaints are justified; the denuded forests are there for all to see and the diversity of crop specialization has never been replicated. And others—the decline in production levels—are untenable. Of course, the hacendado finds it inconceivable that the ejidatario could cultivate the land more efficiently than he had. San Felipeños never confuse lack of opportunity with cultural inferiority. To the hacendado, the Indian was a different order of being who could never escape his former station. The hacendado forgets that when the nerve center of the estate was severed, he was left with the casco, the machinery and the irrigation works, while the Indian was given a raw plot of land which offered limited possibilities of exploitation. In the awareness of new life chances, the awards of the hacendado no longer sufficed for the peasant. And his growing consciousness was interpreted by the hacendado as "personal deterioration."

One can perhaps distinguish a nostalgic tone to the reminiscences of old-timers who lived or worked on the hacienda, but it has never been claimed that the hacienda was the best system of production. Here, too, one encounters a sort of ritual. It begins with the statement that it is all over, the hacienda has irrevocably ended, followed by an evaluation that those were graceful days, and continued by an elaborate description of the great house, the church, the graciousness of the family, the elegance of their fiestas, and the fineness of their horsemanship. Finally, when the description has been exhausted, it is invariably noted that the destruction of the hacienda was inevitable, and rightly so. Don Ernesto lived a good segment of his life on the hacienda and concluded:

> Even if it is true that in those days the hacienda produced a greater quantity in some aspects, today, each ejidatario has a piece of land which he can call his own, where he can build his house, where he can work, and where he can procure the well-being of his family. Before, huge expanses of land were in the hands of a single family. It is lamentable the social transformation of Mexico has caused many deprivations and has also cost many lives. Yet the situation is accommodating itself, resulting in a Mexico that doesn't depend on one man (Díaz) or on various persons, but is already depending on many families who tomorrow will have their tranquility and comfort.

In addition, I have never spoken with a peasant who agrees with the ex-patrons that his life was better in the old days. The peasant may not be enamored of the government, but today he is aware he is a Mexican citizen and the revolutionary government was the source of his small plot of land. Although he still cannot clothe and feed his family adequately, he at least feels that he has his liberty, his own milpa and his own house. To him, his father and grandfather, *viejos antiguos* (old ancients), were "idiots," "slaves," "ignorant," "closed" and "backward." Maximino, a respected farmer in his barrio, put it most lucidly when he recalled the life of his father, an acasillado on the hacienda of La Rosa: "My father worked only to work and he worked every single day of his life. Life is better now–I couldn't say much better–but we are surviving."

4

"WE ARE ALL FARMERS": THE AGRARIAN MYTH OF THE REVOLUTION

> *In regard to the agrarian problem we should not accumulate words and empty phrases and certainly not indulge in demagoguery . . . Today in 1970, the agrarian reform continues to be an active program which revised, refined, and enriched, will permit the Mexican Revolution to confront the future with confidence and work efficaciously and resolutely for the betterment of the peasant class, the augmentation of productivity, and the grandeur of Mexico.*
>
> –Alfonso Martínez Domínguez
> President, PRI

The exorcism of the malevolent hacendado, initiated in 1910 with ideological pomp and effected through the wholesale distribution of land, was for all practical purposes completed by 1940. The hacendado, disenfranchised, sought obscurity in the metropolis, and the estate, eviscerated through the break up of its land resources, ceased to function as an economic unit. As more and more acreage was transferred to the ejidos, San Felipe temporarily reverted to a subsistence-based, monocultural economy. Forest exploitation was abruptly suspended, maguey fields were systematically uprooted in their conversion to milpas, and even barren pasture lands were marked for corn production. Animal husbandry shortly disappeared as a result of severe epidemics of hoof-and-mouth disease and the extermination of surviving livestock. Raíz production sharply declined as the "Banco Nacional de Crédito Ejidal" attempted to organize the newly formed ejido communities of the zacatón zone into local credit societies.

Seemingly, the prime goal of the Revolution had been accomplished–the emancipation of the peon and his transformation into a "liberated" peasant sharing, however precariously, in the national patrimony:

> Land distribution, the first phase of the Agrarian Reform, has not only satisfied an essential demand of the Revolution, to which we owe the demolition of the latifundium, basis of an antiquated regime; it also represents the satisfaction of a secular demand, signifying for each ejidatario, joint-holder, and authentic small proprietor, the reconquest of a fraction of the fatherland, of which the peons of the old haciendas had been deprived [Ideario 1969:41].

The distribution of nearly seventy million hectares to some three million peasants has been rhetorically cited as a unique example of agrarian reform in Latin America. This theme has scarcely altered since the initial cry of "Land and Liberty," and continuously equates land distribution, reform and revolution:

The Party of the Revolution firmly continues to hoist the banner of agrarianism. We reiterate the oath that we will not be satisfied until the Mexican Revolution is a complete reality in all parts of Mexico . . . . The memory of Zapata symbolizes the union between men who served the cause of agrarianism–those within the womb of our party who fought for the enforcement of all the principles of the Revolution–and the common man who sustains them in the search for clear and profound waters that emanate from the 28th of November, 1911 and will not stop flowing until the last peasant has been liberated and the last piece of land distributed [El Universal, October 4, 1969:6].

Land distribution was also envisioned as a catalyst of social justice and the ensuing incorporation of the peasant into Mexican society:

The economic, social, and cultural liberation of the peasants constitutes the fundamental objective of the Agrarian Reform [Ferreira 1970a:4a].

The agrarian problem consists of incorporating a high percentage of Mexicans who live in conditions of underproduction, underemployment, underconsumption, ignorance, and insecurity in the development of the nation [Fernández Ponte 1970:1].

Agrarian reform was later conceived as an integral part of national development, but only within the last few years has this aspect been presented as a bilateral process. "The life of the countryside is the life of the nation, itself," is a frequent expression of those who have looked beyond Phase One, and the symbiotic quality of provincial-urban relationships has been publicly proclaimed. At a recent gathering of the official revolutionary party, for example, the sole presidential candidate expressed the desire that:

. . . peasants, smallholders, graziers, those in the professions and in business, and in general, all Mexicans, not only listen, but also share the responsibility–nondeferrable, patriotic, imperative–of resolving the main questions of the countryside: possession of the land, water and agriculture, rural education and technology. Questions that, among others, are vital for the existence of half our population that lives in the rural zones, as well as the other half that works and lives in the urban zones articulated to an incontrovertible question . . . . Everybody, absolutely everybody, should understand that the progress and sustenance of the nation depend upon the resolution of the problems of the countryside [Fernández Ponte 1970:1].

It has also been recognized that the only feasible method for achieving the integration of the rural sector into the national economy is through agro-industrialization:

. . . small private property and the ejido, the forms of land tenure Zapata fought for and the Revolution succeeded in raising to the category of a constitutional precept, have not only been and are instruments of economic justice and the foundation for a more equitable distribution of the national income, but also the basis upon which a system of modern agrarian exploitation must be promptly constructed [El Universal, October 4, 1969:6].

Yet agrarian reform has been identified so vigorously with land distribution that its flexibility as a panacea has been adversely affected; now it has been superseded by "agrarian revolution" as the concept in current vogue. "Agrarian reform" has come to symbolize justice in whatever form–social, economic, political–and "agrarian revolution," the whole complex of agro-industrial innovations which will buttress the reform:

Without agrarian reform one could not speak of agricultural progress in Mexico. Without agrarian revolution, the agrarian reform would be stunted and precarious. Social justice without abundant production and high work yields would be mere expectancy and poverty [Ferreira 1970b:19].

Despite more than fifty years of uninterrupted exposition of a series of principles, ranging from land distribution to rural technical improvement, all loosely categorized as ongoing aspects of the Agrarian Reform, the contrast between a capital-intensive industrial sector and a labor-intensive agricultural sector is still perceptible. Most speakers confine their comments to safe generalities, and avoid specific accusations. One can thus skirt the truth without being slanderous. But occasionally some muckraker will raise his voice, especially during a campaign year, and the local region will be thrust briefly into the limelight, only to return soon afterwards to its previous complacency. This was the situation of San Felipe del Progreso, when the irony of the municipality's name was publicly used for its shock effect:

INIQUITOUS EXPLOITATION OF 300,000 MAZAHUAS
STAGNATE IN CONDITIONS OF EXTREME MISERY IN "EL PROGRESO"

The situation of the largest municipality in the state will be exposed to Echeverría

These were merely the headlines of a commonplace story repeated in numerous rural regions formerly lauded as models of agrarian reform:

> The social, ethnic, and cultural segregation in the state, of which the Indians of San Felipe are victims, will be discussed with Licenciado Luis Echeverría Alvarez, presidential candidate of the republic, when he visits this important zone of our entity. More than 300,000 Indians, principally Mazahuas, including many who speak only indigenous languages, live marginal to progress and development, vegetating in conditions incredible to those residing in the urban zones.
>
> In the municipality of San Felipe del Progreso, one of the most important indigenous centers in the state, the Mazahuas live without electricity, without schools, and without factories. They are exploited and censured, above all, by monopolists of raíz de zacatón who pay 2 to 3 pesos per day to extract this product.
>
> Through the auspices of the Center of Political, Economic, and Social Studies of the state party, this problem will be presented to Licenciado Luis Echeverría Alvarez, so he perceives the necessity for uniting the efforts of private initiative, the municipality, the state government, and the federation in incorporating the Indians into the development of our state.
>
> This ethnic group has remained at the margin of all the benefits of progress, due principally to the isolation they are found in and the disinterest of the authorities in their integration.
>
> The discussion will proceed from the point of view of the formulation of projects that will permit integrated development—the establishment of industrial plants of raíz de zacatón controlled by the state—to eliminate intermediaries and end the exploitation and victimization of these Indians [El Sol de Toluca, May 16, 1970:1].

Ardent followers of Mexican parlance will recognize that this "exposé" conforms admirably to official rhetoric. It is repetitive and tends to focus on a single theme—exploitation—in order to attract the superficial scrutiny of a momentary audience. It is exaggerated; almost all the statistics are incorrect and are reproduced for effect rather than factual accuracy. It is evasive; in the search for explanations, a culprit is always sought—here, the middleman—although his visibility in political, economic and social spheres is completely tangential to the basic problems of the rural zone. It is based upon faulty logic; in assuming that the victimization of the Indian populace will cease with the elimination of the intermediary, one is led to the erroneous conclusion that the local situation is a function of local irregularities rather than of national policy.

Nevertheless, the indictment of San Felipe contains some pertinent facts: rural development is inseparable from balanced economic growth; the "agrarian revolution" or "integral agrarian reform" is still an illusion in many parts of Mexico; economic inequities are not simply a matter of skewed income distribution, but are coordinates of social and ethnic discrimination as well; no one village or town is independent or autonomous, but part of a larger regional economy; and implicitly it acknowledges that the only partial integration of the regional with the national economy is a supralocal phenomenon related to the meager existence of infrastructures.

The present discussion does not presume to evaluate the success or failure of the Agrarian Reform, a theme which has occupied such diverse Mexicanists as philosophers, social scientists and politicians. Not only has "agrarian reform" been dissected with redundant regularity, it has also been elucidated in as many styles as there are authors (Albornoz 1966; Durán 1967; Romero 1963; Stavenhagen et al. 1968; Tello (1968). These variant interpretations stem from the ideological implications of the concept, from its unequivocal identification with the Revolution, and from the basically retrospective analysis of a concept which has subtly and continuously changed in context. What they do imply, however, despite the numerous spectacular examples of agricultural modernization in Mexico, is the persistence of the contrast between a society that has been transformed into a modern industrial state and certain local sectors of the society, particularly the densely populated "indigenous areas," which have not received feedback from the national level.

Most simply, this juxtaposition has been described as a dichotomy, whether between national and indigenous cultural groups, developed and underdeveloped, industrial and agricultural, or urban and rural. Inevitably, the dichotomy is one of superordination-subordination, perpetuated through relationships of dominance and exploitation. This situation has generally been categorized as "plural" or "dual" and explained as a prolongation of colonial characteristics into the period of political independence, in spite of the later institutionalization of a revolutionary movement. Modern Mexico has variously been depicted as a dual society, a dual economy society, a plural society with plural cultures, and a monistic society with plural cultures and a dual economy. At times, the total Mexican society has been characterized as dual or plural; at other times, the regional society has been so characterized. These permutations do not exhaust all the possibilities by any means, but they are the most freely manipulated designations. "Plural" and "dual" have also been used interchangeably and indiscriminately:

> The plural structure of society in reality goes far beyond the dichotomy of national and indigenous culture groups. The country's development itself is dual or plural in that, as is typical of all colonies, there is a group that participates in the benefits of development and one that does not. Today the proportion of participants is greater than in the case of colonies and includes groups that are diverse in nature and immensely numerous, in comparison with the favored few who participate in the benefits of colonial development; but Mexico still has, however, the structure typical of colonial develop-

ment; an immense sector participates in development and another is left on the sidelines, while the relations between the one and the other continue being those of colonizer and the colonized [González Casanova 1968:479].

Elsewhere, González Casanova subsumes the two concepts under an entirely new category, "internal colonialism," in reference to the chronic decapitalization of the Indian communities subjugated by a Mestizo population. Although he continually oscillates between "plural" and "dual" as one and the same phenomenon, one can also discern a more specific application of terminology. Mexico is still regarded as both a plural and a dual society, plural in relation to the existence of distinct and culturally heterogeneous ethnic populations, and dual in regard to the structural inequalities between Indians (all indigenous ethnic groups) and the national group, particularly in the sphere of economic "dependence" and "monopoly" (1969:126-139). González Casanova bases his definition of pluralism on cultural heterogeneity, yet "internal colonialism" makes no allowances for differences within the Indian population—all Indians are treated as bearing the same structural position in relation to non-Indians—or for similarities between Indians and Mestizos.[15]

Other theoreticians have rejected the "plural society" theory for Mexico, while retaining the concept of "cultural pluralism" in conjunction with societal dualism. This interpretation has been most systematically elaborated by Aguirre Beltrán. Although he initially acknowledges the existence of cultural pluralism—cultural diversity not only between Indian and Mestizo groups but also among the many Indian groups—his analysis of dualism is almost completely in structural terms, concentrating on the political, economic, and social relationships between a dominant Mestizo metropolis and an exploited Indian hinterland. He differs from other proponents of dualism in his rigorous application of the concept, restricting its occurrence to a prescribed number of "refuge regions," rather than to an entire country or all Indians.

The "refuge region" is viewed as a biotic community inhabited by two groups and composed of an intrusive center (the provincial capital) and its dependent villages and hamlets. One group, the *Ladino*[16] representatives of the national culture, has exclusive occupation of the metropolis and control of the hinterland, which has been since pre-conquest times the domain of the Indians and their defensive terrain for the conservation of archaic life forms. Both Ladinos and Indians retain their societal identities because of the limited (but necessary) number of structured communication channels; although they live in socioeconomic symbiosis, it is a hostile symbiosis, characteristically tense and discriminatory, burdened by colonialistic, interethnic relations of superiority-inferiority. Just as intergroup relations are not geared to the modern society, so too, technological innovations have lagged behind with minimal alteration of the original habitat. If human relationships are hostile, the "refuge region," itself, is equally hostile—physically inhospitable, isolated, geographically marginal, and undesirable in the opinion of the Ladinos (1967:11-41).

In addition to its physiographical marginality, the "refuge region" is further described as an underdeveloped pocket of an industralized nation. The regional economy in its totality, the interaction of Indian and Ladino economies, is considered a backward colonialistic remnant, and more precisely, an impediment to national modernization. Indian and Ladino economies are perceived as two distinct systems, each uniquely organized and differently oriented. In reality, neither system conforms exactly to the model as each has been modified through constant contact with the other, yet never to the point of obscuring the oppositions: subsistence versus capitalistic, primitive versus industrial, exchange versus money, prestige versus impersonal market, and emotional versus rational. The indigenous economy, while highly autonomous, is a dependent economy,[17] but the extent of market relationships with the local Ladino economy varies in accordance with the degree of acculturation (1967:110-127).

The one explicit conclusion that may be culled from these interpretations is the prevalence of social and economic inequities and the reality, palpable and undeniable, of the impoverishment of many Mexicans. Yet rather than clarifying the obvious, these models often obscure the situation because they are constructed on the basis of assumptions that are simply not valid; they then lose their significance and relevance as a result of the often subtle contradictions that are involved in their formulation. The basic assumption is that an Indian group exists in Mexico. Clearly there are Indians in Mexico and to deny their existence would be absurd. What is reprehensible, however, is the manner in which Indians are referred to the public by Mexican speakers; their analyses of dualism and pluralism ultimately depend upon the conceptualization of Indians as a discrete society. Yet, the identification of Indians, what is Indian and who are Indians, has been one of the major themes in Mexican anthropology for the past fifty years. The controversy has lost its vitality, but has by no means been resolved. The Indiàn population has been demarcated in relation to other groups by a potpourri of cultural indicators, social-racial factors, and structural situational positions. Yet "Indian" continues to be a variable concept, depending on the emphasis given to any one combination of variables.

An inevitable consequence of the "Indian society" hypothesis is the skewed portrayal of Indians that has little bearing on empirical reality. Although cultural heterogeneity among Indian groups is acknowledged and oblique references are made to different stages of acculturation (Aguirre Beltrán 1967:111; González-Casanova 1969:134), this diversity is thereafter ignored and Indian groups are treated not only as cultural equivalents, but also as sharers of the same structural position in relation to non-Indians. This is a static approach that draws upon the model of the closed corporate community: Indians who no longer conform to the ideal type are classified as non-Indians and no allowance is made either for individual Indians or for Indian communities that are undergoing a strong transitional process, although at present they may still be identified as Indian. Even in the refuge regions, the special focus of proponents of dualism, Indians are not immune to this process.

The Indian society has then been singularly equated with the exploited, dominated society, while its "marginal" position within the national context has been approached almost completely as an "indigenous problem." The innate conservatism of the Indian community–its tendency to preserve traditional forms–is viewed as an impediment to national integration. The Indians are dismissed as a mass that "produces little, consumes less, and contributes almost nothing to the progress of the country" (Ochoa 1970:1). González-Casanova has partially surmounted this tendency when he treats internal colonialism primarily as a structural phenomenon in which various groups, including the Indians, share the same subordinate structural position in relation to certain privileged groups in the total society (1968:480). Yet his thesis is greatly weakened by its inherent contradictions; despite the propensity for a structural analysis, he wavers between defining internal colonialism on the basis of social structural relationships among groups and on the basis of cultural distinctions between Indians and non-Indians. He opts for the second in his emphasis on the Indian' magico-religious culture, prestige economy, aggressiveness, traditionalism and conformism (1969:135-139).

In the duality between Indian and Mestizo or Ladino societies, the Indian society symbolizes rurality, underdevelopment, and subsistence agriculture, while the non-Indians are identified with urbanism, industrialization and modern capitalism. This situation is usually explained by invoking colonialism–the persistence of obsolete, feudal-like relationships on the regional level. Apart from Indian conservatism, it is the local Mestizos, particularly the provincial elite who are held responsible for the lack of dynamism in the Indian sector. Rather than seeking an explanation at higher levels, the local Mestizos are seen as the most persistent and insidious exploiters, notably in their monopolization of the regional economy.

While accepting the existence of economic and other forms of repression on the regional level, one cannot conclude that a monocultural and decapitalized "Indian economy" is solely the consequence of Mestizo machinations. As Stavenhagen has emphasized, internal regional relationships lose their rigidity when analyzed from a more inclusive perspective:

> In the more underdeveloped regions of the country which have been called its "internal colonies," the oppositions and contradictions between social classes at the local and regional level very often lose their importance as compared with the larger opposition represented by the subordination of the region as a whole to the dominant centers or "metropoli" of the country, that is, the large cities and the areas of rapid economic growth [1970a:267].

One must also acknowledge the more subtle existence of "institutionalized" discrimination at the national level, a pernicious indifference that has revealed itself in a total disinterest in the regional development of areas inhabited predominantly by Indians. It is only reasonable to expect that a locally based elite would fulfill essential functions and perform numerous services that a revolutionary government had promised but rarely delivered.

Most theoreticians have drawn heavily on field data from southern Mexico for the construction of models of both Indian-Mestizo relations and Indian society. A series of interrelated variables have been extrapolated and presented as characteristic of and peculiar to Indian society in general, although they actually refer to the highland communities of Oaxaca and Chiapas. In these areas, the Indian community or ethnic group is coincident with the municipality, while the Ladino minority is concentrated in dispersed provincial cities. Since the Revolution, these regions, at the perimeters of the nation, have been partially integrated into the national structure in terms of communications, commerce, and services. Of course the provincial city is the prime recipient of nation-level action, therefore accentuating the decapitalization of the rural communities, which are invariably Indian in these regions.

All the "dichotomy" models have some relevance for these highland areas, but empirical reality is not so facile that they can accurately be applied to Mexico, Indians or Mestizos. Examples exist of Mestizos who have retained a community-based isolation and a subsistence-oriented economy; they have similar structural relationships with neighboring ranchers as the Indians of Chiapas have with the Ladino elite (Taylor 1933). Along the Mayo River, Mayo Indians and non-indigenous *Yoris* live in villages dispersed throughout the rural area; continued intermarriage has resulted in a shallow semblance of former group cohesion (Erasmus 1967). Many Indian groups of central Mexico consider themselves nationals, wear no distinguishing costume, speak and understand only Spanish, and have virtually abandoned the so-called "prestige economy." These people continue to be identified as Nahuatl or Tarascan because they originate from a village that was at one time an Indian village or because they are recently descended from speakers of Indian languages. In the state of Mexico, Otomíes, Matlatzincas and Mazahuas live in close proximity with Mestizos, sometimes in the same municipality or community; they are often indistinguishable from one another. Despite some cultural diversity among these groups, they share a broad cultural base, participate in the same economic system, and are equally subordinate to other segments of the wider society.

Let us consider the municipality of San Felipe. Before the Revolution, Mexico was steadily progressing toward fulfilling the essential requirements of a dual economy society,

> a trend toward fixed (or presumed fixed) technical coefficients of production in more and more capital-intensive enterprises on the one hand, and toward variable ones in more and more labor-intensive activities on the other, together with the peculiarly lopsided pattern of investment, productivity, and employment which flows from this steadily widening disparity [Geertz 1968:62].

A quagmire had been deliberately and consciously encouraged in which a privileged oligarchy identified with foreign capital and extractive industries entrenched itself while the multitudes not only did not participate but were segregated under the "benevolent" guardianship of a rural plutocracy. In San Felipe, the capital-intensive sector was represented by an intrusive population of large landowners, the fortuitous beneficiaries of governmental policies which fostered the development of industries and secondarily stimulated market opportunities. They dominated and controlled the commercial sector, as well as the subsistence sector of their wards. At their best, they were interpolaters between the indigenous population and the national society of which they were a part; at their worst, they were interlopers who caused drastic permutations in the indigenous economy, stultifying it by maneuvering its most valuable components–land and labor–so that it not only failed to grow, but began to wither. These privileges were righteously defended, however prejudicial, since they were rooted in a legal caste system that placed the Indian completely outside of Mexican society and treated him as an inferior and uniquely motivated being.

Since the Revolution, this system of colonial relationships has ceased to be universal. The hacendados, prime abettors of neo-colonialism, are no longer powers to be reckoned with. The Indian peon is no more a separate entity; he has been ideologically incorporated into Mexican society and takes his place as a peasant or ejidatario along with non-Indians who are also peasants or ejidatarios. The focus of economic activity has shifted from the estate to the town, and in this process, the town-based elite began to perform comparable but not necessarily the same functions as its landowning predecessors.

These historical events clarify yet do not entirely explain the present conditions of San Felipe. The poverty cited by San Felipeños and its lagging development compared with other regions are not the natural consequences of the continuation of colonial relationships between two discrete and hierarchically arranged societies with distinct economic systems based upon different rules and motivations. If any viable contrast exists, it is between the region and outside units rather than within the region. San Felipe exhibits a single, somewhat diversified regional economy, with differential participation by the various social segments. Although two subjectively determined social categories, "gente de razón" and "inditos" are recognized and employed by local inhabitants to distinguish Mestizos from Indians, they neither indicate bounded societies nor cohesive groups. The use of stereotypes obscures a number of social positions which do not conform precisely to one or the other. Similarly, there is no dichotomy between a self-sufficient, prestige oriented subsistence economy and a rationally oriented money economy, each pertaining to a particular society.

The two principal economic activities, maize production and zacatón exploitation, can neither be correlated with distinct ethnic groups nor different economic systems. Maize, commonly equated with subsistence agriculture, is both a staple crop and a commercial crop. Subsistence production and commercial production follow virtually the same procedures, nullifying the accepted dichotomies of traditional-modern and labor-intensive–capital-intensive. A single producer may variously be engaged in subsistence farming or subsistence-commercial farming depending on momentary conditions. Given a finite number of restrictions, he may be forced to produce primarily for family consumption; at other times, he may manipulate his crop in the market, with the intention of amassing capital. The exploitation of raíz de zacatón, regarded locally as an industry, bears scant relationship to a sector generally characterized as urban, dynamic, developed and heavily capitalized. The local industrial sector can be distinguished from the agricultural sector primarily by its export emphasis and its supra-familial productive unit. Raíz processing is an under-capitalized industry and will survive only in a decapitalized milieu.

The economic bipartition in San Felipe exists between the vast majority of San Felipeños of whatever social segment and a small number of Mestizo intermediaries who are vitally linked to extra-regional productive processes. When the estate system was finally emasculated, the former peon continued to do what he was most proficient at–planting corn. Yet he is no longer engaged in the type of subsistence agriculture that accompanied hacienda agriculture; the land tenure system is unique, distinct from past forms of landholding, and technological innovations have altered production methods and output. Most farmers, ostensibly involved in subsistence agriculture, are motivated to move their crop into the commercial market. With this orientation, they find themselves with a whole new series of problems, ranging from the financing to the marketing of their crops, which they cannot resolve independently. Since the only effectively implemented aspect of "integral agrarian reform" has been the wholesale distribution of land and San Felipe has usually been treated as a "badlands" by outside functionaries, the local intermediaries perform special and necessary roles. Of course they have taken advantage of the deficiencies of the agrarian program and clearly they have profited. The intermediary, because he is locally-based, rarely acts with disinterest. It is always the intermediary who has expanded most successfully in commercial endeavors and revived certain economic activities that were the underpinnings of the estate. Although the farmer's entry into the commercial sector was at first facilitated by the local elite, it was later restricted by the same elite, not necessarily intentionally, but often because of a biased view of economic priorities. Yet it is a distortion and gross oversimplification of a rural situation in which the government has followed a policy of denial to denounce the intermediaries as "despoilers," "human plagues," "swarms" and "enemies to be combated," and to blame them for hindering or obstructing agrarian reform. As for the farmer, he is confronted with these impediments–social, ecological and institutional–which constrain him to a precarious existence. Over 90% of the economically active population of San Felipe is employed in agricultural pursuits; the primary identification of this group, before nation, state, village, ethnic origin or social class, is as farmers. The dilemma of these farmers can no more be considered an "indigenous problem" as it can be considered a problem of the regional community blighting national dynamism.

The farmers of San Felipe reside predominantly in the rural zone, while non-farmers are concentrated in the town. But even in town, over 30% of the actively employed adults are farmers.[18] Agriculture is not an exclusive activity; farmers, through necessity, have secondary and tertiary occupations, and townsmen who would never identify themselves as farmers also farm. What is it that distinguishes the farmer, who receives higher cash returns from a secondary activity or devotes more time to that activity, from the non-farmer who dabbles in agriculture yet produces a larger crop than the farmer? Although agriculture is not a prestigious occupation to the townsman, it is positively valued as important, pleasant and honorable. Townsmen, especially those who farm as an avocation, have a healthy respect for farming and its problems. Various townsmen are intimately associated with farmers through the siphoning off of surplus produce, the distribution of requisite goods, and the performance of services, and have their own commercial interest in mind in their approbation of farming. They have a totally pecuniary attitude toward crops, perceive them as assets, and calculate in terms of capital gains. Sowing a crop is more than an occupation for the farmer. Cultivating the land connotes a common way of life, conditioned by specific attitudes toward crops which non-farmers do not have. Farmers of whatever class or ethnic identification tend to act and react consistently; they share basic techniques, are subject to similar ecological conditions, and have the same problems.[19] The farmer's principal crop is a life-giving force. Corn is food and money; it can be both consumed and sold. Corn is indispensable, while money is dispensable; corn is security, money is ephemeral. As one farmer noted, "in spite of the conditions we live in, here we have a milpa and corn; if I were in Mexico City and had no work, I could not eat." As long as the farmer has a land base that will permit him to renew his crop, he will not willingly abandon his burden. The one certainty that agriculture offers is the repetitive, recurrent nature of the farmer's performance. Just as he knows he will marry, bear many children, and die, the farmer will sow his milpa every year and hope to be rewarded with an adequate harvest. Ideally, his harvest will provide him with a full storehouse as well as a saleable surplus; frequently he is disappointed.

When the farmer says he is poor because the government does nothing to help him, he is not necessarily being fatalistic, but rather expressing a realistic assessment of his predicament. Farmers who came to maturity under the auspices of "Agrarian Reform" have been incessantly indoctrinated to have certain expectations. Ideologically, they were promised "liberty" and "independence" and guaranteed "social justice"; concretely, they were assured of land, water, credit, fertilizer, machinery, technical assistance, schools, roads, electricity, health and recreation centers, and bureaucratic institutions which would function in their interests. It was the state that transformed itself into a patron and created a waiting clientele, the "pequeño proprietario" (small-scale proprietor) and the "ejidatario." And it is the state that has programmed "integral agrarian reform" with its repertoire of infrastructures, while the client listens to ineffectual pronouncements which merely intensify his disillusion.

"Pequeño proprietario" and "ejidatario" are nearly synonymous in San Felipe. More than 75% of the farmers are "ejidatarios" (11,353), having usufruct rights to a plot of land, as well as ownership of their house plots. The remaining farmers reside in villages whose ejido applications are still pending and own at least their house plots. The area of the municipality is 74,619 hectares, of which 53,763 hectares correspond to the ejidos; yet only 17,047 hectares of ejido property and 5134 hectares of private property are cultivable. Noncultivable lands are divided among forests, pastures, totally unproductive terrain, and according to census statements, "uncultivated, but capable of being productive" fields. In actuality, there is no available land in the municipality. Land officially classified as "uncultivated," 28,889 hectares (IV Censos Agrícola, Ganadero y Ejidal 1960), is either deforested and unsuitable for lower altitude crops, violently eroded and studded with limestone outcroppings, or covered in zacatón bush.

Land distribution was virtually completed by the late forties although some additional expansions were later made; since then the population has more than doubled, rising from 38,781 to 87,173 inhabitants (VI, IX Censos Generales de Población). Farmers were originally donated plots which fell below the stipulated minimum,[20] and the plots have been reduced to even smaller proportions as the first ejidatarios divided them among their sons. The average ejido plot is now 2.7 hectares, while private property averages under 1 hectare. Ejido plots tend to be relatively intact, ranging from 1 to 2 hectares in size, but private property is extremely fragmented. Most farmers have accumulated land little by little in a haphazard manner and neighboring milpas rarely belong to the same person. Farmers are now reluctant to divide their fields into yet smaller units which cannot sustain a family. The second generation of ejidatarios managed to come to terms with an inadequate land base through technical applications that have doubled crop productivity per hectare. For those without

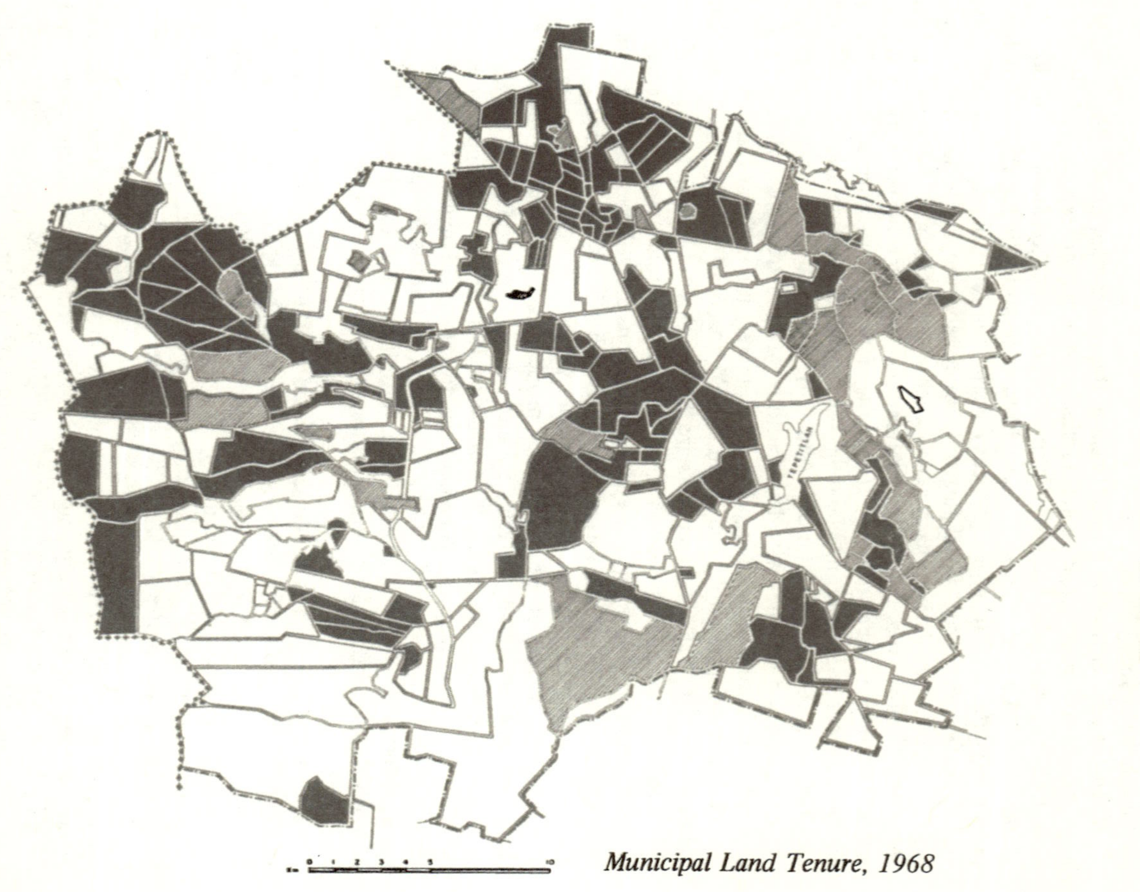

Municipal Land Tenure, 1968

ejido lands, there was still the possibility that pending grants would be approved. The remembrance of the hacienda was fresh and some land was better than none:

> . . . the subsistence munifundio, even though marginalized from the process of economic development, fulfills a function at the present historical moment: it contributes to fix the population on the land to provide minimum subsistence to those who otherwise would perhaps have none. As long as present incongruities in the use of the country's financial resources continue, and as long as the present economic system continues to favor the city over the countryside, the prosperous areas over the poor ones and the upper social strata over the low-income groups, minifundio subsistence agriculture will remain, and perhaps extend itself indefinitely [Stavenhagen 1970:257].

The third generation of ejidatarios, excepting lucky sons, find themselves without land and without memory; it is for these prospective farmers that the rhetoric of "integral agrarian reform" has a peculiarly hollow ring.

In 1936, the "Banco Nacional de Crédito Ejidal" was specifically created to subsidize ejidatarios, principally in the form of loans with crop as collateral. The bank presently has relations with "selected farmers" from the town of San Felipe. Most people are bitter about the bank; their first experience proved to be the last. The bank is remembered as an incorrigible bureaucratic maze which "didn't fulfill its part of the bargain." In the late forties, the bank provided the ejidatarios of three barrios with seed and fertilizer, and agreed to purchase their harvest. A disagreement soon arose over the arrangements for storing the maize. At that time there were no government granaries in the region and the bank did not want to receive the maize when they lacked convenient storage facilities. Of course, the bank refused to pay for the crop until it had received it. The ejidatarios, on the other hand, needed immediate cash and began to sell maize to local dealers. When the bank was ready to accept the crop, it had already been sold. The ejidatarios had also been given Canadian bred sheep which shortly began to die of worm disease. The bank ignored requests for a veterinarian, insisting that the barrios owed them money. The barrios still owe the bank money and the bank declines to do business with the ejidatarios. The ejidatarios, for their part, have little confidence in any programs emanating from the bank.

In 1939, the "Comité Nacional Regulador de Subsistencias" was established. Presently known as CONASUPO (Compañía Nacional de Subsistencia Populares), this federal institution sets standards of quality and regulates the value of maize by purchasing at a guaranteed price. The maize is then stored in the granaries of ANDSA (Almacenes Nacionales de Depósito), operated by the ejido bank.

The farmers of San Felipe dislike dealing with CONASUPO. Frequently, they are unable to. Since the rupture of relationships with the ejido bank, it is not unusual for a farmer to borrow seed and fertilizer from local merchants; before the harvest, they are already obligated to return the crop to the creditor. Even when this is not the case, farmers prefer the local businessman to the "red tape" of ANDSA. ANDSA accepts maize only during a five month period at the fixed price of 920 pesos per ton (1000 kilos). They receive maize by the ton only and the farmer is responsible for its delivery. It is often necessary to wait several days for the reception of one's crop; for those farmers who must transport their crops from the interior of the municipality to Atlacomulco, approximately ten miles from the town, the "wait" is an effective deterrent. Once attended to, the farmer is given a receipt and told to come back the next day after the maize has been weighed and valued. A discount will be subtracted from the fixed price, the exact amount depending on the quality of the maize, and careful consideration is taken of the percentage of humidity, impurities (other seeds, pebbles, dust, dirt), rotten, moldy or insect-damaged maize. When the farmer returns, the weighing may not have been completed and he will have to make another trip for his money and the final receipt.

CONASUPO does not acknowledge the selling practices of the local farmer. Rarely is the farmer capable of selling in units as large as a ton; he prefers to hoard his corn and sell it bit by bit as the season proceeds. He hopes he will receive a better price when corn is scarce, but then he finds that the price fluctuates, not to his advantage or even freely, but according to the manipulations of the black market.

CONASUPO is presently financing the construction of a federal granary in the municipality, which will be paid for by the farmers through a tax on each kilo of maize. The granary is expected to sell hybrid seed and fertilizer at cost, and to serve as a meeting place for farmers to discuss their problems. It is promoted as the eliminator of the intermediary. The local intermediaries are unhappy, but not unduly worried. They still count on the persuasive power of personal relationships and on the many related services they perform for the farmer. They may well be right. CONASUPO has become well known in the municipality since the opening of a price regulated general store two years ago. Although it sells small quantities of grain, farmers prefer the likeable corn merchant to the sterile turnstile and patronizing attitudes of CONASUPO employees.

The farmer is always confronted with a variety of uncertainties regarding his growing crop. If a frost falls unexpectedly early or late, the plant is likely to be burned; if a hail storm occurs when the ears are green, they may be lost; the roots may be attacked by spiders or the stems, leaves and ears by worms. No preoccupation is as crucial, however, as "the rains" which eclipse all other problems in importance. What at first appears to be a relevant issue is turned into an obsessive concern as farmers either lament the suddenness of a torrential storm or wait expectantly for showers which do not fall. To speak of too much rain or too little rain would be an inaccuracy. Rarely is there excessive rainfall, although a heavy storm can result in the decomposition of young plants or adversely affect the germination of recently planted seeds. Nor is the total amount of rainfall revealing; when farmers speak of the "lack of rain," they are not referring to inadequate precipitation, but to its irregularity and unpredictability.

In the tierra fría of San Felipe, two seasons are recognized by farmers—the dry season and the rainy season. The growth cycle of corn corresponds exactly with the full rainy season, characterized by frequent heavy showers from May until September. Ideally it will rain sporadically both before and after the full season, first to facilitate plowing and germination, and later to allow the corn to dry before harvesting it. When these conditions are not met, the results can be disastrous. In 1969, for example, it rained lightly in March and April while May and June were dry months; it did not start raining steadily until late August and

—photo by B. L. Margolies

breaking up the soil before sowing

—photo by B. L. Margolies

sowing maize

—photo by B. L. Margolies

cultivating the milpa in Palmillas

then it rained violently for six weeks. During the last part of September, an early frost fell. By late October, when the crop was harvested, farmers had lost from 60 to 75% of their expected yields. The following year, farmers were warier. Again it did not rain. Many farmers simply left their fields lie fallow; some planted despite their doubts that the growing season would not be long enough; if frost were to fall before the harvest they would again lose the crop. Others simply vacillated, waited too long, and finally broadcast their fields in barley. Barley is not a staple food, but serves admirably for fodder and as an ingredient in brick making. Barley does not require cultivation and these farmers left the municipality to look for temporary work in the city.

Almost all eventualities that jeopardize the corn crop can be controlled. Both insect pests and viral infections can be fought; hail is an infrequent threat, and the peril of frost could be avoided if corn were planted on schedule. Only "the rains" are seen as a capricious hazard. The "lack of rain" is the most distressing problem faced by farmers. In the incessant preoccupation with rain—why it has not arrived, when it will arrive, how much will fall—the farmer will comment, "if God succors us, the rains will come." This statement will be repeated by various farmers with a slightly different twist—"if God wishes," "if God helps us." Never is it said, "it is as God wishes," a comment reserved exclusively for post-mortem jeremiads. Just as in crises relating to birth and illness, the appeal for rain is to an accessible God. The farmers believe their hopes will not be in vain.

Farmers have few rituals devoted to the agricultural cycle. The "old customs," if respected at all, have been deemed the responsibility of women or children. Before sowing, some families still carry assorted seed to church for the

—photo by B. L. Margolies

the entire family works in the milpa

benediction. And after the harvest, just as their ancestral Mazahuas offered the fruits of the earth to the goddess *Madre Vieja* (Carrasco 1950:136), some farmers send the *diezmo*[21] to the priest. The only occasion when the farmer actively participates in ritual activities, is in the propitiation for rain. Farmers, on their own initiative, organize and pay for Masses held throughout the agricultural cycle. These Masses are generally planned by barrio neighbors or co-workers in the taller de raiz and draw large crowds despite their early morning occurrence. They are held in honor of *Nuestro Padre Jesús*, the titular patron of the town and its barrios, and famous throughout neighboring municipalities for his preternatural powers. In 1970, farmers waited uneasily through April in expectation of rain. By May, several farmers were noticeably disturbed and initiated collections for a Mass. The image of the patron was removed from the church and carried aloft by a procession to the barrio of Calvario. Mass was led by the priest in the barrio chapel and the image was then returned to the church. People proceeded to their normal activities, yet waited with anticipation. Late in the afternoon, the sky darkened, thunder roared, and a brief, swift, but heavy shower fell. The people said it was a miracle from "Nuestro Padre."

The farmer knows he cannot domesticate the rainfall, but he also realizes that the problem of "lack of rain" can be mollified. He has been told this by the government through ejido representatives; in fact, he has been promised this. Where before, he was merely resigned, now he is openly wrathful. "Lack of rain" and "lack of water" have been transformed into the specific complaint of "lack of irrigation." In 1964, the dam of Tepetitlán was inaugurated. This was a long awaited event and was touted as the salvation of the municipality. With a capacity of 22,000,000 cubic meters of water, Tepetitlán was ceremoniously

photo by B. L. Margolies

corn is harvested manually by work parties

delivered to the people in the name of agrarian reform. This honorary transfer was attended by the President of the Republic, the state governor, the secretary of Hydraulic Resources, cabinet members, and representatives of the "people." According to the inaugural speeches, the opening of the dam was viewed as an act of liberation:

> They are a people of difficult expression. Their introspective temperament prevents them from showing their true sentiments; they do not brim with ostensible manifestations, but know how to feel the most noble sentiments. I speak for the Mazahua Indians who express their deepest gratitude to you (President López Mateo).
>
> During long centuries of their existence, this ethnic group, whose ancestors were hunters of venison—as the Náhautl root of their name indicates—has lived in ignorance of its own history, and the knowledge that we have of them from the texts is laconic and sparse . . . .
>
> The Mazahuas, traditionally disdained by scholars, have consistently been ignored; these circumstances have been accentuated by their state of submissiveness and their subjection to frequent exploitation. The northern zone of the state of Mexico has been their principal locale, and they are the first inhabitants of the present municipalities of Ixtlahuaca, San Felipe del Progreso, Jocotitlán, Atlacomulco, Temascalcingo, and El Oro.
>
> Now the Mazahuas are being granted the greatest act of social justice since the agrarian distribution with the inauguration of the new dam of Tepetitlán, credited by the government of the republic to the tenacious and forceful determination of Alfredo del Mazo, esteemed collaborator in the task of bringing water to the people of Mexico.
>
> The fluid and contortive contour of the "dam of hopes" will irrigate the surface of the uncultivated valley, similar in the winter season to the steppe—desolate and grim. Through the miracle of water, this valley will be transformed into promising meadows to elevate its low economic level, to ameliorate its ancestral deficiencies. . . .
>
> You (President López Mateos) have left here, in the dams José Antonio Alzate and Tepetitlán the solid base for the agricultural development of this zone, depositing the seed of progress in these lands. That Ehecatl, our ancestral god of the winds, scatters the seeds to the four cardinal points, so that they germinate and multiply in promissory fruits.
>
> This day is one of liberation for the Mazahua Indians, and you, Mr. President of the Republic, are the author [Colín 1964].

At present, Tepetitlán irrigates several villages in the immediate vicinity as well as the ejidos of Palmillas and Jalpa which occupy a continuous area south of the town. What is the situation in other parts of the municipality? In the town and its adjacent barrios and villages, there are three primary sources of water: the dam of Obraje irrigates approximately 100 hectares of town ejido lands; the reservoir of La Cañada is closed one year and opened the next to flood the ejidos of both the town and La Cabecera; Embajomuy, with a capacity of 300,000 cubic meters, supplies the remaining ejido lands of the town, the private property of townsmen located near the ejido, as well as the residential sites of the barrios, La Cabecera and Tunal, and the villages, Jalpa and Obraje. The ejido of Tunal has a rudimentary irrigation system in which water is pumped from several ponds. In the interior of the municipality, however, conditions do not compare favorably. Here there are two sources of water—the numerous rivulets that flow into Tepetitlán, and scattered springs. The rivulets are dammed and overflow during the rainy season, while the springs are used principally for domestic purposes and tapped occasionally to irrigate pastoral lands.

Although 16% of cultivated lands is officially classified as *tierra de riego* (irrigated land) (IV Censos Agrícola, Ganadero y Ejidal 1960), this statistic glosses over the intermittent character of local irrigation systems. None of the irrigation works includes storage tanks and following a prolonged period of drought, water sources rapidly go dry. Then the seeming advantage that the valley town and barrios have over the interior is easily nullified. In 1969, for example, Embajomuy was opened and allowed to drain completely. It did not rain again and farmers were unable to irrigate during the cultivation. The next year, the water level was extremely low and the farmers held a raffle to select the users of its waters. Even when there is a heavy rain, water is lost because of the time-consuming task of closing the dam with staves.

The principle adhered to regarding water rights is one of spreading. Rather than a few farmers receiving a full share of water, a large number of farmers receive an insufficient amount. Farmers speak in terms of riegos–a half riego, a riego, two riegos or three riegos–to designate the number of times a field is irrigated. Each crop requires a minimal percentage of humidity, that is, X number of riegos, to reach healthy maturity. Farmers receive only a half riego for corn before sowing, a practice which is merely prejudicial to the crop. Of course, if it has been a dry year and he receives no riego (as in the case of those who lost the raffle), he may not plant on fields he has been accustomed to irrigate. A half riego, however, effectively eliminates the possibility of crop diversification. Wheat, for example, needs three to four riegos, one before sowing and the others throughout the winter months of cultivation. Wheat is planted almost exclusively by the ejidatarios who receive water from Tepetitlán; an insignificant amount is planted in the seasonally watered lands of the zacatón zone, moisture-retaining because of the loaminess of the soil. The calcium rich soils of the town provide ideal conditions for the growth of alfalfa, and several farmers have experimented successfully with small garden plots. But alfalfa requires even more riegos than wheat, and large-scale cultivation is precluded by the "lack of riego."

Despite the inauguration of Tepetitlán in 1964 and the panache with which it was christened, farmers were skeptical–but still ready to admit the possibility of irrigation. During the next three years, the municipal president devoted a disporportionate amount of his time to soliciting the Secretary of Hydraulic Resources for irrigation. When he left office, he sent a seething report to the governor, enumerating the municipal facts of impoverishment and concluding:

> Since taking office, I have repeatedly petitioned the federal government for the canalization of the Valley of San Felipe, so that it might benefit from the waters of Tepetitlán. Until now, I have not even received the consideration of an answer regarding the completion of the necessary studies.

He and his fellow San Felipeños did not realize that Tepetitlán and Alzate were constructed specifically for the purpose of generating hydroelectric power in the state of Michoacán. "If we wait for the dam of Tepetitlán, we will just be left waiting," is the expression of one but the sentiment of many.

Whereas the acasillados of the hacienda were deliberately restricted to domestic production by their patrons, contemporary farmers are determined to produce for both "consumption and sale." The agricultural cycle itself has not changed, but numerous technological innovations have been accepted in the interest of greater efficiency and higher productivity; these include the adaptation of metal tools and alternative instruments for sowing, more frequent tractor rentals, and the application of chemicals–insecticides, herbicides, and fertilizer.

Chemical fertilizer, applied sparingly in the forties, has been in general use for the last twenty years. Its rapid acceptance has been furthered by the scarcity of organic fertilizer and the poverty of the soil. Farmers do not need a soil analyst to tell them that the shallow topsoils and argillaceous deposit of San Felipe are of poor quality. They also prefer to "work" their parcels season after season and plant maize rather than rotating with barley, beans or peas. Every few years farmers do rotate or permit fallowing, but they can postpone this through the regular application of fertilizer. Although the manufacture of fertilizer is subsidized by the federal government, it is distributed by retail dealers; the farmer pays approximately 500 pesos ($40) to fertilize each hectare, but he feels that the heavy expense is justified by a larger "sale product."

Farming is a more costly proposition than ever before. When favorable conditions prevail, the farmer comes out ahead; when it does not rain, he not only loses part of his crop, but is unable to recoup his basic investment. For many aspects of financing, one can appeal to relatives. Relatives will lend work animals, seed, and sometimes land, if they are working out-of-town. Young men, even those with their own land, rarely own the necessary tools of the trade and are generously aided by fathers and older brothers. Relatives, however, cannot underwrite a farmer; they cannot buy one's fertilizer and they cannot market one's crop. For this, the farmer must rely on outsiders.

"Outsiders" refer, not to any official or governmental agency, but to the locally based Mestizo merchants, the *comerciantes*. "Comerciante" is a loosely applied term in San Felipe, precisely because it denotes a prestigious occupation. A comerciante may be the man with a vegetable stand in the weekly market or the owner of a tiny store or a door-to-door peddler of notions. The comerciante who establishes business relationships with farmers, however, is one of two types. He is either the owner of an impressive general store or he is a dealer, buying and selling both grain and animals. Several store owners are also dealers, and both types farm and are thoroughly cognizant of agrarian problems.

Several years ago, various merchants were conspicuous money-lenders. The professional money-lender, however, is considered a despicable figure, and has been involved in so many notorious tales that he has since gone underground. People still lend money at usurious rates but try not to do so as a constant practice. Usurers with reputations are avoided as farmers realize that they do not have to fulfill exorbitant conditions. Money-lending is still practiced in the interior, but often with unpredictable consequences for the practitioner. Recently, for example, an ejidatario from Santa Ana Nichi balked at the continued harassments of a local usurer, the widow of a prominent merchant. The village delegate ignored his appeals; finally he went to Don Ernesto who put his complaint into good Spanish:

> Desperately needing to buy fertilizer for my planting, I went to Señora C., one of my neighbors. She offered me a loan of 400 pesos ($32), telling me she would charge a monthly interest rate of ten percent. As the sowing was almost completed and I had to

apply fertilizer, I accepted her conditions—only that, in 1968 and 1969 I lost the harvests, first because of torrential rains and then because of prolonged dryness. I could not pay the señora back completely, although I have since given her 324 pesos ($27) in interest. On the 30th of January, I returned the 400 pesos, as noted in the receipt she gave me.

I ought to point out that when she lent me the money, I signed a receipt. When I asked for its return, she told me it had been lost.

On January 14, she arbitrarily went to my house and attempted to steal a filly. But my wife stopped her. Words were passed and she, the Señora C., threatened my wife with a 22 caliber pistol. Realizing that she couldn't take the filly, she left and went directly to my fields to remove a calf, which she still has and refuses to return, claiming that I owe her an additional 200 pesos ($16).

Since I consider the actions of this woman unjust, I am soliciting the authorities for her appearance before the judge—to exact the return of the calf and in addition, to explain the reason for charging this class of interest. According to what I have since been told, such interest is completely unjustified.

Aware that they are liable to be dragged into the district court, most merchants protect their commercial interests by providing financing without actually handling any money. This is accomplished by exchanging fertilizer for maize. The "merchants" buy fertilizer at wholesale prices in Mexico City. A portion is sold to other local retailers or directly to farmers. But it is far more profitable to lend fertilizer and contract for later payment in the form of newly harvested corn. Whatever the specifics of the transaction, the farmer usually returns twice the value of the fertilizer. While the cost of fertilizer is strictly linked to the national market, the price of corn varies locally from year to year. Let us say that it has been a season without disasters; the price of corn will first vary and then settle as the merchants reach agreement. In an average year, recently harvested corn ears will be valued at 45 cents per kilo. Fertilizer is lent at 650 pesos per ton. The farmer will return 650 pesos worth of corn at the rate of 45 cents per kilo, a total of 1444 kilos of ears. Yet if he had sold his dry corn, in the form of grain, to CONASUPO, allowing for an approximate weight loss of 30%, he would have received 92 cents per kilo for slightly more than 1000 kilos. The more usual contract, however, is to deal in *costales* rather than in kilos. A 50 kilo sack of fertilizer will be returned in the form of two costales of corn ears (140 kilos). The fertilizer is worth only 33 pesos, while each costal is valued at 31.50 pesos. If a farmer borrows a ton of fertilizer, he will often find himself returning 40 costales worth 1260 pesos at the official price.[22]

Even when the farmer does not borrow fertilizer, he is dependent on the middleman to market his crop. The local merchant is very obliging. Like CONASUPO, he also discounts for impurities, but he will buy all year long, ears or grain, large or small quantities. He will even relieve the farmer of transport, and he will weigh, evaluate, and pay for one's crop efficiently and without paperwork.

Every farming family knows who the important merchants are; as businessmen, there is a certain amount of rivalry between them. At times even their relatives can be seen accosting peasants in the streets, asking them to whom they are taking their corn, and reminding them that they will receive a good price if they change their minds. The merchant himself tends to rely on sound tactics to hold and enlarge his clientele. He will rent the necessary tools at a reasonable rate; he may be generous with drinks at the proper moment; he may cash a check or explain an official paper, purchase milk, eggs or cheese from a customer although he has no genuine need, or give away roughage or leftovers. He permits his customers to charge goods and will wait until after the harvest for a payment which may run into several thousand pesos. He genially accepts requests for godfathership and tries to present himself as an affable personality. In short, he wants to be thought of first when a client or potential client is ready to sell his corn.

The merchant has a perfect understanding of both the farmer's attitude toward corn and his selling habits; with this advantage, he not only manipulates the price of grain, but also controls all grain movement—out of the municipality and into the national market, and redistributions to the original sellers. The merchants first assess the price of grain on the national market and then adjust this figure intermittently according to local supply—the availability or scarcity of corn. Immediately after the harvest, they purchase corn at rates 10 to 15% below the official price. As long as CONASUPO remains open, the local price remains fairly stable, perhaps rising once or twice. After April, however, when CONASUPO closes, the price spurts steadily upward until it has more than doubled by seeding time. When the merchant sells corn, he is more autonomous; lacking outside competition, he sells grain at the price he judges the farmer can bear. In 1969, for example, merchants received corn at 80 to 85 cents a kilo; by January, the receiving price had risen to 94 cents. In April, it rose to 1.05 pesos and by the seeding period had reached 1.95 pesos. The merchant then resells the corn locally at 5 to 10 cents above his receiving rate. He, himself, will store the corn in his private granary. He may sell to CONASUPO just before it closes or he may wait until after April to transport it directly to the industrial sector of Mexico City, selling to feed processing plants.

Merchants know that the farmer is more interested in corn in his storehouse than money in his pocket, and that after April he will buy more grain than he will sell. The merchant therefore makes the majority of his purchases when there is an abundance of corn and the majority of his sales when corn is scarce. While he thinks in terms of money, the farmer calculates in reference to corn. What Beals has stated for the farmers of Cheran is equally pertinent for the farmers of San Felipe:

> The farmer does not count interest and wages; the measure of his effort is maize in the storehouse to feed his wife and children. It is useless to point out that he could earn enough wages for the same amount of labor to buy two or three times as much maize as he can produce, for he will not be convinced . . . the calculations made on the basis of our economic viewpoints are relatively valueless. Profits, interest, deprecation, and wages do not enter into the farmer's calculations (with the exception of a few large farmers). Rather would the typical farmer calculate that the maize obtained in this case would, with a family of not over five, feed the family for a year by exercising due care. If he had two pieces, each of a hectare or a little more in the area, he could count with some security on feeding his family [Beals 1946:66].

The farmer's grain supply is manipulated somewhat like a checking account. The principal deposit is made with the harvest after X amount is set aside for immediate conversion to cash. Weekly withdrawals are then made for the family's personal consumption, while sporadic withdrawals may be necessary for further conversions into cash. If it has been a good year, the farmer will still have some credit at the time of the next harvest deposit. But in a bad year, even if he does not convert corn, his account will empty rapidly and he will have to buy to keep it open. In order to buy, he may touch his savings—turkeys, pigs, milch cows or sheep. If he had previously contracted to sell his crop, he may find himself slowly going bankrupt as he loses his work animals or a piece of privately owned land.

The farmer does not plan on buying corn; consuming and selling are his aims. The farmer intends both to stock his storehouse and to sell at least half of his crop. With an average yearly consumption of seven to eight cargas for the family (1050-1200 kilos) and an average production rate exceeding one ton for each hectare, this goal is feasible under favorable conditions. The post-harvest sale is the major sale while remaining sales are spaced throughout the year and consist of small quantities. Although prices are lowest following the harvest, the farmer generally requires immediate cash. Normal conditions are less than favorable, however, and the farmer has two choices. He can either cover his consumption requirements by not selling and looking to outside sources for cash remuneration, or he can sell two or three cargas (300-450 kilos) and supplement his home stock later with minor purchases before sowing. During an unproductive year, the farmer may not be able to cover his consumption requirements and will begin a series of purchases shortly after the harvest. The exact consumption-sale-purchase pattern varies widely not only from year to year but from farmer to farmer. Because of the multiformity of soils, the inconstancy of rainfall, and the fallibility of rudimentary irrigation systems, production averages per hectare range from twenty to seventy costales within a given season. A farmer rarely exploits all of his fragmented parcels. His decision is contingent on momentary circumstances and while he voluntarily may allow a parcel to lie fallow, he is also faced with the possibility of forced fallowing. One year he may hold his own, while the following season finds him precariously attempting to live on a total harvest of several hundred kilos of corn. Where the farmer had expected to convert maize into money, he must now convert money into maize.

In times of scarcity, the farming family mobilizes its resources through a series of expedients, some of which are practiced on a regular basis and simply intensified, and others which are merely temporary measures, activated under duress.

Before the harvest, numerous families will economize by restricting consumption. Families will first stop eating; where previously they had eaten two or three meals, they will now sacrifice one; where previously one meal contained a meat or stew dish, other substitutes will be found. It is not unusual for a family to spend five months subsisting on household garden crops or wild greens. The house site, never more than six cuartillos, is bordered with maguey plants and fruit trees, and intercropped with broad beans, kidney beans, squash and corn. During a poor season, the family will rely heavily on garden produce, supplemented by gathered mushrooms, turnips, mallow, tuna, nopal shoots, and a variety of herbs such as *quelites* and *quintoniles*. With the exception of occasional trips to buy provisions—chiles, tomatoes, onions—market visits are sharply curtailed. Home products which had previously been consumed or utilized—milk, eggs, some pulque and sheepskins—will now be hawked in the

—photo by B. L. Margolies

spinning wool

market or from door to door. When the family needs a particular item, it will either postpone its purchase or devise a substitute; if wool had been spun to be sent to the weaver, the family will postpone a new blanket for another season; if a bowl breaks, concave maguey leaves serve admirably; should one's preferred fuel supply diminish, animal dung will be set aside and dried. Finally, those farmers with religious cargoes may simply suspend participation in the titular fiestas until they feel they can adequately endure the expense.

Children, once they have attained the age of fourteen, may be sent out of the municipality to earn three or four times the local salary. Their destination is, invariably, Mexico City. Girls easily find employment as servants at the rate of 300 to 400 pesos per month, while boys start the climb through the construction trades with a starting salary of 80 pesos a week. These children are expected to support themselves as well as contribute to the family coffers. Every farmer has at least one son or daughter working in the federal district. If he is fortunate, his child might even find a "patron" or "patroness" who takes more than a casual interest by becoming involved in family affairs. The farmer, himself, may leave the municipality and commute on a seasonal basis; he must devote approximately a month and a half to each hectare cultivated. Those who do not engage in a local secondary activity complete the first plowing in the fall, dry and sell some corn, wait for the passage of the high festive celebrations of January, and then spend the remainder of the dry season in the capital, returning in the spring to plant their fields.

Farmers also participate in independent activities or engage in secondary occupations. In the interior of the municipality, where local opportunities for wage employment are minimal, various villages have become known for their specialists–weavers, charcoal makers, firework makers, musicians, knitters–or their cultivation of fruit trees or potatoes (a crop that grows well in the high altitudes of the northern corridor of the municipality). Circumjacent to the town, two secondary occupations predominate, the practice of a skill learned in Mexico City such as bricklaying and carpentry or the running of a small-scale commercial enterprise. Several farmers have opened shops in their barrios. These stores are managed by family members and stocked with a small selection of comestibles, soft drinks, beer and pulque. Other farmers systematically raise hogs; hog raising requires an initial investment of several hundred pesos as well as continued input for balanced alimentation, but the farmer can earn a profit that will adequately cover his daily cash expenditures.

The most lucrative secondary activity, limited exclusively to a few families residing in or near the town, is the management of a permanent stall in the marketplace. These families deal exclusively in perishables, fruits and vegetables or fish, that are not sold in the general stores. Their stalls are run during the weekly *plaza* or full market, during special plazas accompanying religious or secular festivities, and between plazas, weekdays when the number of stalls dwindle to approximately a dozen.

Let us consider the Marcos family–Basilio, the patriarch, his wife, their three married sons and two married daughters. Basilio sells carp and *charales* (small dried fish), and operates three stalls, one for himself and his wife, and the others for his daughters. Each of his sons runs a fruit and vegetable stall. The brothers buy their merchandise in the wholesale markets of Mexico City and rent a truck

—photo by B. L. Margolies

an herbalist demonstrates medicinal herbs in the market

—photo by Graziano Gasparini

a petty vendor greets her compadre in the market

to transport their weekly purchases. Basilio, however, receives his fish from middlemen in Michoacán, ships it by rail, and depends on his sons to transport it from the station. Basilio's dried fish arrives prepared, but his carp must be processed before selling. He manages the dried fish stands with his daughters, while his wife and sons spend the day preparing the carp for the full plaza on Sunday. It must be cleaned, washed, salted down, roasted, cooled and packed. Basilio and his sons lower their prices during the full plaza when they compete with professional merchants, but they still average 600 pesos per week each, placing them among the wealthiest of farmers.

Of course other farmers participate in market activity, but few do so on the scale of the Marcos family. Some manage stands on a regular daily or weekly basis, specialize in candy and notions, and sell just enough merchandise so that they, themselves, can use public transport from Mexico City or Atlacomulco. Others invest mainly their time and labor, preparing coffee, stews, *tamales*, roasted corn, butter and cheese, *tacos* and *enchiladas*. During a poor harvest season, people who ordinarily would not sell arrive in the market, settle on the ground and spread their "wares" on a torn sack or worn shawl. These "wares" rarely require a cash investment and range from medicinal herbs to mountain greens to spiced, baked beef blood.

The majority of farming families enter the market as vendors tangentially. Regulars with small stalls who specialize in a particular comestible expect merely to subsidize their cash income; rarely can they compete with the professional merchant who travels the regional market route and floods the full plaza with a variety of comestibles transported in his own vehicle. Petty vendors enter the

—photo by B. L. Margolies

tortilla vendors

—photo by Graziano Gasparini

pottery vendors from San Juan de los Jarros

market when their corn is spent and do so simultaneously; they hope only to earn sufficient change for the purchase of a few provisions. Market officials have been extremely lax in the past, allowing the market to expand freely as long as the prospective vendor paid his tax and sat more or less in the proper section. The market activity moved with the seasons and was adaptive to the fluctuating buying power of the farmer. But in recent years, the new municipal president felt it was time to put the market in order and make sense out of a chaotic jumble. Stalls were rearranged, streets roped off, taxes were raised and vendors disconcerted. Changes supposedly made in the interest of bringing order to the marketplace had irrevocable repercussions for petty and small vendors. Petty vendors were effectively eliminated from participating in the market while the others weighed the advantages of selling. The pulque vendors, for example, were told they would be moved and the move would be accompanied by a tax rise (from 2 to 8 pesos). They were also told to pay 50 pesos each, although why, they did not know. Together they went to see the president to explain that they only made about 35 pesos during a full plaza, and now it practically was not worth the effort. They had been comfortably settled in the portals of a large house off the plaza; they were now being moved to a service road leading to the barrio of Tunal, in the direct rays of the sun where the pulque would spoil. They again went to the president and he now refused to see them. He let it be known that if the vendors felt it was no longer worth their while to sell pulque, then they could stay home.

When a farmer has not produced enough to feed his family and pay his expenditures, he has one more recourse: wage labor within the municipality. Of all forms of subsidiary employment, this alternative is the least attractive; the

—photo by B. L. Margolies

the husked corn is transported in henequen sacks

available opportunities fall into menial categories and offer small remuneration. The advantage of this type of employment is its flexibility which permits the farmer to occupy himself with his own priorities by a minor juggling of his schedule.

Only the very young and the aged work exclusively for others. Youths are employed as shepherds, household servants, shop helpers and loaders; they treat these first jobs as a learning experience, and once they have reached adolescence, they are off to Mexico City. The old or infirm may work as garbage collectors, street cleaners, municipal gardeners or laundresses.

Temporary employment is readily available throughout the agricultural season, with peak demands for large work parties occurring during sowing and harvesting. Townsmen who farm as an avocation and ranchers generally hire laborers for the span of the maize cycle. Farmers with sons or relatives in the city may also find themselves short of labor; they, too, are compelled to offer wages. Families are able to combine their own farming chores with wage labor obligations because of the staggering of planting schedules necessitated by soil differences. Agricultural wage labor is the one area in which the terminology of the hacienda has survived. Hired laborers are known as peons, while a group of peons constitute a cuadrilla. Cuadrillas are from the same village and readily find work by reporting to the town plaza on Monday mornings and contracting for a six-day, thirty-three-hour week. The corn huskers, whether men, women or children, earn a daily wage of 7 to 8 pesos; corn bearers have a more arduous task and average approximately 12 pesos. The captain is either selected by the milpa owner or chosen by the other members of the cuadrilla; he bears ultimate responsibility for the peons and receives a minimum salary of 12 pesos. The

—photo by B. L. Margolies

the taller–removing outer husks of raíz de zacatón

—photo by B. L. Margolies

washing raíz de zacatón in the taller

cuadrilla is left on its own in the milpa, but owners make frequent spot checks. Townspeople are especially diligent in this respect; they are convinced that mischief will transpire in their absence. Agricultural wage labor is brief and seasonal, a quick and unsatisfactory solution to the problem of ready cash. It is considered acceptable for women, children and grown landless sons; the mature farmer prefers to work in the taller.

The raíz de zacatón workshops still figure prominantly as a source of employment for farmers, although the industry itself has been on the decline. The first severe crisis, precipitated by land distribution and the conversion of zacatón fields into milpas, was stoked by World War II as European markets were cut off. Production plunged from 1,621,000 kilos in 1936 to 472,586 kilos a decade later. By the 1950s the East European market had been lost, and natural bristle brushes were largely replaced by synthetic products and electrical cleaning appliances. Presently, there is a small but steady domestic demand as well as a market in Germany, France and Switzerland. The industry has survived because raíz de zacatón is more economical and durable than synthetics; it can also be reprocessed and pulverized, utilized as a paint base or in the manufacture of canvas. Locally, employment in the industry has decreased by 75%. Not only is there less demand for workers, but the workers, themselves, prefer employment in the capital.

The control of the raíz industry, temporarily severed by these crises, has since reverted to its original monopolists. Although the Fuente family was unable to recover from the confiscation of Providencia, the Díaz de la Fuente branch continued to operate their taller in the town. With the death of Jesús Díaz de la

—photo by B. L. Margolies

talladora prepares raíz for final binding

Fuente, ownership of the taller passed to his five nephews, de la Fuente Díaz. They not only managed to open an annex, but accumulated several hundred hectares of prime zacatón land during the height of land distribution. The taller in San Felipe is part of a complex which includes more than twenty workshops and large ranches dispersed throughout the zacatón region of central Mexico. They control all raíz movement, buy from independent processors, and run the business from administrative offices in Mexico City. During the war, they suspended operations in the annex and later sold it to a group of former employees, all townsmen. After a brief power struggle in 1948, Don Zefarino, the leading merchant, bought his partners' shares. He and four other processors from the zacatón zone proper sell their finished products to the Díaz brothers. Another taller, producing brooms and brushes exclusively for the domestic market has opened recently; it is owned and operated by the López brothers, who learned the business under the tutelage of their father Don Ernesto and through a brief apprenticeship with the Díaz enterprise.

With the exception of the López brothers who have experimented with new varieties of brooms and mechanized manufacture, the industry has not altered since its inception in Providencia. Zacatón exploitation and raíz processing involve a series of manual operations that depend upon cheap labor drawn from the field. The raíz reaches the workshop via middlemen who buy from the farmers of the zacatón zone. The farmer cuts the foliage of the plant with a machete, loosens the earth with an iron-tipped stick, and carefully removes the raíz with a lever. The trunks of the plant are detached with a hoe and the clods of earth removed from the raíz. The raíz is superficially washed, pounded to detach the husks, and tied into bundles of five kilos. It is now ready for the middleman. Although the standard price is 3.50 pesos per kilo, the raíz can be discounted as much as 35% if it is dirty, humid or of poor quality. The middleman will try to obtain the finest raíz–elastic, soft, thin and even lengths–as his selling price of 3.7 pesos is also liable to discount.

The workshop is a simple structure, a large flagstone patio surrounded by galleries which shade the stone washing troughs and wooden work benches. Several enclosed rooms are reserved for offices, fumigating, and packing. Raíz is delivered to the workshop on Mondays, and the first half of the week is dedicated to its thorough cleaning. The crude washing process that had been carried out in the zacatón zone is repeated with care and excessive attention to details. The trunks are snipped with shears while earth and husks are picked out by hand. The bundles are then immersed in the trough and vigorously struck with a wooden pole. The worker next spreads the raíz on the floor; supporting himself by gripping the rim of the trough, he beats the bundle repeatedly with his bare feet. When all the husks are removed, he returns the bundle to the trough and weeds out discolored, stunted or kinky strands. The pile is untied, arranged into uneven lengths, and scattered across the courtyard and through the streets to dry. The raíz is then tied loosely into eighty-kilo bundles and bleached in sulphur furnaces. The clean raíz is again divided into five-kilo bundles and shuffled, mixing long with short strands. The worker gathers the bundle in his arms, places it upright on a stone plank, and sways rhythmically in a circular motion until the bottom of the bundle is perfectly even. He divides the bundle into standard piles of 300 grams, binds them with wire or henequin twine, and trims the bottom strands; the fagots are combed with a steel punch and revised for dark strands. After a second drying, the bundles are submitted to the receiving captain who inspects them, notes the number of kilos processed by the worker, and prepares them for a final fumigation. The fagots are now classified and labelled according to color, quality, and texture. They are pressed into packs of sixty kilos, packaged, tagged, and early the following week transported to the warehouses of Mexico City by company truck.

In the taller, there is a bipartite hierarchy—employees and *talladores* (laborers). This is a division that is occasionally bridged through compadrazgo, although various employees have refused requests of godfathership, claiming that they cannot maintain discipline when they have compadres among the workers. One employee noted, "You know how they are; turn your shoulder a little and they laugh." Yet this division can never be crossed; one starts either as an employee or as a tallador and works his way up within these categories. The fact that these occupational statuses are invariably correlated with social racial concepts serves as a reinforcement of ethnic lines and a quiet condonation of the inequities which exist in the industry.

TABLE OF ORGANIZATION

	General Administrator	
	Chief Cashier	
	Supervisor	
Employees	Secretary	
(Mestizo)	Auxiliary	Administrative Aide
	Assistant Cashier	
Talladores	Classifiers (5)	Patio Captains (2)
(Indian)	Other Laborers	

Employees are either townsmen or outsiders transferred from company workshops who have been with the owners for several years. They earn from 800 to 2000 pesos per month, and those at the top of the hierarcy are also entitled to profit sharing. Classifiers and patio captains are steadily employed talladores with senority and a daily salary of 25 pesos. The classifiers not only sort and label the processed raíz; they are also responsible for a variety of chores—cleaning, sweeping, wire cutting, and paring fruit trees. Captains are essentially vigilantes; they check the quality of the work and the orderliness of the workshop. The other talladores are transient workers from the barrios and villages within walking distance or a short bus ride from the town. There is a constant turnover as workers come and go freely. The processing cycle is a week's duration and workers are paid by the piece at the rate of 1.65 pesos for each finished kilo. If a full week is completed, one can average 150 pesos. Talladores with agricultural or ceremonial obligations are excused for part of the work week; they can skip weeks with impunity, enjoy their pulque breaks just as they do when they are working in their fields, and are permitted the use of the taller grounds for a lunch shared with their families.

The workshops continue to attract labor despite their low salaries, because the raíz cycle partially corresponds with the maize cycle. Raíz is processed primarily from January to June, while the farmer must remain in the muncipality from March through July to prepare and sow his fields. After the rainly season, newly sprouted raíz is difficult to work with because of excessive moisture. By January, however, the raíz has hardened to maturity, weighs more, and is less bulky. Brute raíz now arrives in the taller at the rate of thirty to forty tons a month, compared to ten tons following the rainy season. In December, an average of sixty workers are employed in the town workshops, but by May, the figure jumps to more than 300. May is both a quiet month of the agricultural cycle and a time of intense scarcity. It is in May that farmers must convert money into corn; the taller is the only steady alternative that they have.

Workers are protected by the "Ley Federal de Trabajo," which stipulates employment conditions for women and children, working hours, and minimum salaries. The minimum salary "shall be sufficient to satisfy the normal necessities of a family head in the material, social, and cultural order and provide for the obligatory education of his children" (1970:4). Minimum salaries are determined by the National Commission of Minimum Salaries on the recommendation of a regional committee composed of an equal representation of workers and employees.

In San Felipe, the employment of minors is explained as "helping father," social security benefits and overtime are absent, those working the stipulated eight hours earn far below the minimal salary, while others who obtain the minimal salary must invest double the legal workday. Although workers realize that they earn a higher salary in Mexico City, they do not know what the minimum salaries are for their region. (17 pesos in agriculture and 22.50 pesos in industry). The Commission publishes a booklet, "Minimum Salaries," for the purpose of disseminating this information to employees, employers, and the general public. Governmental officials are admonished to inform and orient the public, and protect legal guarantees by sanctioning violaters. But in reality, the Commission expects the minimum salaries to be taken as a guideline and has no expectation that they will be complied with.

The townsmen who figure prominently in the regional commission often have an unrealistic assessment of the farmer's earning power. The farmer is blamed for his poverty; the farmer's laziness, not the reality of a short agricultural calendar and the lack of local opportunities, is perceived as the cause of his underemployment. Townsmen do not recognize that the average farmer never possesses more than several hundred pesos in cash and contend that the "typical peasant" earns nearly 5000 pesos annually–720 pesos for three months as a peon, 2100 for several months as a laborer in Mexico City, and 2000 pesos for his crop. When the townsmen presented their report to the regional commission, they recommended that the minimum salary should not be raised; a raise would be merely detrimental to the peasant since merchants would automatically increase their prices. At the same time, it was implied that the peasant rarely worked a full eight-hour day and a raise was not warranted. They did, however, assess the situation correctly by maintaining that a token raise in the minimum salary would be ineffectual in altering the economic indigence of the municipality.

The farmer is unaware of concepts of modernization, but he is concerned with the economic security he could attain through increased productivity. The modern farmer is not simply a subsistence agriculturalist with a desultory urge to engage in cash cropping. Confrontation with a multitude of constraints—an insufficient land base for a mushrooming population, unproductive soils, constant hazards which could be eliminated only through large-scale investments and a political policy of superficial interest—functions to stymie the farmer's attempts to find solutions at the same time that it leaves him humiliated by unfulfilled expectations. References to peasant traditionalism, conservatism, leveling mechanisms, and forced expenditures, should therefore be made with utmost care, for they often serve inadvertently to stigmatize. Is it not presumptuous to assume that "It is the social and cultural context of economic operations which keeps the forms of Indian economic organization more or less distinct from modernity" (Nash 1967:101). Just as it is time to revise our concepts of "Indian" and what constitutes a distinct Indian economy, a reevaluation of small-scale farming is necessary with recognition of institutional impediments that prevent the farmer, be he Indian or Mestizo peasant, or struggling rancher, from participating more than marginally in the national economy.

5

PETITIONERS AND PARISHIONERS

The municipality is a school of democracy and an ample opportunity for political participation. Economic activity and simple living together do not suffice for complete incorporation into the destiny of a community. Only a full and conscious political life gives real meaning to personal endeavors and makes us coparticipants in the highest values of our nation.
—Luis Echeverría [1971]

The "free municipality" as a concept of local self-government is a creation of the post-revolutionary federation. Its attributes and functions are clearly stated in the Constitution of 1917; it was intended to exemplify "the most genuine expression of Mexican democracy" (Colín 1949:97). The municipality had existed previously and was conceived as a natural economic and social unit, represented by an *ayuntamiento* (council) acting in the interests of the community. But the municipality tottered into meaninglessness under the vicissitudes of the constitutional regimes, and with the *porfiriato*, it bowed to the central units and the discretion of "political bosses." Locally, the titular officials pandered to the hacendados.

The free municipality would be autonomous, liberated from outside domination and inside submission. It was instituted to rectify a situation in which the municipality had been a tributary of a state government that made local decisions and appointed local officials. "Autonomy" as it finally evolved was a compromise concept, yet the model of the free municipality was surprisingly antithetical to its predecessors. It is the smallest administrative unit in the juridical hierarchy with no intervening authorities between it and the state.[23] It is governed by an ayuntamiento chosen through direct popular election. All literate adults who have resided in the municipality for at least two years are eligible for election. The ayuntamiento is responsible for enforcing national and state constitutions, and has some leeway in interpreting municipal laws. The ayuntamiento is free to administer its own finances, but the source of funds is determined by the state upon an analysis of municipal necessities.

Despite the optimistic legitimization of the free municipality, it is more and more spurned as a mockery of grass-roots democracy:

> The free municipality postulated by the Constitution has dissolved into an inefficacious myth, or more to the point, a pretext for demagoguery . . . the local legislatures do not look at the necessities of the municipality, but at political interests and they consider perorations before municipal services . . . . The ayuntamientos, theoretically free, are enslaved by a penury which inhibits them from discharging their obligations unless they obtain loans granted in exchange for subjugation [Salazar 1969:4].

The municipality, rather than functioning autonomously, is manipulated, while its freedom has been distorted by outside restrictions. The fundamental premises of municipal government—the right to elect one's representatives and the management of adequate funds—have been forcibly abnegated, designated as the domain of the federation and the omnipotent revolutionary party. Those who participate in local government merely retain the illusion of participation and are relegated to the level of formal petitioners.

Although the concept of the free municipality may have been promulgated in 1917, the local government of San Felipe was controlled from higher levels through party officials and on the inside, coerced by a loaded pistol. Throughout the 1930s the inevitable consequence of the increased momentum of land distribution was a more flagrant violence instigated by a small number of prominent peasants. The obvious means of curbing their activities was by placing them in positions of legitimate authority. This imposition came from the PNR[24] and in 1937 the first puppet president took local office. A resident of Tunal, a former overseer in the taller de raíz, Severiano López was neither the choice of the townspeople nor of the peasant loyalists. Severiano had been selected in place of the "people's" candidate. He held office less than a year when the expected crisis exploded openly in the town. Apparently Severiano and several other men were swigging liquor in the main cantina when Carlos, the rejected candidate, dropped in. Carlos still had designs on the presidency and felt he had been the rightful candidate. Calm reigned despite the tension and then the discussion became heated. Pistols were drawn, men began to fire indiscriminately. Francisco Téllez, a prominent townsman, former secretary of the ayuntamiento, and chief of the Receptoría de Rentas began to exchange bullets with his nephew Carlos. Francisco died instantly while Carlos stood by dazed, only to be cut down by Severiano. One of Carlos's cohort fled from the store and hid behind the largest tree in the plaza. He, too, failed to escape and later died of wounds; in the confusion witnesses could not identify his assassin. Nobody was imprisoned, nothing was said, and Severiano continued as president. He had an arrogant spirit and was now extraordinarily confident. He wanted to govern independently and increasingly opposed state officials. "Justice" came several months later. One morning, Severiano was out riding with state surveyors and was felled by a distant bullet. The townspeople surmised that the surveyors were merely a subterfuge to lure him away from town limits, where he was dealt with by the governor's henchmen. Severiano was followed by Mateo, also a ruthless killer. But Mateo behaved discreetly and carried out his duties like a gentleman, to the satisfaction of both the state and the municipality. He, in turn, was followed by Macario, another peasant leader; while there were still scattered tradegies during his term, they were not as blatant as previous bloodbaths. As land distribution neared completion, violence was aborted, and the imposition of atypical candidates in a period of momentary and special circumstances abruptly ended. In 1943, Don Ernesto was unanimously elected municipal president, unanimous because his father had been an illustrious regional politician and he, himself, was respected and admired throughout the municipality. Since his term, nine other municipal presidents have held office; none has been elected directly, and perhaps three have captured the support of the local people. When the violence that served as a pretext for the imposition of municipal officials abated, the juggling of local elections continued to be the subtle mechanism for curtailing the autonomy of the municipality.

Every third year, with the occurrence of municipal elections, politics is embraced as the all-consuming issue. Politicking takes place under the umbrella of PRI; there are no opposition candidates, there is no campaigning and there are no platforms. The elections are a signal for the release of pent-up energies, a brief interregnum for discussion, dissection, manipulation, and total devotion to the kaleidoscopic events which might culminate in the success of the town's candidate. Although elections are for the ayuntamiento, the star is the municipal president.[25] He is not only the supreme local authority; he also bears an extremely personal relationship with his constituents, that is, unless there is sympathy between them, he will accomplish nothing. The election is a contest between personalities rather than a contest between issues. Everybody is intimately aware of the municipality's principal problems and each potential candidate promises to solve them, although his order of attack may differ.

The municipal president should be a man of intelligence, with "preparation" (a combination of education and practical experience) and a genuine interest in local problems. He should be economically comfortable and should place public interest before private concern. Previous political experience is unimportant. As long as he is untainted by personal scandal and knows how to deal jovially and frankly with different types of people, he is eminently suitable. Naturally he should be a member of the community; only if he has lived municipal problems will he be sufficiently induced to solve them. It is felt that if he is conferred an honor only one out of 90,000 municipal residents can have, then he is absolutely obligated and responsible to his constituents. A clear statement of the qualities a municipal president should embody was made by one townsman:

> Certainly the municipal president who is going to be effective must project the concern he feels for his own people. An individual who has the interest to serve–this is what we need–a person who has the desire for his people to improve, not only and exclusively with words, no, but with deeds. As for his personal circumstances, ideally, he should be a person who is prepared and he should enter office without economic problems. The municipal presidency is an honorific position. One can accept gratuities or a sort of salary, not as municipal president, but as judge of the civil register. He receives a minor sum for official expenses. He can also charge a certain amount for civil marriages, for example, and after remitting x sum to the municipal treasury, the rest is a retribution for his work. But in reality, his post is honorific. Therefore, if he holds an honorific post, he should not have economic problems. His principal ideal should be the benefit of his people. Second, political dexterity. Here I refer to his ability to control the people so that in the moment when he calls them, they respond with affection and sincerity, or if not this, at least in a way that they are with him. . . . There are persons who have absolutely no business in seeking the municipal presidency–those with no preparation, those who are irresponsible. Never! But unfortunately, political situations and situations of convenience often intervene.

The formal procedures pertaining to the election of municipal president are few and unfold in the course of a few weeks. To these must be added the secret meetings, the deliberate gossip, the hushed conversations in passing, and the strategies, maneuvers, and intrigues which contribute to the gusto of the elections. Political events officially begin with a meeting in the town hall, open to all residents of the municipality. This is attended by prominent townsmen, members of the ayuntamiento, prospective candidates, and their sponsors and claques. The prospective candidates introduce themselves and summarize their platforms. It is often cynically noted that whether it is Señor X, Y, or Z, he offers the work plan that all offer since the municipality "lacks everything." The six men who are nominated have a week until the convention to gather support and signatures. At the convention, three forerunners are choses as *precandidates.* Each must prepare a curriculum vitae and a letter of registration, and collect a minimum of 300 signatures. He must also formulate a *planilla*, a list of co-ayuntamiento members. He is helped by his clique, a temporary coterie composed of his unofficial sponsor and two or three other individuals who solicit signatures, drum up publicity and, in short, function effectively as public relations experts.

The period preceding registration in the PRI office of Toluca is a time for quiet machinations and incessant sounding of opinion. The precandidates are in the limelight and their names, personalities and characters are scrutinized, evaluated, reexamined, asserted and confirmed. One, of course, discusses the good points of his favorite precandidate and sometimes tries to glorify him, although never to the extreme of adulation. One is also critical of the others, but never to the point of slander or vindictiveness. One simply makes a statement that cannot be proven, by exaggerating a known weakness or making derogatory references to the precandidates' associates.

During the elections of 1969, two of the precandidates were residents of San Felipe town, had either held political office or committee membership, were steadily employed–one in the regional ejido bank and the other in the taller de raíz–had subsidiary incomes either from commerce or small-scale ranching, and were well known and generally respected. The third, although born in San Felipe, had been a long-time resident of Atlacomulco. He owned a sheep ranch in the municipality and was an unknown except in the vicinity of his ranch.

Juan B., the taller employee, was effusively commended by his supporters:

> Don Juan is the best of the three. There's not a bad thing about him. He's a diligent man and is completely devoted to his work. I don't think it's possible for anybody to find fault with him–he just doesn't have any defects . . . He isn't vicious. He has always been an honest man, 100 percent honest. Nobody can say he's a thief (an accusation made to emphasize his unsuitability) when he has worked constantly for forty-two years. They say he's a man advanced in years . . . . Don Juan will be sixty and possesses all of his faculties. . . . Surely it's often preferable that the leaders are older. Their decisions are more serious. Their behavior is more serious. They're more mature and won't commit the errors of a young man. Don Juan is the ideal person to lead here in the municipality. Apart from this, he has good intentions and he has great *arraigo*–they know him, they esteem him; he has the people's sympathy and he alone has it. And he has a thorough knowledge of the problems of the municipality. He was 2nd regidor in 1942, then 1st regidor in '47. In '54, he was juez conciliador. He knows, then, the needs of the people, he's immersed in their problems. Only those who understand our problems can solve them, and those who refuse to recognize our problems simply ignore them . . . Don Juan has the support of all the people, literally, all! He has the support of the young people, the greater part of the feminine sector, the popular sector, the raíz industry–all the *zacatoneros* support him–and the middle class here in town. He's known in the ranches and the humble class, the poor people, feel a great sympathy for him. Even the dogs know him. In short, he's highly regarded and whoever passes him on the streets inevitably salutes him.

Juan B.'s severest critic was the sponsor of another precandidate. He claimed that Don Juan was too old to serve, had little education and even less culture, and was of Indian origin—100% Indian—while his followers were also Indians and his friends, politicians with bad reputations. He also insisted that Don Juan owed the bank 80,000 pesos. Noé M., the other townsman, he dismissed as an alcoholic with an aggressive character, supported by old-time politicians who enjoyed little popularity in the municipality. Few of these comments were essentially accurate, but the critic did succeed in casting doubts on his targets' integrity. His own precandidate was described as a native of San Felipe, and extolled as a rancher who applied modern farming techniques, a model family man who did not drink, was financially well-off, and had the support of the most important people in the countryside. His lack of political experience was considered a virtue because he would be free of obligations to the politicians of the town.

Most people made realistic assessments of Juan B. and Noé M. and neither vilified them nor glorified their capabilities; they felt that Juan B. probably was not the perfect precandidate and knew that Noé M. had failed to capture the candidacy in previous elections. People who spoke up, however, were totally antagonistic toward Tomás O., whom they considered a die-hard and an introvert. But the anathema was situational rather than personal. Although Tomás did have a ranch in the municipality and was technically eligible for office in San Felipe, he had resided in Atlacomulco for fifteen years, was employed by the bank in Atlacomulco, and had married a girl from Atlacomulco. His qualifications and personality were not at stake; he was simply considered ineligible by San Felipeños who did not want their affairs manipulated by an outsider.

For many years there has been a definite animosity between the two towns. Atlacomulco is a district seat, which has sent local sons into the national political arena, including the illustrious diplomat Isidro Fabela and the present state governor. Atlacomulco has received what other towns believe to be disproportionate benefits because of its hierarchial connections. San Felipeños refer to natives of Atlacomulco as *mezoteros*—scavengers who burned maguey leaves because they could not afford carbon fuel—to assure themselves of the town's humble origins. And the mezoteros dub San Felipeños *zopilotes*—vultures which infested the town's barrancas, the dumps for festering carcasses. Yet despite the harmless competitiveness of these nicknames, San Felipeños have been especially angry since the construction of a paved road that forced them to detour through Atlacomulco to reach the state capital, when there was a perfectly adequate and repairable "colonial road" in the municipality which cut directly south to Ixtlahuaca and Toluca.[26] San Felipeños also feel the residents of Atlacomulco denigrate them, are unfriendly, absurdly proud, and convinced of their superiority. As open and receptive as they feel their town to be, the idea of a municipal president from Atlacomulco was absolutely insufferable.

Tomás O. was sponsored by one of the town doctors and Consuelo, rancher, restaurateur, boardinghouse owner and widow of a man who had served many years on the ayuntamiento. Consuelo sincerely admired Tomás and knew he was a serious boy who had worked his way up. She and her grown children were total zealots in their devotion to Tomás. She ignored the men who contended that a woman had no business mixing in politics and was even goaded by their criticism. She held private meetings with the doctor in his Atlacomulco office, away from preying eyes. She corralled several friends and relatives into attending an audience with the deputy of Atlacomulco. After a few awkward moments, he put the women at ease, listened to Consuelo's eulogy of Tomás while the others sat silently by, and assured them that he would do everything within his power to guarantee a favorable reception for Tomás.

Registration day shortly arrived and the precandidates, their sponsors, and representatives of the various sectors joined the thronging crowd outside the PRI office in Toluca. The competitors from San Felipe recognized each other, but did not speak. When it was Tomás's turn, he was summoned into the chambers of the general delegate of PRI. The doctor gave a short speech, pointed to his companions–his secretary, Consuelo, her son, one of Tomás's peons–and emphasized that Tomás had the support of all the sectors. The delegate nodded, received the registration papers, thanked the group, and accompanied them to the door. Consuelo unobtrusively withdrew and headed straight for the local newspaper office to make a statement:

> Diverse groups from the municipality of San Felipe del Progreso registered the precandidacy of señor Tomás O.V., as aspirant to the nomination by PRI for the municipal presidency.
>
> At this publication were señora María del Consuelo Real representing the feminine sector, señora Guadalupe Chávez, Doctor Joaquin Briz de la Fuente representing the professionals of the municipality, señor Efraín Granados Arriaga of the "Unión de Introductores de Granado y Tablajeros," and Austreberto Real for the young people.
>
> They said they registered this precandidacy with the support of more than 3000 members of the peasant and popular sectors [El Sol de Toluca 1969].

She then rejoined Tomás, the doctor, the deputy of Atlacomulco, and several other politicians from Atlacomulco and Toluca for a leisurely luncheon at a local restaurant. It was late in the afternoon when the group finally dispersed.

The formal announcement of the candidate was delayed a week, yet everyone seemed to know beforehand that Tomás had been nominated. Of course since he was the only candidate, there was no point in voting. The townspeople were incensed, refused to acknowledge Tomás's candidacy, and emphatically stated that they would not accept the decision. They were not alone; PRI was besieged with telegrams and telephone calls from over 100 municipalities: "The offices of PRI in Toluca and Naucalpan have been converted into conductors of the wrath and general dissatisfaction of the municipalities, roused by the imposition of candidates for municipal president" (El Heraldo de Toluca 1969:1).

It was only following the official announcement that public paroxysms became abusive. People claimed that they had the right to elect their own ayuntamiento; that the problem with San Felipe was the preponderance of municipal officials who accomplished nothing, were disliked, and were imposed on them. They then began to malign the municipal presidency, insinuating what a fine opportunity it was for padding one's pockets:

> The income of the municipality is quite large, but it is not proportionate to our problems. Many times various presidents have taken office without the initiative to do anything. They don't have the volition because the people don't speak out and say, "Mr. President, what has happened to the municipal funds; where are they?" Each time a president comes in, he's a cipher and there's no progress. What we need now is a good president who is responsible and knows the problems of the municipality, who works

and doesn't wait for money, a president who uses funds for our well-being and progress and knows how to influence Hydraulic Resources, the Secretary of Roads. . . . And it's not only his responsibility; the responsibility also falls to those who form the ayuntamiento as well as to a people that make demands.

And then the commentary became increasingly vehement as it centered on particular individuals:

> There has always existed *caciquismo* here. We have Don ________, Don ________ , and others who are the *amos* of the pueblo–those who command. Just because they have money or are more alert than all the Indians, they've been influential . . . Another cacique is Señor R.B.. This man lives in El Oro, but he has properties in the municipality. He has money, power, and support from the political acquaintances whom he's helped. He's influential in the villages and has pressured people to give signatures, signatures by force. He obligates them, he pays them . . . .
>
> The municipality is still forsaken and the people don't protest because they're not united. The ones who have wanted to govern have always been men with money. Between them there is social familiarity. The middle people, the poor people–they don't take them into consideration.
>
> Look at our actual president. He's well-off. He has money, property, and rents, but he hasn't shown any integrity. People have clearly seen that if 1500 pesos enter, these funds are not passed to the treasury; the robberies are openly committed. The people can't protest because nobody will stand up and confront him. The budget of the municipality probably exceeds a million pesos annually. Nevertheless, the president submits a budget of 350,000 pesos and we don't know exactly where the money has gone. He's sponsored projects, but he doesn't care if he leaves a huge deficit for the next president . . . .
>
> Tomás was nominated because others with money, property in the municipality, and political connections intervened. R. B. gave 50,000 pesos and Dr. ________ another 20,000 pesos. The present municipal president also helped with 20,000 or 30,000 pesos–either with his own money or with what he robbed from the presidency–because he doesn't want others to enter and discover the bad things he did; the incoming president will cover up his bad actions . . . .
>
> To obtain his signatures, Tomás and the deputy of Atlacomulco completed the list with names from Atlacomulco–which has absolutely nothing to do with what's going on here. It isn't legal. Today it appeared in the paper that Tomás O. has the support of 3000 people. And tomorrow ask anybody from the pueblo what sympathy they have for him. Nobody wants him in the pueblo and they don't want him by imposition. Tuesday is the day of the commission, the day when the Partido Revolucionario Institutional of Mexico supports a single candidate. An envoy from PRI will come here and say, "Señores, the party supports Fulano de Tal, the party supports Tomás O." No! It seems the pueblo has already begun to wake up–democratically. They no longer want impositions. Then what's going to happen is that we may have a calamity. What's going on isn't legal politics, but a *cochinada* (foul play).

The initial indignation was rapidly expended, however, as townspeople realized that accusations would lead nowhere. By now the various factions had united in their common bond against Atlacomulco. They chose a totally new precandidate to proffer as a replacement for Tomás and they obtained the support of a representative selection of the various sectors. Within a week, a caravan of twenty cars departed for Toluca to make a formal protest. They were received by a minor official of the PRI and left a written proposal. After a suspenseful wait of several days, the delegation repeated the visit, but went straight to the governor. They gave him a formal petition, asking rather than insisting, apologetic in tone, and reiterating loyalties to the party fold:

Several days before Tomás O.V., a native of this municipality and for the last fifteen years a resident of Atlacomulco, was declared candidate for the municipal presidency by the partido REVOLUCIONARIO INSTITUCIONAL, a large commission of neighbors from this locality was named to interview you. In your absence, it was not possible to personally deliver a proposal we had formulated. It was tendered to one of your employees.

The letter and object of our presence was to inform you personally of our disagreement with this selection, made by the general delegate of our state party with the marked intervention of the district deputy. They neither considered the sentiments of the people nor the illegality of the circumstances surrounding the designee. As we noted, this person has lived in Atlacomulco for fifteen years and precisely because of this absence, ignores the necessities of the peasant sector and the specific problems of the town. Of course we do not disavow the honorableness of this person, but in the present case consider that the candidacy for municipal president ought to fall to a person more intimately tied to the people and their needs.

The only persons selected to serve as delegates to the convention were exclusively those who held offices of municipal delegate, small proprietors of the hamlet La Ciénega, and workers of Tomás O.V. The work of the convention was done with these elements. Legitimate delegates, such as the peasant sector and the popular sector, were not allowed to enter the precinct. They were ready to block the nomination because of his lack of residence and his total ignorance of the necessities of the collectivity of our municipality in general. Before this arbitrariness and demonstrating one more time their discipline to our party, these people withdrew without committing any act of violence.

The only aim of this exposition is to do justice to a municipality that has been silent, but authentically PRIISTA and DISCIPLINED, and to avoid defrauding the expression you mentioned on so many occasions, 'the authorities will be elected by the will of the people and with the support of our *partido revolucionario institutional*,' and not by five or six opponents who lacking residency in this municipality and ignorant of our problems try to hinder our progress and create dissatisfaction in a people that will suffer the consequences unjustly.

Considering the above and remembering that a reproach is not being made to particular persons, but directly to the people in general, we come with all respect before you, Señor Prof. CARLOS HANK GONZALEZ to implore in a most attentive manner that the designation of Tomás O.V. be reconsidered. Certainly for our part, it is not our purpose to create problems, but to collaborate, work, and fortify ourselves–to improve our conditions of prosperity for the benefit of the collectivity–and as it's natural, seek progress and the tranquility of the municipality for the good and aggrandizement of our beloved state.

We are with you, Señor Governor, in every moment, which we demonstrated during your campaign and now, under your governorship, we are at your respectable commands, to procure the betterment of our municipality so that it will be consonant with its name of PROGRESS.

We have only one desire: THE WELL-BEING AND PROGRESS OF THE LAND THAT BORE US.

We declare to you, Señor Governor, our sincere adhesion and respect.

Two weeks passed before a final decision was handed down. The nomination would stand, although after a brief conference between the deputy, the sponsors of the rejected candidates, and the municipal representative of PRI, the plan was adjusted to permit the participation of more townspeople in the ayuntamiento. The elections had formally terminated and the townspeople reconciled themselves to the compromise. They were still loyal partisans at the same time that they were also frustrated contenders. They accepted the decision by emphasizing its temporary nature and skipping to the future—"the party won again, but just wait until the next time around." They would conform, superficially and briefly.

Several townspeople believed that if they were to accomplish anything in the town, it would have to be at their own initiative rather than at the half-hearted intervention of an outsider, "with the mentality and social attitudes of Atlacomulco." They were determined to form a club. The former sponsors of Noé M. and Juan B. made discrete inquiries and decided that the many positive responses warranted the calling of a formal meeting. A week after the new president had been definitely nominated, the first meeting was held. Only eighteen persons attended—the leading merchants, the priest, the primary school director, the disappointed precandidates, their sponsors, and the replacement candidate. The discussion revolved around a single theme: why had so few shown up when at least fifty people had expressed a spark of interest? Was the political crisis so fresh in people's minds that they did not want to become involved? Guillermo López spoke up. He had been active throughout the elections as Noé's principal supporter; he, himself, had been municipal president and was the son of one of the municipality's most revered ex-presidents. He opined that the "entire town" should be invited to the next session and that it was somewhat premature to complain that the club wasn't functioning:

> This club isn't a political thing, but a beneficial thing. We're going to have our youths involved in tournaments instead of drinking in the cantinas. We need a community center. The trouble with San Felipe is that there's no place to go except work and home. We need a center with a library, dance hall, theater, game room, and maybe a swimming pool. We'll make the petition for the land in accordance with the agrarian and ejido laws. We'll ask the government for construction materials, but the town will do the work. This will be a town project. The purpose of this organization is to build works. What's the matter here? It isn't a lack of cooperation, but inertia. Why haven't the members of the ayuntamiento come to the meeting? Why haven't the people come? They're all waiting to see what's accomplished. We need a publicized reunion. Politics is finished; its time for the town to unite.

Invitations would be reiterated; the next meeting would be convened promptly, and the organization and functions of the society would be written into the bylaws and carefully explained.

Not everyone was convinced by this pep talk. Between meetings, there was a good deal of amusement on the part of elder townspeople who felt they had the proper perspective. One woman conjectured:

> So they think they're going to make public works. You'll see what will happen. Nothing! To build public works, one needs money and this is a poor town; the families here are poor. Yes it's true they need such an association because the ayuntamientos are famous for accomplishing nothing. When was the last time a president accomplished something for this town.

She laughed as she commented, as though predicting the inevitable outcome.

The "entire town" was not invited to the next meeting, but forty-two of the fifty-two individuals that had been asked to attend appeared. The incoming ayuntamiento was conspicuously absent. Guillermo stated the object of the meeting:

Now we have dropped politics. We have the obligation to work together for the well-being of San Felipe. Our goals are for all of us. Let us work and see if it is possible. We need to take an active part so that San Felipe del Progreso lives up to its name.

He emphasized that the meeting was not merely a casual gathering, but would be run according to parliamentary procedure. The group would be legally registered as an association in the district capital and members would be obligated to abide by the statutes. Guillermo, the acting chairman, was easily elected president and was joined by a board of directors. The members were requested to contribute 10 pesos to the treasury; to solicit funds, and to participate not only in meetings, but also in civic acts and social affairs. The functions of the association were formulated:

(1) This association has been organized on the basis of unity, enthusiasm, and strength for the benefit of San Felipe del Progreso.

(2) This association solicits the collaboration of all those who seek the material, civil, moral, and spiritual progress of San Felipe.

(3) It is not identified with any institution, creed, or organization of whatever type.

It does not attempt to supplant obligations or responsibilities which specifically correspond to other institutions or organizations.

Its members are affiliated on the basis of good will, specified in these statutes.

Various club names were then bandied about, which played on the words "progress" and "unity." "Progreso de San Felipe Unificador. A.C." was preferred; it intimated that unity was an ongoing process. To conclude the formulation of the association, a motto was selected. Again suggestions ranged widely, but always within the same theme: "Progress is a minimum of promises and a maximum of realizations," "Unity and progress," "For the betterment of our small country." "Unity and work" was chosen as a succinct reflection of the realistic aspirations of the members.

During the first two months of the association's existence, the members met seven times. These meetings drew a substantial audience in addition to the formally enrolled members and were chaired briskly and efficiently. At times the discussion floundered over details which were trifling in their repetitiveness—reappointments necessitated by the absence of several members of the board, exhaustive explanations of bylaws which had not yet been duplicated and distributed, and analyses of the appropriate time for future sessions. Yet the group accepted subcommittee responsibilities and planned celebrations for the major national holidays, ran chess and dominos tournaments, organized basketball and volleyball teams, shamed neighbors into painting their houses and sweeping their sidewalks, and obtained the land for the proposed cultural center. This was all accomplished without the slightest dissension. People were disposed to be agreeable. Amicably inclined, they knew they were there for a common goal. Those who were prone to dissent, as in the case of the incoming ayuntamiento and their friends, were quietly absent. When they did comment, it was to denigrate the plans for a community center, which they felt would suit the old men who wanted a hangout to play dominos. But inside the meeting room and among the associates, there was perfect harmony. Anybody who wanted to speak was given the floor, discussions were allowed to run a natural course. The chairman would then summarize the main points, present a conclusion and ask, "are we all in agreement?" Almost imperceptibly the elders in the front row would nod their heads in unison and murmur one by one, "that's fine," "exactly," "clearly," "that is it." And the rest of the audience promptly followed with a chorus of "yes, yes" and "fine." The issue was settled.

And then the crisis came. People did not exactly dissent but they were obviously worried that they would be asked to perform duties of which they were incapable. The board proposed that for the first large project, the community center, they should petition the governor. They said that it was absolutely necessary to approach him as a legally notarized group. They began to push the matter of the notary, a problem which had been pending for several weeks. Again the president emphasized that each member of the association would be legally required to fulfill his responsibilities. Some members were wary and simply stated that they did not want to feel obligated to pay the quota and whatever other expenses the project might entail. Others plainly panicked, rose, and declared they had nothing and therefore could contribute nothing. Guillermo exhorted the audience to calm down and assured them that their economic participation would be minimal and certainly reasonable. What he wanted was their active participation and their moral support:

> You, tomorrow, have a friend, for example, and you tell him, 'we have an association in San Felipe; give us two shovels or five shovels or two wheelbarrows.' This is the labor, exactly, we want from our members. We're not talking about donating a set sum, because, in this case, knowing the economic potentialities of each member, surely it would be audacious to plan a project of this magnitude. What we're discussing, exactly, is work we can do with our friendships, people we can count on, friends who in reality can help us. Yes, they exist. I've had the chance to talk with a man, and I'll say his name–R. B. And he told me, 'As soon as necessary, come and see me. It will be a pleasure.' And as we have him, we have other friends–lawyers, doctors–people who can help us, people who have the necessary means. And therein lies our labor. It's not to contribute cents, ourselves, but to try and raise them so we can direct and project them to an end.
>
> . . . and if after taking the necessary steps, after registering properly, after going to the governor, we find we can't do it, then we'll look for something else within our capacity.

The members were given a chance to reconsider and to declare themselves if they wished to end their affiliation. No one stood up, but then no one was enthused. An indefinite acquiescence was reestablished with the plea that it would be "distressing" to walk out at this point. The members agreed that they would not leave capriciously; they would speak to the president privately and make any resignations in writing.

A month passed swiftly without a meeting; townspeople were occupied with Christmas festivities and the yearly religious rites honoring their patron saint. The next meeting was disappointing; attendance had dropped by more than 50 percent. Those present were dejected and tried to convince themselves that twenty functioning members were better than fifty apathetic chair warmers. The priest had earlier maintained a neutral role, but now he offered his advice. He observed that previous meetings had been lackluster because people wasted time in endless chatter. He prodded the group to move ahead, to be more agile, more spirited. He noted that he had recently seen a man who had left San Felipe twenty-five years before; this man had commented, "San Felipe is the same." He said the town would change only if principles were applied with enthusiasm. He consoled his listeners, "what difference does it make if we are only twenty; twenty people can change a town. You shouldn't be discouraged if only a handful showed up today. Sunday is a bad day anyway; everybody stays home on Sunday. If we are fewer, we'll just have to work harder."

Despite the priest's spiritual counsel, the meetings petered away. Guillermo contended that there was no point in convening for mere appearances; when he had something to report, he would hold a meeting. He did not want an "elephant" on his hands and promised to seek an immediate response from the governor. The board requested an audience with the governor, were received, and presented a written proposal. They claimed that they did not come as politicians, but as a municipality with problems–they were concerned with all social classes in the community and wished to promote a continuous dialogue among the different sectors. The governor liked the project and agreed to put an engineer at the town's disposal. The scheduled date came and passed, but the engineer did not appear. A second appointment was made; the incident was repeated.

Perhaps, the associates thought, if they cooperated with the new president, they might be able to coordinate their priorities. A discussion was held in the town hall and the problems of the municipality dissected. Yet the board was not satisfied with the meeting; the municipal president had been gauche and showed his ennui. They personally would never agree with his policies. Behind their annoyance was the knowledge that the incoming president refused to recognize the association as such. He resented its leaders who he felt were not only usurping his functions, but doing so outside the formal power structure. He doubted that their motivations were humanitarian, and believed their inclusion of the peasant sector was a simple political tactic. In many respects, his analysis of the situation was correct. The board was composed of political rivals who felt that they had lost the opportunity to govern themselves because of petty factionalism. If they could train the townspeople in formal associational procedures, in three years they would stand solidly behind one candidate–their candidate. If they were legally incorporated, the wrath of their opponents could not be vented on individuals; it would be diffused through a group that personified the town. They knew that during the interval they would have to cooperate if not collaborate with the ayuntamiento, but they accepted this for business reasons. Meanwhile, they would lay the groundwork for their own participation in local government. Their town would govern, rather than be governed. And then they became genuinely interested in a community center, but confronted much the same obstacles that ayuntamientos had been plagued with for years.

Since the institutionalization of the free municipality, it has evolved more as an administrative than a political unit. Its autonomy has been restricted by state priorities; it is the state government that determines both municipal laws and the proportion of municipal monies which may be retained. Yet the illusion of autonomy is maintained; the state rarely interferes in the daily administration of the locality. Only in emergencies such as an outbreak of violent deaths, does the state actively intervene; under normal circumstances, the muncipality is ignored.

The state government does not make specific provisions for the municipality (excepting campaign promises); the responsibility devolves on the municipal president who, as chief administrator, must petition the state. He is free to manage municipal funds as he sees fit, but rarely does he control a sum which will permit him to make even the most modest modifications.

The municipality has at its disposal revenues varying between 20,000 and 35,000 pesos per month. The largest revenues are returned during festive periods with the marked increase in commerce. The municipal budget represents only 25% of the municipality's income; an additional 25% is collected by the state government through a branch of the "Receptoría de Rentas"; the remainder is remitted to the federation by the local "Oficina Subaltera Federal de la Hacienda." Federal revenues derive primarily from taxes on business establishments, commercial sales, extractive industries (raíz de zacatón), and diesel engine vehicles. State income is obtained almost entirely from property taxes on houses and land (valued at more than 500 pesos), and graduated mercantile taxes. The municipality has the right to collect a large number of minor taxes specified in the "Municipal Law"; they are difficult to enforce and are frequently evaded. These funds enter the municipal treasury, but a 25% surcharge is automatically set aside for future transfer to the "Receptoría de Rentas." After normal administrative expenses have been met, the municipal treasury is left with a surplus averaging between 50 and 100 pesos per month.

The ayuntamiento, when confronted with a problem, cannot resolve it internally since the majority of revenues are allocated for maintenance. Municipal authorities are relegated to the position of suppliants. They must petition outside, in state and federal dependencies, and they must petition from within, among those who originally expressed concern. The problems of the municipality are multifarious. They range from education, communications, electrification and irrigation in the rural zone to an adequate water system, sewage systems and an indoor market in the town. These problems are all the more burdensome because the municipality is the largest in the state. Various villages in the northwestern portion of the municipality have repeatedly attempted to separate, but the municipal authorities were strong enough to block these movements. They knew the municipality would lose its principal source of public income–obligatory certification fees. Commercial relationships have declined with these villages as they look more and more to Ixtlahuaca and Toluca, but the ayuntamiento has preserved an arrogant pride in governing an ungovernable municipality.

Projects of whatever class are realized through the system of "cooperation." The initiative and a minimum of 33-1/3% of the cost must come from the municipality, while the state and federation equally underwrite the remainder in the form of construction materials, technical assistance and labor. Should a proposed project be out of vogue in state realms, as a private school or community center, the municipality will be forced to bear the brunt of the burden. Petitioning for a project is an onerous task which can keep the municipal president commuting between town and state capital while the regidores run the municipality. A municipal president with foresight will first try to lay a firm groundwork for future requests by inviting the state governor to visit the municipality. The governor will be regally welcomed, dined, and courted with expressions of fidelity, while the municipal president attempts to ferret out his pet interests. Once the president is aware that the governor has reserved funds for X project, he will then try to interest the village delegates, although they may have had another priority in mind. In most cases, however, it is the village that goes to the municipal president. The president keeps a running diary and a file of written requests in which the responsibility of the village is clearly delineated–what form of cooperation will be given, whether cash or volunteer labor and the amount. The president will then make his petition all together to coordinate the delivery of construction materials and visits of state technicians. He will make his petition directly to the governor at a semiweekly audience.

The governor is the ultimate state authority–the "boss"–and the only person who can authorize public projects. If he approves the project, the municipal president is informed by the general secretary to appear before the appropriate dependency–the state office of the Federal Commission of Electricity, Public Works, etc. The president's task will be facilitated if he has the proper connections, a network of contacts which can be mobilized on his behalf:

> When I was municipal president, I had friendships with quite a few people, such as the deputies of the Chamber of Deputies. I had relationships with several people connected with Gobernación–the private secretary of the governor, local deputies, federal deputies, certain relations with friends through whom I could reach the federation. Yes, there were friendships and certainly, it makes the task of the municipal president more effective. It's like everything else. One has to have relationships to do things; any other way, it's impossible. If you're alone, you walk alone. In the political field, we have to have relationships, the help of people who function inside organizations. It's very important because you can arrive more easily. You can speak more clearly, you can explain problems more exactly without so much protocol–*oye, mira, fíjate; pasa esto, esto, esto* (listen, look, this, this, and this is going on), help my people in such and such form. Then, these people are better connected and they can go to other contacts they have. Without a doubt, things function better this way.

Once authorization has been granted, the president must return to Toluca, accompanied by the commission that originally solicited the project. The delegation will be informed of the details of the project–its estimated cost and the respective contributions of the state and federation. They will be told when they can expect the materials and what aspects of construction their village will be responsible for. After matters have been clarified with the state, the commission must begin fund raising, a process which can often be prolonged for several years.

Fund raising is a tedious chore which requires knocking on doors and asking for a few pesos, reiterating the request a week later, and then spacing one's entreaties further apart in the attempt to keep those doors from slamming in one's face. As one tired fund raiser noted:

> If we want to dress well, it's going to cost us. If we want to travel, it will cost us. And certainly if we want to live better, the same. It's not that people don't want progress; they do, but they don't want to pay the price.

There are also other customary mechanisms for raising money, through dances, raffles or kermises. These events take place every few months and provide meager profits of 200 to 400 pesos. The most effective means remains the constant pestering of contributors; and attempts to institute other informal systems have proved futile. The priest, a relative newcomer in the community, left himself open to criticism by his drive to raise funds for church repairs. He held block meetings with the family heads to explain his need for approximately 120,000 pesos. He said he found the old system of contribution degrading both for himself and for the townspeople. He intended to set a deadline of six months, after which he would formally contract for the work. He would send a sheet around in which the family would specify the amount they could contribute. People, he believed, should not be obligated to declare themselves in public; these methods were for the old days. Only he and the chairman of the committee would revise the lists; this way, one would answer to God alone and not be forced to make invidious comparisons. But when the townspeople estimated that the sum would come to 800 pesos per family within a period of six months, they were scandalized and convinced that the priest's plan would never work. It seemed much more reasonable to hire contractors each time a small sum was available; people would feel that the project was progressing without costing an outrageous amount. So it will sometimes take more than ten years to raise funds because people frankly admit they are incapable of contributing. A successful collector must wait an appropriate interval for people's memories to fade and then renew the request at a propitious moment.

Although fund raising may proceed smoothly, a project is likely to be delayed when the promised government support is not forthcoming. The municipal president or the committee in charge of the project must again appeal to the governor, "respectfully" remind him the project has been authorized, but the materials have not yet arrived, wait for a response, and repeat the route among the different dependencies. The chairman of the private school committee once noted, "what one has to do, exactly, is ask and ask and ask. And I'm sure that many times, they (the government) must tire of the person who keeps asking." He, himself, had collected the respectable sum of 250,000 pesos since the project had been supported by many of the wealthiest townspeople. He then found that the government ignored his requests for more materials when the project neared completion after six years. He finally finished the school by "borrowing" materials from the proposed secondary school site. He hired peons to steal over early one morning and cart away the materials brick by brick. He does not condone his actions, but he is highly satisfied he was able to complete the school.

Once a public work has been completed, it requires maintenance and personnel; government funds are never dispensed for this purpose. Schools, for example, have received top priority both within government circles and among municipal residents. Villagers not only believe that education provides the basic skills with which one can defend oneself, but also realize that it is the only secure ladder out of the agricultural trap. Townsmen contend that "progress" and "civilization" are the products of a fundamental educative process, which provides not only basic knowledge, but "prepares" the masses by inculcating the general national "culture." In the field of education, then, the interests of the rural zone and the interests of the town have converged. Whereas in 1936 fifteen schools functioned in the municipality, by 1970 there were more than sixty rural schools (half primary schools of three grades), as well as two full primary schools and a secondary school in the town. Twenty villages received minimal aid from government sources and built their schools through sheer grit. Villagers made personal sacrifices in order to contribute funds and volunteered to work one or two days a week. The completed school stands as a symbol of progress, and villagers have even made provisions for the bathhouses, bathrooms and lights they hope one day to obtain. Schools built principally through state or federal subsidies are also supposed to be staffed by state or federal teachers. In the federal facilities, one-third of the twenty-five schools are not functioning because teachers have never been assigned; in the state system of twenty schools, twenty-four of the eighty-three instructors have been placed in the town's primary school. Villages which have constructed their schools through their own initiative are also obligated to subsidize the teachers. This burden can be sustained only under the most propitious circumstances and schools open and close frequently in response to the rhythm of the farming cycle.

Townsmen wanted a secondary school for the same reasons that villagers sacrifice for primary schools. San Felipeños' claims that they had to send their children away were indeed valid, but they also felt that a municipal seat, and certainly the seat of the largest municipality in the state, should have a secondary school. The completed school is a modern building with ten classrooms, impressively situated along the town's main entrance. But it has been plagued with problems, principally its inability to attract pupils. The townspeople who previously sent their children to outside schools continue to do so, maintaining that the school is understaffed and the facilities mediocre. And village children who manage to complete three years of primary school generally do not have the opportunity to continue their primary education in town. The full primary school graduates an average of 120 students annually, yet registration in the secondary school varies between thirty-five and sixty-five. Although the school is incorporated by the state government, the state is not obligated to provide either maintenance funds or grants for school materials when there are fewer than 300 pupils. The three full-time staff members, graduates of normal superior colleges, are paid by the state for six hours of instruction weekly. They and a part-time staff recruited from Atlacomulco are subsidized by the parents for additional instruction. The school does not have a library, teachers conduct science courses without a laboratory, and the secretary does not even have a typewriter. When the new director arrived, he was surprised to find two desks in the administration office; records were stuffed into desk drawers or filed haphazardly on the floor. He purchased secondhand furniture and built shelves, which he then stocked with his own books. All funds—whether for overtime, sports equipment or office supplies—are obtained from a tuition charge of 35 pesos monthly, and kermises and dances organized by the students. The school is barely solvent and most of the classrooms are now used by the overcrowded primary school.

Villagers often complain that their interests are not represented justly by the ayuntamiento. The ayuntamiento has traditionally courted the peasant sector, yet with the exception of a brief period of agrarian unrest, the ayuntamiento has always been composed of townspeople or ranchers. Many town dwellers forget that local government is municipal government and not just town government. Their attitude is, "never mind the municipality; do something for us." The municipal president frequently shows preference to the town; not only is he among his own kind, but if he does not push through at least one blazing project and a few minor items, he is subjected to continual harassment and behind-the-back criticism. Townspeople thus receive disproportionate benefits which nevertheless fall short of solving their special problems; at the same time, they are offended by their association with "the most backward municipality in the state." The president, then, must balance his decisions carefully. He is, after all, *municipal* president and must give evidence of his expertise in the form of progress reports on rural projects to the state governor. He must also raise standards of living in the rural zone.

Previously, it was the practice for municipal delegates to keep the municipal president informed of village problems. The municipal delegate served and continues to serve as the effective communication link between village and town. Although the delegate was selected by villagers, he had absolutely no authority to initiate action, act independently, or make decisions. The delegate's only recourse was through the municipal president: was it not easier for the municipal president to represent the interests of ten or twenty villages than for villagers to attempt to take their particular problems directly to the state? The delegate's speech and comportment would immediately mark him as Indian or peasant, and he would be left waiting in the governor's waiting room. Municipal delegates are still mainly recipients of information rather than initiators, yet some have worked closely with ejido officials and members of the "Junta de Mejoramiento" of their villages, forming commissions to go directly to Toluca. In the last few years, several villages have obtained land and materials, and constructed schools on their own initiative. At times, this type of independence has arisen from the total indifference of municipal officials. The barrios, for example, have been legally incorporated into the town since it was promoted to the level of *villa* in 1877, but have always made their supplications directly to Toluca or worked privately through prominent townspeople. While barrio residents often identify themselves as residents of the town, townspeople consider *el centro* the town. During the recent gubernatorial campaign, the candidate promised to install potable water systems in all towns with populations exceeding 2500. Settlements containing less than 2500 inhabitants would be eligible for a well system. El centro already had a potable water system that regularly broke down but would not be eligible for a new one because it scarcely counted 1000 residents. Statistics, townsmen claimed, did not tell the truth: "what about the floating population–those who work in the taller, go to market, the 1500 kids who attend school and eat, breathe, and defecate on town property." The townspeople decided to include the barrios in their petition for potable water; with a respectable total of 4500 residents, they were sure they would have no difficulty.

The numerical predominance of the peasant sector in San Felipe cannot be ignored by politicians. Townspeople feel that PRI exploits the peasants and capitalizes on their ignorance by lulling them with words, not acts. Whenever a public project is completed and regardless of the proportion of aid donated by state or federal dependencies, it is inaugurated with ostentatious flourish by an assortment of political figures. The peasant is lauded and congratulated on how well he has lifted himself up by his own bootstraps:

In few places, it is true, does one see such courage, enthusiasm, and eagerness to excel, and the desire to develop for the good of its children. Today this school is a symbol for all of you and the municipality; you should not forget that it is a positive activity and the product of the efforts which each and every one of you has demonstrated to endow your village with a cultural center where your children will be able to acquire the *culture* necessary to be useful citizens–for the village, for the state, and for the good of the entire fatherland. It is also significant that your presence today is evidence of your eagerness to continue improving and progressing in all aspects of your community. The authorities designated by you have carried through a magnificent labor. It is also evident you have known how to value the efforts of the state authorities and governor, the Director of Education who through the different dependencies has given his help and impetus, as well as the aid of the municipal president. Congratulations are due not only for this occasion, but for future occasions–to continue fighting because each step is a progression to a superior level, a higher cultural level. This is what each and every corner of the municipality needs–active people, resolute people who do not allow obstacles to conquer them, but on the contrary, are determined to overcome these obstacles and succeed as they have succeeded with this school.

Before national elections, peasant support is actively solicited and consensus reaffirmed by stressing the continuity of the Revolution. When Luis Echeverría spoke in Atlacomulco shortly before he was elected president, municipal delegates were informed by the municipal president to attend, accompanied by delegations from their villages. Fifty buses, chartered by PRI, transported the group from San Felipe to Atlacomulco; each delegation was given a poster and treated with a free box lunch. Luis Echeverría called on the peasants to act "with energy, imagination, and decision, the same qualities they demonstrated in the defense of their rights as revolutionary combatants" (Ferreira 1970c:1). He claimed that liberation from peonage was not enough, and in the future, the peasant would be able to live with decorum, a revolutionary objective. Only when all objectives of 1910 had been fulfilled, could one cease to speak of the Revolution. He urged the peasants to vote. In the days proceeding the elections, posters were plastered on the most visible walls:

It is a privilege to decide. Vote!

We must perform our duty in the name of the fatherland. You? 1910. 1970.

1910. Yesterday you were needy. Today vote. 1970.

You write the history. 1970. Vote.

Telegram. July 5, 1970. Urgent. The best governors will be those whom you elect today. Vote.

Election day came and barely caused a ripple. The voters were primarily government employees, pensioners and a small segment of townspeople who felt it was their duty to vote. Many townspeople were still bitter over the recent local elections and contended that there was no point in voting since the outcome had already been determined. Politics was simply a game, "played out by deputies who weren't worth five peanuts." As for the villagers, they remained as always, a silent majority.

The lucrative process of evangelization was, ultimately, a salvational program of subjection, in which the Indian encountered the justification of his earthly misery in the call for humility.

–Graziano Gasparini [1971]

Religion plays a tangential role in the lives of many townspeople; with the exception of a minority of "zealots," townspeople accept their Catholicism as casually as they do their nationality. This is not to say that townspeople do not participate in religious activities; they cooperate in national fiestas, attend Mass on Sundays and occasionally present themselves for weekday ministrations. But formal Catholicism is not a preponderant force that can succor or incumber; townspeople are neither supplicant nor oblivious. They merely feel that formal participation has little relationship to one's personal faith.

Just as every proper municipal capital is the seat of the municipal palace, so too, it is the seat of a spiritual leader and his parish house. The priest and his assistants, the deacon and vicar, are considered religious mentors and accorded the required respect. The priest is greeted with a handshake by his male parishioners, and a bow and hand kiss by women and children. He lends his spiritual presence to all national civic ceremonies and is usually asked to speak a few words. If food is served at any of these celebrations, it will not be eaten until the priest has pronounced the proper blessing. When one has a new car or home, he will not be able to enjoy it until the priest has recited a benediction. Whenever he presides at a baptism, marriage, fifteenth year coming-of-age, or funeral, the priest will invariably be invited to partake of a sumptuous meal. He is frequently urged to dine privately with leading families, is always offered a drink on unexpected visits, and even has his own day when he is honored by townspeople with a festive dinner.

The priest must also court the town. He is, after all, an outsider and like all outsiders, open to criticism. He will accept all invitations with obvious pleasure and will voluntarily reciprocate. The priest and his assistant clerics will celebrate their birthdays and saints' days with the town by sponsoring an open house in the parochial building. He may ask some of the families to bring dishes, but often will throw a supper himself, dispense liquor, and arrange for entertainment—a band, singers, a poetry reading or folk dancers. The priest is supported by his parish in more than spiritual ways, and he must maintain the best possible relations. If he transgresses a town custom, he will be censored either through lack of cooperation or through quiet commentary made behind his back. The status of "vicar," for example, does not give one the license to flirt with town girls when they are involved in religious activities. Parents will withdraw their daughters without explanation once sufficient gossip has aroused their irritation. When the priest called the block meetings, people were generally shocked, not only because he asked for excessive contributions for church repairs, but also because he was bold enough to read the parish budget aloud, something which no priest had ever done. People were stunned that the purchase of a new jeep and an expensive mimeograph, both within a few months, had left a sizable deficit. The priest told the people they were misinformed if they thought he was robbing the parish; a large parish did not necessarily indicate a large budget. He was not bringing this matter up for himself alone, but for future priests that would be sent to San Felipe. He claimed that he never received more than 25 pesos of alms for a Mass, which barely paid for lighting and the sacristan. One should train oneself to leave at least a peso during the Sunday Mass and teach the children to do the same. He assured the townspeople the church repairs would bring them satisfaction and he would fight a transfer until the work had been completed. His audience listened respectfully and attentively; each agreed to contribute from "embarrassment." But after the meetings people began to express their negative reactions. Of course the priest heard about the backlash and was offended. The matter of church repairs was inconspicuously dropped.

The spectrum of religious participants ranges from those who admit to having entered the church a few times over the last decade—they feel uncomfortable, they don't know how to confess—to regular attenders who wish to set an example for their children to a few enthusiastic devotees of religious associations. Only at the level of the association are townspeople forced to participate more than passively. Although associations have existed as religious fraternities in San Felipe since the late eighteenth century, they have been revamped during the last twenty years as a consequence of structural changes in the Church itself. Where previously the association was almost entirely occupied with the sponsorship of the fiestas honoring a particular saint, Christ, or the Virgin, it now has a more inclusive significance. This is in line with townspeoples' contentions that they seek personal satisfaction from life and the attainment of a higher state at each stage of one's development. Such well known organizations as "Acción Católica" have recently been dismembered and deprecated by the clergy as mere "associations of devotees within the Church hierarchy, with social and religious significance." Today the association is considered an extension of the religious order, concerned not only with personal salvation, but also with serving as attestations to the others. The members participate in various monthly practices and exercises, attend Masses and Rosaries, all in the interest of encouraging the proper attitude toward life. Some of the associations also sponsor nationally celebrated fiestas which members must not only pay for and organize, but also prepare for spiritually through confession and communion. The associations theoretically encompass the parish (San Felipe and the circumjacent twenty-three villages), but of the eight associations which are presently functioning, officership is held by townspeople and only two involve significant participation by villagers. Membership and leadership of six associations are exclusively female. Women are considered the moral guardians of the community and are encouraged by the men to join. Religious activity is also a unique occasion for a woman to participate publicly without risking criticism for meddling where she does not belong. The other associations are presided over by artisans—men with a reputation for being religious and for sprinkling their conversations with sublime words. They are on the lower end of the town scale, socially and economically; they would never have a chance in the political arena and yet they are constantly in the public view together with the priest. They have religious prestige, especially in the opinions of their village followers.

With the exception of the communally celebrated ceremonies of Christmas and Easter, the national fiestas commemorated in San Felipe are devoted to the distinct images of Christ and the Virgin. At their simplest, these celebrations involve the singing of *mañanitas* (a birthday song), an early morning Mass, and a procession in the atrium of the church. Participants are devotees of the image and members of the name association. Other associations, however, celebrate a series of Masses solemnized by the presence of three ministers. The "Hijas de María," for example, consecrated to the "Santísima Virgen," is noted for the profundity of its devotion. Open primarily to *señoritas*, members are required to live seriously, abstaining from dances, liquor, flirtations and provocative clothing. The fifteen members, now reduced from fifty, are required to sponsor a Mass on the eighth of each month, financing it through the system of cooperation. On the fourteenth of August, they commemorate the ascension of the "Santísima Virgen" by keeping a nightlong vigil in the church; the devotees pray and sing, and take turns leading the group. The following morning a Mass is celebrated, followed by a procession in the atrium led by the standard-bearers. Members can be identified by their azure belts and large medallions. In celebration of "La Purísima Concepción de María Santísima" on December 8th, an expensive Mass is held, officiated by a triumvirate of priests. Before the coronation of the "Santísima" at the end of May, thirty Rosaries are scheduled, paid for by donations solicited from townspeople; an outdoor Mass is held on the thirty-first and attended by a sizable congregation drawn by the presence of allegorical cars. In addition to actual ritual activities, associates attend monthly meetings in which they discuss the preparations for fiestas, arrange for the admission of new members, organize charitable works, and confer with the priest.

Other associations are devoted to the adoration of abstractions. The "Vela Perpetua" sponsors a monthly Mass in adoration of "La Divina Providencia." During Lent and other occasions which can range from local droughts to an earthquake in Peru, members are obligated to "make visits to Nuestro Santísimo." The "Adoración Nocturna," the one association open exclusively to men, holds three vigils each month in adoration of God. Members are divided into three sections, each responsible for a monthly vigil broken by a midnight Mass and terminating with a morning Mass.

A recently formed association, the "Congregación de la Doctrina Cristiana" is neither concerned with vigils, adorations nor religious holidays. Its members are a small group of teenage town girls who serve as voluntary instructors of the catechism. Formal religious training had been virtually nonexistent in the municipality and it was well known that villagers were totally oblivious to the formal religious calendar and indifferent to such concepts as "eternal life." It was even rumored certain priests had slapped their parishioners in the face because of their neglect in attending scheduled Masses. Although San Felipe is a *foránea* in the church hierarchy and divided into four parishes, each priest is capable of holding a maximum of fifteen weekly Masses, heavily concentrated in the parish seat. Religious instruction, before the formation of this association, was also offered exclusively in the parish seat. Attendance was limited to children of poorer town families and barrio children. Instruction was erratic; teachers would prepare one group for their first communion, move on to a second group, and later to a third. When they finally returned to the original group for further instruction, the simple catechism had already been forgotten. Approximately twenty instructors are now giving weekly instruction in nine villages. They hope to attract enough members to organize religious classes corresponding to the primary and secondary school grades. The burden will fall on the Church; most parents, both in town and village, feel that religious instruction is not their job. The priest has had to contend with the children's high rate of absence and their parents' complete disinterest. Teachers still find that several days before the ceremony, children have not learned to pray. Teachers have repeatedly visited homes, but the hassle between home and church responsibility has not yet been resolved.

The associations are also used by the priest as a *palanca* (a means) for obligating people to participate in the celebrations of *Semana Santa*. Not everybody who takes part is a member of an association; it is simply easier for the priest to approach people through the association. The distinct acts, however, are not sponsored by the associations, but by particular *cargueros*. The *cargos* are not considered vows, but obligations accepted on the invitation of the priest. Cargos do not involve heavy expenses and are generally shared by several cargueros. Don Rubén, for example, is a vigilante; he is responsible for organizing the image-bearers, checking that the procession proceeds on schedule, and maintaining order. The twelve apostles who partake of the Last Supper are men who ordinarily do not attend services. They are the leading citizens of San Felipe—the merchants of the large general stores, the principal grain dealers, and solid governmental employees. They have to provide their own costumes, are obligated to take communion and attend the dinner in the parish house. Their wives are responsible for preparing ceremonial dishes, setting the table and serving. The cargos of the sermons (Las Tres Caídas, La Crucifixión) are almost always shared by several persons and amount to no more than a contribution of a few pesos. Bakers also accept cargos, donating special breads throughout the week. Easter Week is the opportunity to advertise that one is a serious townsman and "cargueros" such as the ayuntamiento and important commercial houses figure prominently among the sixty participants. Even the normally apathetic participate passively as members of the audience.

Until recently, Christmas was largely a family celebration although the Masses of *Nochebuena* and *Pascua* were enthusiastically attended. The traditionally exuberant *Posadas*, one of the most popular fiestas of the Mexican ritual cycle, had gradually petered into a minor fiesta, slighted by adults, anticipated only by the children. The Posadas had customarily been held in the parish house with each night of the *Novena*[27] sponsored by a group of families. By 1968, the priest, impatient with the poor turnout, decided to hold the Posadas in the streets. For each street or group of streets, he drew up a list of six families, and invited one to be the principal organizer. These families, in turn, were to visit each household in their section, and ask for contributions, either cash or food and beverages. According to the priest, he invited families who had already proven their *arrastre*—respected townspeople who commanded attention and got things done. It was obvious they would be the main force behind the Posadas. The day of the fiesta, streets were washed down and adorned with balloons and evergreens while the Nativity was constructed. The fiesta started in the evening with the chiming of the church bells. By the time a sizable crowd had gathered, sparklers were set off, and anyone who wanted to participate was given a candle and joined the procession led by the priest. The priest chanted the "Santo Rosario," breaking frequently for carols. He then recited the Novena and led songs asking for lodging. With the termination of the religious ceremony, the evening joyfully culminated in the breaking of the *piñata*[28] and a high-spirited scramble for the fruits and sweets. The children were not alone in their enjoyment; they were regaled with party favors, hard candies and peanuts, while adolescents danced and sang at the encouragement of the spectators. Adults milled about chatting and were plied with punch, enchiladas, tacos, *buñuelos* (fritters), sandwiches and coffee. After people eventually dispersed, the priest ended the occasion with a late supper in the home of the principal organizer. Only on the last evening of the Posadas, when families prepared for midnight Mass and private dinners, did attendance wane. As in all public undertakings, there was some grumbling that certain people did not fulfill their obligations; yet most townspeople concluded that the Posadas were actually quite successful. The colored lights and decorations transformed the streets into a gay scene, and a friendly interstreet rivalry enlivened the general festivities. All agreed Bravo Street had given the best Posada; here even the poorest family donated a basket of fruit or prepared a special dish. The townspeople's single regret was that the Posadas and Christmas spirit occurred once a year.

Townspeople also have preferred saints and manifestations of Christ and the Virgin, to whom they are privately devoted. Devotion at its simplest is demonstrated by displaying a pictoral image in the home or making occasional visits to a pilgrimage center. One's favored supernatural is considered a benefactor to be thanked in times of munificence or appealed to in dire stress. When one considers himself particularly fortunate–he has earned a good deal of money, had a windfall of crop, recuperated splendidly from an operation, or barely escaped accidental death–he will voluntarily offer an *acción de gracias* by sponsoring a Mass to thank God or another guardian.

Although benefactors are viewed as general protectors capable of lessening one's anxieties and contributing to one's tranquility, their miraculous powers are actively invoked only during severe crises. Townspeople, however, do not supplicate and never beguile themselves into believing they will receive something for nothing. They make *promesas* to a particular benefactor, in which they vow to perform certain devotions in exchange for the fulfillment of their requests. Promesas are taken seriously, "otherwise they would be a joke, not a devotion." One feels obligated to discharge a promesa whether or not a specific time limit has been mentioned. Promesas are made by adult townspeople for specific reasons. The average townsman will make one or two vows in his lifetime either to help him and his family through economic straits or to combat severe illness, such as childhood diseases, paralysis and infirmities that impinge on working capacity. Most townspeople vow to sponsor a Mass in town or at a nationally famous shrine.

Occasionally a promesa will be carried out before the execution of a request, but this reversal of the normal sequence is considered undesirable; one is liable to become entwined in a cycle of renewing promesas for unfulfilled requests. One young woman, for example, had vowed to don a habit for two months in the expectation that her husband would marry her in church. Her husband did not respond. She was on the point of renewing her promesa, but finally decided he wasn't worth the effort. Esteben, a carpenter, suffered from a stiff and painful leg. He promised to visit the Virgin of Guadalupe and the Virgin of San Juan de los Lagos. His leg is still stiff although he has faithfully complied with his vow for the past five years.

When a devotee has specified a time limit which he later exceeds, he can still absolve himself through a *voto*, an oath to God. The devotee must personally fulfill the "voto" by confessing, attending Rosary consistently, and visiting the benefactor's shrine. The average person ordinarily fulfills his promesa since he obligates himself under the most exceptional circumstances; he protects himself, however, by only vaguely divulging when he plans to complete the vow.

The most religious townspeople commit themselves to numerous and elaborate promises. These parishioners are also zealously active in associations, willingly accept cargos imposed by the priest, and conscientiously attend scheduled rituals. They own a variety of pictoral images, are devoted to several benefactors, accept the responsibility of completing vows of close relatives, and frequently make vows as acts of contrition for venial sins. This vow consists of a strict dedication to a particular benefactor. The repenter must sponsor a Mass, adorn the house altar with fresh flowers and lighted candles, hold a private novena, confess, take communion the first Friday of each month for nine months, and practice abstinence at designated times for the duration of the vow. These townspeople also make long-term vows by translating associational membership into devotional obligation, which incorporate them as laymen in the Church hierarchy; not only do they have constant access to a supernatural guardian, but they acquire considerable social prestige as adjunct officials and a serene sense of power over their religious charges.

Twenty years ago, a Protestant missionary arrived in the municipality, settling in Jalpa. She brought not only a new religion, but medicines, food parcels and a determination to learn Mazahua and village customs. She avoided the municipal seat and before municipal officials realized what had happened, she had small, but active congregations in several villages. She encountered little competition since orthodox religious activity was confined predominantly to the town. Inevitably, the new proselytes entered into dissension with their Catholic neighbors. The few brisk skirmishes that occurred in Jalpa were quickly quenched when the converts were escorted to the town jail. They were released only because the assistant postmaster threatened to bring the case to the district authorities. The postmaster, an even more outrageous blasphemer, was determined to retaliate by publicizing his promesa–a vow to remove the sacred image of "Nuestro Padre Jesús" from the altar and conduct business from this consecrated place. The other townsmen, totally opposed to the evangelical movement, reacted by planning to lynch the postmaster. They headed for the post office and were so incensed by his rapid flight, that they burned down his office and home. Then, as now, certain people believed there are only two religions–"one that embraces the Virgin and one that does not." The townspeople decided that something must be done to combat evangelism. Their vehicle would be "La Pía Unión."

At this time, the association of "La Pía Unión" was dedicated exclusively to annual pilgrimages to Tepeyac in honor of the Virgin of Guadalupe. Don Rubén, the president of the association, is proud of his role in the resurgence of *local* homage to the Virgin. He joined the association simply to participate in the pilgrimages and explained how he obtained his first post as delegate:

"We were sprawled out in all directions. Then a brother of the board of directors spoke to me."

—photo by B. L. Margolies

pilgrimage honoring the Virgin of Guadalupe

—photo by B. L. Margolies

the image of the Virgin of Guadalupe is led into the church

"Little brother," he said, "which section do you belong to?"

"The third."

"Who's the delegate?"

"I don't know, but we're wandering like a flock of sheep."

"You're going to be delegate."

"They're not going to obey," I replied. "They're 'inditos,' you know how they are." Yet Rubén began to command his group and they fell into line. Soon his position was formalized and he later became president. It was Rubén who suggested local pilgrimages and open-air Masses as a more manifest devotion to the Virgin. The matter was taken up in Toluca and the bishop selected the ninth of each month as a pilgrimage date. According to Don Rubén, "we hold a Mass to see if the Santísima María moves their hearts and brings them back to their own religion."

Don Rubén is responsible for organizing the pilgrimages and is required to attend plenary sessions held in Toluca. He is assisted by four collaborators who are fellow townsmen, and twenty-five delegates, one from each participating village. The delegates are not only members of the association; they are also fulfilling a promesa—a continuing devotion to the Virgin of Guadalupe. They are expected to live exemplary lives and serve as an inspirational example to the pilgrims. When Don Rubén discovered that a delegate had abandoned his wife and was living "openly" with another woman, he went to Chichilpa to confer with the municipal delegate. Certainly this was a case of moral turpitude and a denigration of the "Santísima Virgen." After a brief consultation with the pilgrims, another devotee was selected to replace the delegate.

With the exception of a small group of pilgrims from San Felipe, members of the associations are villagers. In contrast to the other associations, members consider themselves perpetual devotees bound by the obligation of a continual vow. Although the ceremonials are officiated by the priest, they are held according to peasant tradition and involve lengthy processions, lavish decoration of the Virgin's altar, the burning of incense, incessant exploding of firecrackers, chanting and festive meals. The pilgrimages are always well attended with an average of 200 participants and attendance climbs sharply with the addition of the men during the agricultural season. Each month a different village is responsible for sponsoring the fiesta; the devotees must pay for the Masses, jubilantly welcome the other pilgrims, and host a dinner. The pilgrims leave their villages early in the morning and assemble at a designated meeting place a short distance from the host village. The actual procession may not begin until midday since the etiquette of homage stipulates that pilgrims arrive by foot. When all pilgrims have finally tottered in and the priest's jeep is sighted in the distance, Don Rubén habitually shouts, "get in line," "over there," "the other boys behind," "let's go pilgrims." The pilgrims unfold their standards and file into position behind their delegates. Firecrackers are set off to signal the commencement of the peregrination and the group repeatedly sings, "Let us go, let us go, let us go, let us go walking to the brown Virgin, she is waiting for us; you are awaiting us with great fervor that we come to see you and receive your love; the brown Virgin is calling us, let us go, let us go, let us go walking." The pilgrims are met by their hosts a short distance from an outdoor altar and a succession of firecrackers are exploded in welcome. The sponsoring group is headed by the

—photo by Graziano Gasparini

las pastoras dance and sing for the patron image

village fiscal, bearing a censer and followed by the candle-bearers, flower-bearers, standard-bearers and image-bearers. Only the imagination limits the elaborateness with which the framed image of the Virgin of Guadalupe is adorned, and the pictoral representation may be hidden behind multicolored balloons, tinsel, crepe paper, plastic fruit, biscuits, special breads, and *cempoasúchil*, strung and brightly colored flowers. The fiscal sets off another round of firecrackers while Don Luis (Don Rubén's collaborator) kneels and kisses the image of the Virgin. He then repeats a series of *vivas*—"Viva Cristo Rey, la Santísima Virgen de Guadalupe, el Santo Papa, el señor Obispo, el señor Cura, la Pía Unión de Peregrinos, la Peregrinación de la Concepción (or whichever village is sponsoring the fiesta), viva México, viva México, viva México"[29]—repeated in unison by the pilgrims. Led by the sponsoring group, the pilgrims now proceed to the altar, covered with a lattice-work of evergreens, wild flowers, paper flowers and crepe paper. Don Luis delivers the Mysteries and blesses the kneeling pilgrims with the sign of the cross made with the censer. Alms are deposited in front of the image and the pilgrims advance to the village chapel. They pass through a series of pine arches singing "La Guadalupana," the story of the Indian Juan Diego and Tepeyac. The church bells are rung to connote happiness, more firecrackers, the air is filled with smog and the scent of incense, babies hidden in their mothers' rebozos react with wails, and the prosody is lost in a cacophony of competitiveness. The procession circles the chapel and is rained with confetti and animal crackers as it enters the building. The Mass has finally begun. The pilgrims are in the house of God.

The priest explains that the walk and songs have prepared the pilgrims to be

—photo by Graziano Gasparini

Nuestro Padre Jesús, the patron of San Felipe

close to God, with dignity and sanctity. He requests a moment of silence for the pilgrims to ask God for particular necessities—that he send rain for the milpas, blesses one's family and children, and remembers the sick. The priest recites the penitential rites and proceeds to the various orations. He explains the meaning of Christian life: We have left our houses to come on a monthly pilgrimage. During the walk we should have been thinking about the significance of a Christian life. It is a continuous progression to God who opens the road to heaven for us. God sent his only son to the world for its salvation. Christ came to make a road toward Father God; Christ is the only one who can redeem us. This journey is never completed; it is continuous and each day more beautiful. This progression is made possible by means of our good works, by means of our faith in Jesus. These works are a testimony of our faith. To believe in Jesus is more than simple acts; it is the transformation of our faith to daily life so that our works are a confirmation of that faith. For example, any outsider who was unfamiliar with our peregrinations and saw our banners impressed with the image of the Virgin, would immediately think, this is the "Pía Unión de Peregrinos." The banners are a symbol of our annual pilgrimages and a testimony of our love for the Virgin of Guadalupe; it is the same with other good works which confirm that we are servants of Christ.

The priest leaves quietly after the Mass and the pilgrims linger for a late meal. Hosting villages will make the effort to offer at least rice and tortillas, but some excel in hospitality, serving tamales and beans. Village authorities and association officers are toasted at a full ceremonial dinner of mole and pulque in

—photo by B. L. Margolies

the firework-maker finishes the castillo

the parish house. By the time they have sated themselves, most of the pilgrims have dispersed and there remain a few straggling vendors waiting to sell a final trifle.

The priest does not condone what he considers the frivolities of the pilgrimages, yet it is his amplest opportunity for maintaining access to villagers. The pilgrimage is the appropriate occasion for teaching religious songs, receiving confession, formal instruction, the implantation of Christian values, harangues against pulque, cigarettes and meat during periods of abstention, and such worldly advice as cooperation with census officials ("for our own welfare") and the virtues of being prompt. The priest deplores the expense of explosives, yet the villagers overcompensate with alms. Not only do the pilgrims sponsor the fiesta, pay for ministrations, and swell the parish's budget, but their "material symbol" of devotion is welcomed at the level of the bishopic. Every year, the image of the Virgin of Guadalupe, also known as the "Peregrine Virgin," is removed from its niche in the cathedral of Toluca, and circulated throughout the state of Mexico. Every fourth year, the image is brought to the foránea and spends one or two weeks in the participating villages depending on the movement of alms. San Felipe has a dependable reputation for contributing an average of 20,000 pesos for the support of the Toluca seminary.

Despite the priest's emphasis on penitence and salvation, villagers are not so much interested in redemption as in protection from latent misfortunes. Villagers believe God makes the final decisions and is unique in his ability to foresee the future. Christ, the Virgin and the saints, although not endowed with prophetic capabilities, are perceived as potent mediators; the villagers expect these preternatural beings to care for them, with God's approval. Although a villager might make an after-the-fact promesa–an appeal to a specific supernatural for a specific reason (such as illness)–obligating himself to perform devotional rites, his approach to the supernaturals is generally prevenient. The villager supplicates rather than manipulates; he does not ask a favor and promise to give something in return. He performs recurrent rites and cares for the images of the supernaturals in the hope of preventing imminent misfortune. Villagers have three primary fears validated through repeated experience: fear of not eating through harvest failure, fear of rapacious illness which can cause one's sudden demise, and fear that one's animals will be similarly affected. Villagers thus surround themselves with images, conspicuously displayed either in small oratories close to the house or on a table altar in the main living room. Compared to townspeople who rarely have more than three or four pictoral images hanging in their homes, villagers own from ten to twenty images, including distinct images of Christ and the Virgin and a repertoire of saints. Villagers decorate their altars with crepe paper, elaborately embroidered tablecloths, holy water, and paper or plastic flowers. They will "light a vigil" every two weeks, light a candle in church, and offer alms on the supernatural's name day. They will also visit the supernatural's shrine, not as a promesa, but as an act of "volition." For images considered especially miraculous, their owners will plan on encasing them in wooden and glass niches; a friend or relative will be invited to be the godparent of the image, and both owner and godparent will carry the image to the church for the priest's benediction, celebrating the event with a festive dinner.

—photo by Graziano Gasparini

a major-domo prepares to announce the completion of the castillo

—photo by Graziano Gasparini

a compañía carries their castillo to town . . .

The highest form of adoration is the acceptance of a lengthy or lifelong promesa to feast the supernatural. In contrast to simple volition the promesa is obligatory, and noncompliance can precipitate an unknown punishment. The most common vow is the assumption of a cargo to participate in the sponsorship of an annual fiesta, while others involve the offering of special services—dancing and music—in honor of the supernatural. The sponsoring group, known as a *compañía* is headed by one or two major-domos and composed of a variant number of *socios* (partners). The cargos are theoretically hereditary, passed on from father to elder son in the event of death or when the father feels incapable of efficiently performing his duties. Sons are not obligated to accept the cargos, while cargueros may feel their sons lack the "proper attitudes" and are unsuitable. A widow may also accept her deceased husband's cargo, but she, too, is not obligated and can pass it along to an outsider if her sons have not reached maturity. Compañías are continually losing prospective members who are eligible to receive the cargo through inheritance but did not accept it or were considered unacceptable. The socios must then invite an outsider to join the compañía. Unlike members by inheritance, invited members have the choice of making a terminable vow or accepting the cargo as a perdurable vow. He is subtly encouraged to opt for the latter through the mechanism of compadrazgo which pairs him off with a working partner and burdens him with an entirely new set of personal responsibilities.

The images of the supernaturals celebrated in this manner are owned privately and housed in their own chapels. With the exception of the "Virgin de la Concepción," whose celebration dates from the formation of the ejido, the

—photo by Graziano Gasparini

. . . and hoists it into place

images of these saints have been venerated for several generations, although ownership and sponsorship may have been passed from family to family. At its most elaborate, the fiesta may endure for more than a week and include pilgrimages and visits of the image to neighboring villages. The image of the Virgin of Loreto, for example, is owned by Gregorio Hernández of the barrio of Calvario. He and his fifteen socios honor the Virgin with celebrations lasting from the thirteenth to the twenty-second of August. The compañía of Calvario maintains relations of "correspondence" or compadrazgo with the compañías of the four villages visited by the Virgin; these compañías are composed of devotees who vow to venerate the image of the Virgin as their own during its sojourn in their villages. They must lead prayers and songs, sponsor a Mass, hold vigil, and prepare a festive dinner for their guests. The Virgin is accompanied in its peregrination by representatives of the compañías that have already been visited; what begins as a small procession in Calvario augments in each succeeding village as it is joined by the custodial compañías. When the image is finally returned to its own chapel, it is convoyed by several hundred devotees. A double Mass is held in welcome return, followed by a dinner composed of the full complement of traditional dishes. The fiesta terminates with the "farewell"–the compañía of Calvario formally expresses its thanks and renews its "correspondence" with the other compañías by embracing and kissing compadres.

The fiesta in honor of the Virgin of Loreto is exceptional in its complexity; private devotionals to supernatural guardians have either been simplified, confined to the family unit, or live on in the memory of the image owners who no longer commemorate name days. Compañías now contend with the waning interest of the younger generation and their rejection of the obligations entailed in a lifelong vow. As one socio noted, "the young men don't take any interest in the customs which had been left by their ancestors." Attendance at the fiestas has also declined; a decade ago, devotees from the interior of the municipality regularly honored the Virgin of Loreto and offered her money, flowers, candles, and ceremonial breads. Only one village still participates but attendance has declined by 75%. Several priests have also been vocal in expressing their distaste for the fiestas: "What are the demonstrations that have been made in these religious fiestas? Discharge rockets! Drink pulque to excess! Spend huge amounts of money on things which serve no purpose! In no way is this satisfactory for the venerated Virgin and for the cult of God in general." Invited to officiate a Mass, the priest chose to deliver a sermon, exhorting the audience to change their customs and honor God in a less "barbarous" fashion. These sermons have generally been ignored, but the priest does have the power to bar dancers and musicians when he thinks the fiesta is too close to an orthodox holiday. Other elements of the fiestas have gradually been eliminated–the exchange of chickens by compadres, the beheading of chickens and the associated horse races, and certain ritual foods from the traditional dinner.

Some fiestas have become strictly family affairs, sponsored by the owners of the image and the godparents of benediction, and attended by family members. Juan Ruiz, whose grandfather built a chapel in adoration of San Ramón, continues to celebrate the name day (Domingo de los Ramos) although the fiesta is not as elaborate as previously. He sponsors a town Mass according to the orthodox calendar and later holds a second Mass when the image of the saint is returned to the chapel. Several musicians still accompany the procession, but the dances have been eliminated and dinner invitations limited to devotees who participate in fulfillment of a promesa. San Cayetano, formerly the object of intense festive rituals, is now honored only in spirit. Two pictoral images of the saint are owned by Guadalupe González and lodged in a chapel built by her great-grandparents. The godparents of the image customarily sponsored a Mass in town on the saint's day, while the owners feted the saint with a dinner attended by musicians, dancers, and devotees from neighboring villages. Guadalupe has not held a fiesta for San Cayetano since her parents' death and former devotees have looked to other saints. She not only assumed the responsibility for a younger sister and two brothers, but also mothered three illegitimate children. The family lives on an income derived from the boys' shoeshine business and occasional contributions from the father of Guadalupe's children. Although her house is in total disrepair, Lupe refuses to move and abandon the chapel. She has vowed to hold a proper dinner and despite her indigence, is optimistic that "one day" she can honor her saint with probity.

Although the apostles Felipe and Santiago are the titular saints of the town and barrios, "Nuestro Padre Jesús" has superseded them as the unofficial patron of both the town and the villages of the municipality. The image of "Nuestro Padre Jesús" occupies the sacred altar; he is revered in every household and his image is prominently displayed in the center of the family altar; he is commemorated with a communal fiesta on the third Wednesday of January, which draws devotees from all parts of the municipality as well as various regions of the state. Parish records indicate "Nuestro Padre Jesús" has had

—photo by Graziano Gasparini

the afternoon before the castillos are burned . . .

—photo by Graziano Gasparini

. . . and the morning after

Masses sponsored in his honor since the mid-nineteenth century. According to villagers, the image was brought to the municipality in the distant past and shortly became the center of a communal cult. Basilio Marcos, one of the eldest major-domos explained:

> Many years ago, some foreign soldiers arrived in San Felipe and they brought "Nuestro Padre Jesús." Our ancestors adored him because he performed many miracles, improving their harvests and protecting their families and animals. It is said that on one occasion, they wanted to take "Nuestro Padre Jesús" to Celaya, but they couldn't remove him from the temple. He was very heavy and was guarded throughout the night by the animals who came down from the mountains.

Townspeople regard "Nuestro Padre Jesús" as their titular patron, yet their participation in festive activities is minimal. In contrast to national civic celebrations when the villager is merely a spectator, roles are reversed in the principal religious spectacle; the townsman is the onlooker, while the villagers take the responsibility for major preparations. Townspeople cooperate financially through their associations to offer Mass and Rosary the actual festive day, but the majority of orthodox rituals are sponsored by villagers. The *Novenario* preceding the fiesta is pledged by twenty-six villages of the foránea, while the continuous Masses scheduled for the festive week are undertaken by the compañías of the barrios. Of course, the townspeople enjoy the fiesta; for them it is both a bazaar and carnival. The full plaza held throughout the week offers an alluring array of foods, regional sweets, and miscellanea, items which are not normally sold in San Felipe. And two weeks before the fiesta, the carnival comes to town, advertising its presence with blaring "ranchero" music, rides, and game concessions, all competing for the townsman's peso. Cockfights and an elegant dance are an additional inducement for forgetting one's regular activities; even the busiest townsman will devote time to amusements. Local merchants also benefit tangentially from the huge influx of people, but are generally slighted for the exotica of a temporary world.

What the priest has termed the "profane fiestas" is for the villagers the culmination of religious expression. The twenty-four compañías which sponsor both the solemn Masses and the "profane" celebrations consider the fiesta the annual climax of their continuing devotion to "Nuestro Padre Jesús." Their activities start the week before the fiesta when a socio from each compañía goes to Mexico City to buy "holy candles" and flowers, and offer a Mass to the Virgin of Guadalupe. They return to San Felipe by train, stopping at Tepetitlán to spend the night and "guard" the holy candles. They then proceed to Jalpa where they are met by their fellow socios. Another vigil and the first dinner of the fiesta are held in Jalpa. The following day, the candles and flowers are delivered to the parish house. A schedule is worked out with the priest, so that processions are staggered by barrio during the high festive days. The firework makers and musicians are contracted to appear in the major-domo's house two days before the compañía's grand entrance into town. During these two days, wives are occupied with dinner preparations, while the men divide up assorted tasks–some buy liquor, while others help the firework makers complete the *castillo*, an intricate pyrotechnic tower. The remainder make the rounds of each socio's home, announcing their arrival by exploding rockets, stopping for a pulque and brief chat, and requesting a contribution for the Mass. The afternoon of the compañía's entry, a festive dinner is held, attended by socios and musicians while the firework makers reinforce and revise their work. Reluctantly, the dinner ends with the repeated warnings of the church bells. The compañías of the barrios meet at the edge of town, where they are joined by *Las Pastoras* and *Los Santiaguitos* who have promised to dance in the atrium for the duration of the fiesta. Barrio residents carrying decorated images to be placed beside "Nuestro Padre Jesús" complete the procession. The evening of the procession, the castillos are burned in a glorious show of light. The compañía's work is terminated, but the socios do not feel they have complied with their vow until they meet in church to give formal thanks. They approach the image of "Nuestro Padre," splendidly festooned with popcorn, adorned with a heart-shaped bread, protected in his niche of colored ribbons, and kneel on a floor splashed with coins. They tell him they are competent men and will continue to follow in his path. They turn from his image and awkwardly embrace, whispering their mutual thanks and promising to cooperate again the following year.

The villagers, like the townspeople, are both petitioners and parishioners. Villagers and townspeople are persuaded by arguments of rhetoric and propaganda which pretend to convince, while merely creating illusions, which promise delivery, while repetitively appealing for patience and obedience. Both groups are devoted to images, the one to the saints and the other to an amorphous political party. The Indian may be motivated by his fear of misfortune and the Mestizo by his quest for power, but they have both been reduced to compliant suppliants in their entreaties to institutionalized authorities.

6

"WE ARE ALL MESTIZOS": THE PARADOX OF EQUALITY

The whole history of Mexico, from the Conquest to the Revolution, can be regarded as a search for our own selves, which have been deformed or disguised by alien institutions, and for a form that will express them.

–Octavio Paz [1959]

Every week, without fail, Macario came to San Felipe to buy hides from the farmers. He did not do much business, but he was attracted to San Felipe because he had been born in Palmillas and eventually expected to return there. A bachelor, he lived in Ixtlahuaca with his mother and married sister. His brothers, still residents of Palmillas, and his mother spoke Mazahua fluently, but he himself claimed to understand only a few words. He always dressed like a charro with a brilliant bandanna around his neck, sported a silken Pancho Villa mustache, and conducted himself audaciously.

"Why is it," he commented, "that in the United States, the houses are so much cleaner. I worked several years in Tijuana once I found myself a patron. Worked only eight hours a day, five days a week and had time to buy a little house and fix it up–the floor, new curtains, windows–the works. Now I have no time. After the market, I have to salt down the skins–will barely have time for supper."

At this point, an old lady approached Macario with some sheepskins.

"What will you give me, María," he asked, using the personal "tu" form.

She didn't respond.

"Look," he reasoned, "the skin is already going bad. I'll give you ten pesos."

She remained silent. "Fifteen," she finally whispered.

"I'll give you twelve and not one cent more."

She wrapped up the skins in an old sheet, but did not move.

"Well, María, I'll give you thirteen, but not a cent more."

She untied her sheet, accepted the four bills and quietly disappeared.

He continued the conversation. "I'd live across the border if I could, but I don't have the papers to pass. It isn't only a question of earning more money; the way of life is different. The only thing which doesn't please me is that a man has less liberty. Here a man tells his wife what to do; there, the woman says she's going out and leaves the husband with the kids."

Another old woman approached, and her walnut face wrinkled into a smile. "What will you take, María?"

She responded softly, "six pesos."

"No," he said, "look how small the skin is. Two pesos, María."

She neither spoke nor moved, but just nodded no.

Anxious to wrap up the sale and continue the conversation, he said, "Well, María, three and not a cent more. Here's your change. Now be on your way."

We were standing in CONASUPO's new general store, admiring the long rows of carefully placed tins and the colorful array of household wares. Yet despite a heavy advertising campaign and regulated prices, the store had few customers. People were intimidated by the turnstile, hesitated in front of the store and then without a loss of step, continued on their way. Don Pepe, the manager, was emptying cartons when he glimpsed a prospective client.

"Come here, Mariquita," he called out in a loud voice.

She intrepidly stopped and stared at him.

"Mariquita, come here. Mariquita, Mariquita," he was now shouting. Don Pepe kept repeating himself, as though to appreciate the crescendo of the "quita" rolling from his lips. He stopped when he realized that his audience had disappeared.

Antioco was enjoying the last few minutes before closing his store. He had just sold some drinks, poured himself a shot, and joined the men conversing at the counter. A woman entered, laden with bundles wrapped in the shawl slung over her shoulders. She waited patiently for Antioco to recognize her.

After she mumbled a few words, he looked up. "What do you want, María? "

"The hour."

"Yah, yah," he snickered, "what do you need to know the hour for, María."

"Oh, tell her the hour," one of the men admonished.

Antioco finally told her the time, but only after he had been properly amused.

The authoritarian and derisive tone with which the Mestizo addresses the Indian, anonymously identified as María in the case of the women, is the most patent aspect of the legacy of inter-ethnic relations molded in the colonial period. Throughout the colonial period, social status was determined by one's legal caste designation. Initially, the caste system was a broadly defined categorical hierarchy, with primary distinctions among Spaniards, Mestizos, Indians and Negroes, but toward the end of the colonial period, it had expanded to include a proliferation of positional types. Although caste distinctions were based upon racial origin, that is, parental ancestry, they were also correlated with physical appearance, occupational status, manners and morals. Each status was associated with legal restrictions or privileges, depending upon its localization in the hierarchy.

In colonial San Felipe, a modified caste system existed–modified because it never attained the complexity of the various ideal systems that were known.[30] In the early eighteenth century when the parish of San Felipe was founded, over 90% of the population was classified as "natural Indians" and bestowed with Spanish surnames according to locality. The Gonzálezes, Tápias, Garcías, Cruzes and Sánchezes preponderant today are derivations of these baptismal and marital surnames. Spaniards, either "naturals of the kingdom of Castile" or "Criollos," were separated from the Indians by the intermediate castes of "Mestisos," "Castisos," "Mulatos" and "Negros" (slaves or freemen). Castes, however, were

—photo by B. L. Margolies

Maximiliano Córdoba and his wife

neither endogamous nor immutable; by the mid-eighteenth century, the blurring of racial lines through miscegenation had resulted in the incorporation of new categories—"Coyote," "Lobo," and "Morisco."[31] Although most marriages were between caste equals, intermarriages also occurred among the intermediate castes, between Indians and all the intermediate castes, as well as between Spaniards and those castes with strong Spanish admixture. By the end of the century, parentage had become a questionable factor; the mixed castes had more than doubled in fifty years and were indiscriminately grouped as "non-Indian castes," identified in parish records by a symbolic cross.

In 1822, the caste system was abolished and the employment of classificatory terminology was prohibited in the attempt to establish racial parity. Locally, the caste system was abandoned by 1833, although classificatory devices continued to be employed. Castes were now euphemistically known as "classes" composed of "indios" and the others who remained unnamed. In 1860, individuals were designated either as "de razón" or "indígena" and those "de razón," whether Criollo or Mestizo, were socially elevated to the category of "Don" and "Doña." Formal distinctions disappeared from parish records by 1878, and donship, which had admirably served to identify social groups, was dropped as a classificatory tool. Yet, in 1900 it was still possible for the parish priest to send a record of "de razón" and "indígena" marriages to the civil register; the surnames which had advertised one's origins a century earlier continued to be viable indicators.

The legal buttresses sustaining the caste system were dissolved, yet social, occupational, and racial segregation continued to be as powerful as before because of substitutive mechanisms that guaranteed the maintenance of a dualistic structure. Despite the protective policies of Maximilian in the mid-1860s authorizing the creation of communal lands for villages meeting specified conditions, practical politics favored the individual accumulation of large landholdings. Indians were still a "caste" apart and treated as brutes whose lives must be regulated; those unfortunate enough to be encapsulated by the expanding estate were subjected to a series of stringent controls delineated by municipal authorities:

> The "peones acasillados" of the haciendas will enter work at 6:00 A.M. and leave at 6:00 P.M., earning 1 *real* (one-eighth of a peso) for journey-work.
>
> The hacienda will give married couples a maize ration presently valued at 3 pesos. . . . The sale of maize beyond rations will be regulated by the market price; the decision to sell or not sell the seed will be at the discretion of the owner or administrator.
>
> Likewise, the owner or administrator will also decide whether to lend money or seed to the peons.
>
> Outstanding debts and debts contracted in the future will be discharged in the form of personal labor. In the case of those peons who leave the hacienda without consent, the authorities are conceded the power to exhort them, using whatever persuasion they deem necessary, to return to the finca and discharge the obligations contracted.
>
> In the free time after agricultural duties, the *naturales* (natural Indians) of this municipality will dedicate themselves to the fabrication of wool and cotton hose (socks and stockings), pottery making, wood cutting for carbon, the rasping of magueys, and hen raising. These products will be sold in the market of the municipal seat. Due to the

numerous abuses committed, the civil authorities will regulate the market (its location and frequency, and the types of products sold) [Municipal Archives 1867].

These restrictions proved so efficacious that municipal authorities were forced to admit that the Indians were living in abject misery. Citizens "with resources" or "fortune" were invited to participate in a commission and cooperate in the foundation of municipal workshops for the benefit of the needy (Municipal Archives 1867). By 1880, privations worsened as village lands were alienated and more and more Indians had usufruct rights to shrunken pegujales. According to an objective observer, "the bulk of the inhabitants of those pueblos (of San Felipe) are engaged in agricultural labors for which they receive a wretched daily wage" (Vera 1880:116).

Although racial classifications continued to be employed in official records, the distinction between Indian and non-Indian was increasingly founded on socioeconomic criteria. The non-Indian, whether Mestizo or Criollo, based his judgments on a consideration of status markers: wealth (property and money), occupation, family background and manners. The Indians, of course, followed customs which precluded an evaluation of their worth in terms of "de razón" standards. Luis Inclán, novelist, native of San Felipe, and one of the most astute social commentators of his time, amply documented Mestizo attitudes toward the Indian population in "Astucia." The daughter of a nouveau riche hacendado (Mestizo) had finally attracted the attention of Atanasio Garduño, Criollo, descendant of a long line of wealthy Garduños, and nephew of the late Archbishop of Mexico. Atanasio narrated:

She began to speak about family and related her ancestry; then she asked about mine and I told her we were reduced to only my father, three brothers, and myself.

–Your father is very rich–she asked–and the principal of the town?

–Those are vulgar exaggerations–I responded,–he has a small ranch, a house, and four animals.

–You are very modest, Atanasio, I know everything very well . . . I don't have any relations here because, and without offense, these untamed people are very unsociable; in vain I have tried to form friendships: they are intractable and live hidden in little hovels in the manner of ferocious savages; if it weren't for the administrator of rents, the administrator of contributions, the military commander, and a few others–strangers that visit us from time to time–we would die of sadness [Inclán 1966:191-192].

Through the civil register, one was officially marked at birth as "indígena" or "no indígena" according to parental origin. At marriage one was additionally identified by occupation, and at death, efficiently buried in the parish cemetery or relegated to the paupers' cemetery, depending on personal statistical compilations. Racial designations were definitively eliminated from civil records by 1893, but as with parish archives which relied on surnames, civil authorities continued to depend on occupational status as an accurate indicator of racial antecedents. The Indian, officially known as "jornalero" (day laborer) but commonly referred to as "peon acasillado," only rarely percolated through the occupational ranks to "artisan."

During the latter half of the nineteenth century, the Indian silently suffered the intensifying aggressions of the hacendado. In some parts of the municipality, his conditions somewhat improved as the hacienda belatedly modernized, but until the Revolution, social stigma immobilized him as effectively as the anachronistic racial classifications which had long since proven valueless.[32]

Post-revolutionary ideologies have been unilaterally committed to the minimization of the cultural and social differences intrinsic to the caste system and its lingering remnants of the Independence period. Autochthonous patterns were glossed over in the perpetuation of the concept of *mestizaje* which has resulted in the popularization and acceptation of various myths, thematically uniform in their references to "equality." The neologism of cultural and racial miscegenation invariably proceeds according to an inflexible formula: Mexico will progress with social justice for each and every Mexican because the nation is egalitarian. No man is indispensable; we are all substitutable and interchangeable for we originate from a womb in which there are neither aristocracies nor oligarchies nor castes. We owe ourselves to the people. Such rhetoric receives its sustenance from a carefully constructed nationalism which stresses the superiority of Mestizo culture and pride in the Mexican's origins:

> We are profoundly proud of our Indian and Spanish ancestors. We are a nation, physically and culturally Mestizo. Fortunately, the intransigent attitudes that censured our Indian ancestors are ending. And those attitudes that with a pseudopatriotism exclusively denigrated our Spanish ancestors are also ending. We should be proud of our double ancestry and its spiritual legacy . . . . He who is ashamed of his mother and father must bear a deep affliction. He will be inhibited from undertaking grand endeavors and will lack vital impetus. We must realize that the conciliation of the factors forming our national being is the point of departure for great national enterprises [Echeverría Ideario 1969:164-165].

The new "cultural mestizaje" is a therapeutic reversal and vindicatory process; it serves to redeem the biologically defined Mestizo and his spurious origins.

Mestizaje forms part of a socialization program begun at an early age under the aegis of educational institutions. In addition to the revolutionary processes of the twentieth century, Mexican history is presented as an evolutionary process in which the conquest and the colonial period are regarded as progenitors of the national culture. The Mestizo is the symbol of Mexican nationalism and the embodiment of a doctrine that stresses "national solidarity as a fundamental factor for the integration of the country" (Ramírez 1948:305). Children are first indoctrinated in concepts of mestizaje with the story of the castes, followed by the postscript of the "mixing" of castes. If they should reach the higher grades, they will then be told to forget what they had learned in primary school; instruction will now proceed from a lesson on race. Children are taught that: races are human groups whose characteristics are transmitted through biological inheritance. The three principal races are the black race, the white race, and the yellow race. Although one race may predominate, regions are not inhabited exclusively by a particular race. Anthropological as well as biological sciences are vital tools in the study of race, since "human groups" have distinct customs and beliefs. No race can be preserved in pure form; each race has mixed with another. The mixture of different races is known as *mestizaje*. Human groups improve through mestizaje; if the Japanese (the yellow race) intermarry with Negroes, then the Japanese will improve their height while the Africans will improve their mental capacities. Countries vary in the degree of mestizaje. In the United States, for example, there is not as much mestizaje as there ought to be as a result of economic exploitation of the blacks by the whites (more than any other reason). We

Mexicans are more like the white race than any other race, but we are all Mestizos.[33]

Rhetoric and formal pedagogy have not been in vain. On all levels of society, Mexicans casually utilize egalitarian designations: we are all Mexicans, we are all Mestizos, we are all the same; even in such rural regions as San Felipe, these expressions are not uncommon; yet a significant segment of the population behaves as though they are more Mestizo than others. In fact, neoracial classifications have experienced a local revival; while a small proportion of the population continues to insist that the masses are "indígenas," symbolized by the numerous "Marías," official sentiment illustrates the confused influence of national propaganda in identifying the majority of the populace as Mestizo. In 1964, municipal authorities conducted a socio-economic census in which they utilized a mestizaje scale suspiciously similar to Jorge Tamayo's (1962). According to the criterion of language, 4646 monolingual speakers of Mazahua were classified as "indígenas" and 13,195 bilingual speakers as "Mestizo-indios." Spanish-speaking individuals, 45,678 "Mestizos" and 2878 "Mestizo-blancos," were further differentiated on the basis of "customs," while the thirty-three "blancos" were not explained (Municipal Archives 1966: Panorama Socio-económico). Both popular and official consensus of the composition of the local population are equally subjective and demonstrate the incongruities of defining a situation in which comparable variables have been consistently disregarded.

Although diversity among Indian groups has been increasingly investigated, a major preoccupation of Latin Americanists continues to be the analysis of a bipartite society, and the contradistinctions and structural relations between Indians and Mestizos. Hunt's discussion of various analyses is pertinent here:

> Essentially, the argument revolves around two basic positions, one of which stresses the differences and the lack of articulation between the groups involved, the other stressing similarities and integration. The arguments have not as yet been presented in such a way that the differences between them can be clearly resolved, and the disputes are probably not as important as the heated arguments might seem to indicate. There is too much that we don't know to choose among them . . . . Some stress economics, some values, others politics; some look out at the world from the Indian village, others stand in the Capitol and look out to the countryside; some stress pattern stability, others change; and some stress degree of integration of the various groups or categories, while others stress lack of integration [1969:549].

Despres has made a similar point in comparing the proponents of pluralism with the followers of the structural-functional model of the homogenous-heterogeneous society. In his opinion, their essential differences derive from a divergent emphasis on integration, the one treating cultural groups as "separately integrated sections," and the other as "reticulated subunits of the total system" (1967:18).

Frequently a particular interpretation is tenaciously defended at the cost of rejecting comparable, but somewhat variant, points of view argued with equal lucidity. Structural relations between Indians and Ladinos of the refuge regions are analyzed as caste relations by Aguirre Beltrán, who perceives the two groups as hierarchically ranked status groups—closed, self-sufficient, and adscriptive. Yet he also acknowledges the complexity of constructing a paradigm when it is not possible to define the Indian with certainty. Cultural characteristics as a basis of identification offer little guarantee, and even territorial localization in an indigenous community is a fallible criterion (Aguirre-Beltrán 1967:171).

Other analysts employ concepts which have been dislocated from their original context, strained and redefined until they bear only a nominal resemblance to the original. An example is the concept of social and cultural pluralism popularized by Furnivall (1944), translated into common parlance with reference to Africa and the Caribbean, stringently purified in relation to British Guiana, and transmuted in its application to the high indigenous areas of Latin America. The classic plural society was a politically integrated entity composed of culturally autonomous groups with distinctive institutional systems in which power was wielded by one cultural section, the dominant minority. Although Furnivall's historical perspective of a colonial economy was detailed and precise, his definition of pluralism floundered in vagueness. In addition to his references to Europeans, Chinese, and the indigenous population as "economic castes," "races," and "sections," the plural society was defined as a "society, comprising two or more elements or social orders which live side by side, yet without mingling, in one political unit" (1944:446). The lack of "common social demand" (1944:447) was further interpreted by M. G. Smith as a "discontinuous status order, lacking any foundation in a system of common interests and values" (1960:769). Smith's conceptualization of pluralism was more rigorous because he based it, not on mere occupational or racial distinctions, but on "formal diversity in the basic system of compulsory institutions" (1960:769). His critics, however, were confused on two points: they did not accept his interpretation of cultural pluralism as a heuristic device in the attempt to distinguish heterogeneous from plural societies (Rubin 1960:780-785); they rejected the distinction between compulsory, alternative and exclusive institutions as spurious in their analysis of institutional subsystems as equally functional (Despres 1967). Despres made a valiant attempt to evade these problems in his reevaluation of institutions as "local" and "broker" and his designation of cultural sections as either "minimal" or "maximal," depending on whether institutions tend to reinforce cultural distinctions at the local level or at the national level (1967:22-23). Yet in his equation of local with basic institutions, minimal cultural sections with heterogeneous societies, and maximal cultural sections with plural societies, Despres does not surmount the ambiguities inherent in other models of pluralism.

Colby and van den Berghe further elaborate institutional incompatibility by defining plural societies in terms of "analogous, duplicatory, parallel, non-complementary, but distinguishable sets of institutions" evinced among corporate groups (1969:7). One is bound to question the relevance of this particular approach to pluralism, when the authors contradictorily state:

> . . . the differential participation of the various groups in *shared* institutions constitutes the very core of a plural society. A plural society is not a set of groups or "cultures" living side by side and "borrowing" traits from each other; it is rather a set of interacting groups which remain distinct by virtue of *not sharing* all their institutions, and which constitute a single society by virtue of *sharing* some crucial ones [1969:20; italics mine].

In fact, the authors' entire analysis of Indian-Ladino relations stresses structural integration rather than structural diversity. "Pluralism" serves no analytic purpose and is misleading as a classificatory tool when a major portion of the study is devoted to the delineation of integrative foci, in which "interaction takes place within the context of an institutional structure which is *common* to the two groups, in spite of internal role differentiation along ethnic lines within this *unitary* institutional structure" (1969:117-118; italics mine). Pluralism is unreliable as a classificatory device because scholars insist on introducing variant criteria in their analyses. What is the purpose, for example, of categorizing internal societal complexities as pluralistic, when two proponents arrive at diametrically opposed conclusions, one depicting the situation of blacks and whites in the United States as an example of cultural pluralism (Smith 1960:771-773), the other as a perfect case of social pluralism (Colby and van den Berghe 1969:9).

The concept of pluralism, when employed in reference to Mexico, has embodied a totality of imprecisions. It has been used to describe colonial society, and in a succeeding extrapolation, applied to modern Mexican society as the characteristic feature of internal colonialism. In its latter usage, social pluralism has been minimally defined as differential participation by groups in developmental processes (González-Casanova 1968:479). Early theoretical studies have also been cited as analyses of plural societies. Although "The Folk Culture of Yucatan" has consistently been criticized concerning the validity of the folk-urban continuum, Redfield is considered an early analyst of a plural society because he "clearly stresses the need to relate the 'primitive isolate' to the large system" (Colby and van den Berghe 1969:5). For Manning Nash, Mexico is a multiple society with plural cultures; his criteria are extent of participation in the national culture and degree of identification with the national polity (1957:1966). Yet differential participation in national cultural institutions has never been a sufficient indicator of pluralism. Like Colby and van den Berghe, he also emphasizes that a single system of economic and political institutions exists. These are the basic institutions discussed by M. G. Smith, who equates institutional homogeneity with social homogeneity.

As Hunt has stated, there is still too much we do not know for us to make definitive statements in terms of pluralism concerning societal organization in Mexico. It is premature to assume that Indians and Mestizos belong to separate corporate groups, when we have not arrived at a satisfactory definition of Indian and have ignored vast sectors of the Mestizo population. It is an evasion of fact to speak of institutional segmentation or distinct cultural traditions when more and more studies have demonstrated that "social and cultural segments" are often subjective perceptions.[34] The preponderance of pluralistic labels, instead of explicating a situation that is genuinely plural, simply signify a plurality of judgments which fail to clarify the subject.

The analyses of Mexico, the plural society, have been based upon a model of Indian society, which itself has been open to question (Hunt 1969). The Indian is presented as a member of a retarded corporate group:

> of language and culture different from the national that as the inevitable residue of their historical development, has persisted in subjection to the exploitation of population groups culturally more advanced, enmeshed in their refuge regions, living a life of bare subsistence and relentlessly maintaining their ancient values and behavioral patterns, in

favor of a tenacious conservatism that creates motivations and attitudes inimical to change and transformation [Aguirre Beltrán 1967:243].

There are, however, "Indian" regions which are not refuge regions where historically derived institutional distinctions have long been erased. We may conceptualize these regions as symbiotic communities in which a bipartite distinction between Indian and Mestizo persists although they share a basic institutional system and broad cultural traditions. The regional social structure is subjectively perceived as a single stratification system dichotomized into two strata on the basis of ethnic criteria—cultural as well as pseudo-racial factors. The two social categories, Mestizo and Indian, are treated as distinct ethnic groups[35] and inter-group behavior is founded on the principle that corporate groups actually exist. Although this characterization of local social structure no longer corresponds to empirical reality, the myth of bipartition is maintained through the invocation of classificatory terminology and associated stereotyped features by those who consider themselves members of the preeminent group. At the same time it is recognized that the Indian sector is steadily moving toward a Mestizo cultural model and that individual and unilateral inter-group mobility is a common occurrence; yet this reality has had such a brief time span that perceptions continue to be phrased in dyads. These groups may properly be considered subcultural units, regional variants of a wider cultural tradition (Wagley 1968).

San Felipeños rarely verbalize distinctions in terms of "Mestizo" and "indígena." Mestizos identify themselves as gente de razón and Indians as "inditos" or "naturalitos," the derogatory diminutives of the classificatory devices used in the civil and parish registers. Unlike their large landholding predecessors, Mestizos do not consider themselves inherently superior to the Indian populace. The Mestizos who today are prominent townspeople lived the revolutionary experience, applauded land distribution, and saw the final destruction of an anchronistic social order in the late thirties. They acknowledge that the Indian peon was oppressed and exploited, and assert that the Indian peasant of the present is not the Indian of 1940. Yet racial prejudices have been transformed into ethnic prejudices because of the Mestizo's composite view of what the Indian once was. Many townspeople have worked their way up to respectable and solid positions from modest origins; they expected the Indian to do likewise, that is, they expected the Indian to disappear along with the acasillado. Not only did the Indians persist, but they doubled in number, a phenomenon which the Mestizo finds abhorrent and resents, but is forced to accept. Were he to compare the Indian with the Indian of a generation ago, he would indeed be enlightened, but the Mestizo often pays lip service in his references to the changing Indian. The Mestizo has an adequate understanding of the regional economy, but only a partial comprehension of the Indian's variant culture. He tends to laugh off, scoff at, or misinterpret what he does not understand. Rather than admit his own ignorance, the Mestizo expresses his concept of Indian culture. He inevitably uses his own culture as a frame of reference in evaluating Indian culture and bases his stereotypes on the degree of correspondence with his life style. These comparisons are perfectly in line with national ideology which has whitewashed Mestizo culture, elevating it to a cult which must be emulated for proper integration into national society.[36]

The fundamental premise of all stereotypes is the contention that Indians are "backward." Backwardness, although sometimes expressed in cultural terms, is more frequently correlated with grinding misery. The Indians are regarded as pestiferous bearers of poverty who have pervaded and debased the municipality. Poverty is not simply a humble standard of living, but an affront to the Mestizos. Indians, because they are poor, do not know how to live in dignity. Mestizos are especially offended when they perceive this "pestilence" invading their town:

> The problem of San Felipe (town) is those people in the plaza. The main street is like a barranca, but then they're accustomed to live in barrancas. The garbage in the plaza is a disgrace–if you want to know what the real garbage is, it's out there in the plaza (referring to the Indians). They put bathrooms in the town hall, but what for–they're accustomed to going outside their front doors. How can you put public washstands in the entry to the town. It's a disgrace! They're used to washing their clothes against the rocks.

Indian homes, as well as Indians themselves, are considered dirty; Mestizos assume that Indians neither wash down their houses nor bathe because they have to lug water from distant wells. Most Mestizos have never been in an Indian home and are not qualified to make judgments, while others marvel at the Indian's white teeth when they are convinced that he has never immersed himself in water. Outsiders are warned not to shake hands with Indians because they are so filthy. Indians do not know how to eat properly because they sell the best of what they have–milk, eggs and meat–and subsist on tortillas and chile; yet they are well conserved, strong and fat. Mestizos do not understand why an Indian will sell what they esteem nor can they fathom the motives behind the sale. They know only that the Indian will squander his pesos.

Indians are blamed for their own backwardness for two reasons: their indolence and their most flagrant vice–pulque. They are considered lazy because they do not work a normal eight-hour day, can be seen "lounging" around their houses at odd hours, and are adverse to accepting menial jobs in town. Townsmen, then, will never hire an Indian as a "trusted employee," for they believe that the Indian will be off greeting passing acquaintances or disappearing into the nearest cantina. For the Mestizo, pulque symbolizes resignation, the poor man's means for drowning his sorrows. The constant vision of the Indian, lolling against the cantina wall with a jug of foaming pulque in his hands is an irritant to the Mestizo. They feel the Indian should be buying workpants and medicines rather than drinking away his money. The Indian who sends his child to work, later spending the child's salary in the cantina, is morally reprehensible. Yet Mestizo critics have capitalized on this vice by opening large *pulquerías* in town. Public drinking for the Indian, however, is an accessory to group interaction. The Indian has a high tolerance to pulque; it is an important dietary supplement which accompanies meals, and a thirst quencher in the fields. Festive activities and Sunday markets are a time of license for the Indian; it is also the only time when his drinking is publicly evident. The Indian never drinks alone; that is a habit reserved for Mestizos.

Occasionally, a perspicacious townsman will attempt to place blame where it is due. He will relate historical fact with present events, explaining the Indian's backwardness in terms of forced submissiveness to the hacendados, a black period in history when Indians were treated as slaves, or he will extrapolate from more recent events, emphasizing post-revolutionary exploitation of Mexicans by Mexicans. Don Ernesto, discussing the inferiority complex of the Mexican, noted: "This has been our history–it's Mexicans exploiting Mexicans–from the *bracero* (migrant worker) to the housemaid, to those people sitting out there. Ask anyone of them who worked as a bracero–who did the exploiting? Who collected the money at the border? We have a lot of misery here (waving a hand at the plaza); they say the best school is hunger, but I don't believe it."

Indians also have "distinct customs," although most Mestizos cannot accurately describe them. But credence is sufficient motive for the Mestizo to either denigrate, distort, deprecate or sneer at the Indian's customs. Mazahua, the indigenous language, is evaluated as a nonlanguage because it is unwritten and has no apparent rules; Mestizos refer to Mazahua as the Indian's dialect. Rituals are interpreted simplistically. All Souls' Day signals commemorative services for the dead, private prayers, a visit to the cemetery, and the offering of ritual foods. Both Mestizos and Indians remember the deceased, yet Mestizos mirthfully insist that Indians actually believe the souls of the dead consume the offerings. Townspeople regard "Nuestro Padre Jesús" as their patron, but acknowledge that the Indians give the fiesta for them; they do not realize what "Nuestro Padre Jesús" signifies for the Indian; they are neither aware of the system of compañías nor the hereditary vows undertaken by socios.

Mestizos believe that they have an accurate acquaintanceship with Indian character; the traits attributed to the Indian, some of which are seemingly positive, are negatively valuated. Wealthy townspeople tend to think the Indian is always trying to put something over on them, while poorer Mestizos resent "those people" practically in their own backyard. Thus, Indians are known to be "listos"–clever. And because they are clever, they are capable of suspiciousness and dishonesty. Indians are suspicious, it is said, because when they make purchases in town, they examine the items minutely; others are incapable of explaining the Indian's suspiciousness, but continue to characterize him as such. Dishonesty, of course, is a natural consequence of distrustfulness and has dualistic implications for the Mestizo. Dishonesty takes the form of petty stealing or lying. Mestizos expect to lose 15% of their seed if they hire peons, and they anticipate that objects will disappear from their homes if they should leave an Indian standing alone in the patio. Mestizos are also convinced that an Indian will never tell the truth–"Oh, you can't believe anything these naturales say; they say everything reversed." Mestizos know that the Indian is probably not married if he says he is, probably earns 5000 pesos if he claims to earn 1000, and probably went to an herbalist when he said he consulted a doctor. Indians are well aware of this mutual mistrustfulness and pepper their conversations with the expression, "Why should I lie; what do I have to lie about." Needless to say, this only strengthens the Mestiso's convictions that he is being played for a fool. Others are convinced that the Indian's poverty is simply a facade which he agilely maintains. One mestizo stall owner who based his opinions on his observations of market interaction contested the pulque interpretation:

> These people are clever and have more money than any of us. They eat their tortillas with chile because they are saving it all for land. They buy a piece of land and in three

years the price has tripled. The money's there–in the land and house. They say they have no money. But if they have to go to Ixtlahuaca to pay a fine, the money suddenly appears. If a man goes to his wife and asks for some change for a 'drink,' she takes out a wad of money. If he goes to the butcher and doesn't have any change, she pulls out a 50 or 100 peso bill. The women are always plucking money out from their breasts. How can you say they don't have any money.

At this point, he interrupted the conversation, drew a roll of bills out of his pants pocket, and vainly searched for change to send his son on an errand. He finally settled on a 100 peso bill and began to commiserate over his own poverty.

In addition to the other aspects of the Indian's immorality–his impudicity regarding drinking, his dishonorableness, and churlishness–the Indian is stripped of all but the basest desires; he cannot live, love and mourn as the Mestizo does. One ex-schoolteacher cited the example of an Indian woman who came to see him, complaining that her husband had another woman and didn't hit her anymore. "Here," he said, "the women are accustomed to being maltreated and when their husbands forget to abuse them, they feel unloved. The men have women only for carnal uses; the women serve for bestial purposes. If the women should arrive at the same level of instruction as their husbands, the men wouldn't be able to control them." Such lack of morality is so ingrained in the Mestizo's stereotype that it is not even necessary to be specific. When he refers to "these people" or "those people," fellow Mestizos know whom he is talking about, and when he states, "but they're Indians" or "those naturalitos are all the same" or "you know how they are," one can simply activate a rich lexicon of stereotypes which will explain everything.

Some Mestizos solve the problem of the omnipresent Indian by pretending he is not there, or if forced to a confrontation, treating him as a nonentity. Upper-class Mestizos are generally polite to Indians whom they know; they are the dons and patrons of the town and are approached respectfully by Indians–addressed as "jefe" or "patron" and accorded the honor of a doffed hat held gingerly in one's hands. Indians who are not known are simply ignored.[37] If a group of Indians are seated along the curb, the townsman will merely weave his way among them, or, if they are lounging in the streets, they will spread apart, yielding the right-of-way. Other Mestizos expect the same proprieties, but do not receive them. They then react by treating the Indian with familiarity, failing to recognize him until a proper interval has passed, expressing annoyance by speaking in a loud, curt voice, slamming a taxi door on his foot, or ignoring his request to stop at a bus stop. Since the Indian is a nonperson, some Mestizos feel they can misbehave with impunity; thus, a contemptuous word or expression might be uttered as though it were meant for the air. A Mestizo might hold his liquor poorly in front of a group of Indians and rest assured that no one had seen him or he might pass an Indian on the street, pause in search of a surrogate victim, and kick a stray dog energetically in the ribs. The animal, yelping and screaming in pain, limps rapidly away, while the Indian turns to acknowledge the commotion and continues serenely on his way.

Just as the Mestizo's stereotypes are based on an incomplete knowledge of Indian culture, his identification of an Indian corporate group is facilitated by the employment of "indicators," readily visible cultural characteristics perceived as peculiar to Indians. These indicators were viable factors a generation ago and are still considered pertinent although not totally accurate. The Mestizo can stereotypically *define* an Indian group, but he is hard-pressed to *identify* this group. He manipulates each of the indicators individually to verify the ethnicity of the Indians and justify his perceptions of a distinct Indian group. When he uses them collectively, the Mestizo discovers that his tight, deceptive model of the Indian disintegrates. He cannot identify "Indians" by a series of rigid, correlated traits because he does not encounter a group which unilaterally conforms. In his personal experience, he realizes that different individuals exhibit variant characteristics. He continues to hold suppositions in reference to Indians, at the same time recognizing that he cannot validate the ethnicity of particular "Indians." The indicators are also ranked in importance; when the Mestizo is unable to identify individuals by the most substantive traits, he retreats, using the label, "medio indio," in acknowledgment of idiosyncracies which distinguish one from the denomination "indito."

Language, a precise indicator in the past, continues to be the most significant characteristic of the indigenous group, according to Mestizos. The Mestizo, when venturing into the plaza on Sunday or passing a pulquería, frequently hears Mazahua spoken; he then says all Indians speak Mazahua and all people who speak Mazahua are Indians, although he can cite examples of Mestizos who speak Mazahua and Indians who do not speak Mazahua. The Mestizo's contentions would seem to be corroborated by statistical evidence; although monolinguism has steadily declined to an insignificant proportion,[38] bilingualism has increased along with the population rise and the decline in monolingualism. In 1940, there were 13,652 monolingual speakers and 8,309 bilingual speakers among the 37,781 inhabitants; by 1950, 38.4% of the populace (15,818) was bilingual and by 1960, 57% (30,957)[39] (VI, VII, VIII, IX Censos Generales de Población). These statistics, however, obscure certain facts. The census figures measure ability to speak Mazahua, not the extent to which it is spoken. Many individuals who can speak Mazahua do not generally speak it, either at home or in public. Whereas twenty years ago, a woman from the interior might have walked into a store in San Felipe and asked for an item in Mazahua, this would be a rare occurrence today. Villagers know that to speak Mazahua is to be stigmatized not only in town, but certainly in the city. Even stall merchants who can speak Mazahua conduct their market business in Spanish, although they are perfectly aware their customers can also speak Mazahua. The majority of bilingual speakers are also past the age of thirty; although parents may speak Mazahua among themselves, Spanish is the chosen language in front of children. Parents realize that all but one or two of their children will leave the municipality; they prepare them for school and their eventual exodus by speaking Spanish. Even in the most physically inaccessible villages of the municipality where over 90% of the adults are bilingual, the children cannot speak Mazahua. Parents generally make the deliberate decision to speak Spanish shortly after the birth of their second child; the eldest child may understand Mazahua, but he will never speak it, while the youngest children will be totally ignorant of all but the simplest salutations. The younger generation knows that the label "indígena" ultimately depends on the ability to speak Mazahua. If they cannot or do not speak Mazahua, then they cannot be Indian. They may have Indian parents, but will no longer consider themselves Indian. Approximately 10% of the townspeople who consider themselves Mestizo and are regarded as Mestizos can speak Mazahua; they do not advertise this ability and sometimes suppress it; through intermarriage and movement into the town they disassociated with anything Indian; if their ability cannot be proven, then neither can their ethnic origin.

Until the ejidal lands were distributed, physical appearance was a viable indicator of ethnic origin. Although Mestizos contended that Indians were darker and shorter than they were, they were justified in their claims that the Indians "all looked alike." Indians had a distinctive attire which distinguished them from even the poorest Mestizo. Men wore long and narrow muslin trousers, a long-sleeved muslin shirt with a "Mao" collar, a woolen belt woven with stylized animal motifs, leather sandals, a wide-brimmed straw hat, and a woolen *serape*. The women dressed in several ankle-length muslin petticoats, the outer one elaborately embroidered at the hem, a woolen bell skirt, an embroidered muslin blouse with a square neck and short loose sleeves, a narrow belt wound several times around the waist, and a woolen *quexquemitl* (poncho). The women walked barefooted, and adorned themselves with plaited ribbons in their braids, numerous strands of glass beads, and silver earrings. With the exception of the belt which is donned infrequently, the men's garb has been totally abandoned. Men presently wear dungarees or chino pants with matching jackets, sport shirts, cotton hats and workshoes. The only notable characteristic of the man's dress is its obvious wear and tear; clothing is worn until it has faded to a dingy white, and is patched and repatched. Wool clothing has been abandoned by women and the quexquemitl and bell skirt are stored as costumes to be worn by dancers during the principal fiestas. Women from the interior may still be distinguished by their homemade cotton skirts and blouses, and their *rebozos* (shawls), used for carrying the youngest child and assorted cargo. Women still go barefoot in their homes, but wear inexpensive plastic shoes in public. In the barrios and villages near town, the predominant attire is a skirt, blouse, and sweater purchased in the local market; younger women have bobbed their hair and own an assortment of costume jewelry. Parents make every effort to send their children to school properly dressed, in freshly starched clothing and presentable shoes; the preponderance of *descalzos* noted by the Mestizos is often the result of parents' admonishments to save footware for school. Rebozos, braids and serapes are common to Mestizos also; only the belt is a distinctive remnant of an Indian costume. When a Mestizo spies the belt, it indicates that he is confronted with an Indian without knowing whether the individual speaks Mazahua.

Another indicator which served admirably in the past was place of residence. Every Mestizo believes he knows where other Mestizos reside; the town was the exclusive preserve of gente de razón, hamlets like La Cienega and ex-railroad stations like Carmona were settled by Mestizos, and ejido villages had been invaded by Mestizo merchants whose obvious prosperity attracted additional waves of Mestizos. If an individual lives in a village known to have been incorporated into the hacienda and lacking what the Mestizo considers the basic necessities of town life—a plaza, concentrated houses, electricity and drinkable water—he will be identified as Indian. In villages which have recently obtained basic facilities, the townsman will remember it as it was; its residents must be Indian although they do not evince any of the usual indicators. Townsmen born in a barrio or village often hide their place of origin, claiming they were born in San Felipe and availing themselves of the resulting confusion between San Felipe, the town, and San Felipe, the municipality.

Other indicators included a series of cultural traits which in coordination with language, appearance and residency, assured one's identification: thus the Indian lived in a one-room adobe house with a packed earth floor, slept on a straw mat, ground his own corn, maintained a peculiar meal pattern, and cooked distinctive food over carbon fires. These traits, however, are no longer employed either as correlates or as diagnostic attributes of an Indian group. Mestizos still refer to them not in verifying ethnic identity, but in estimating socioeconomic status. Borah's once controversial statement is now applicable to a situation in which individuals do not identify as Indians and are uninterested in maintaining the "customs" of their parentage, although they are still ethnically differentiated by equivocal indicators:

> The backwardness of the people denominated Indian–and such it is since it vanishes in most instances whenever and wherever economic circumstances permit–is imposed in some instances by isolation but almost invariably by a grinding poverty. It thus appears that the basic criterion is economic, and that the term Indian today designates in Mexican popular and even learned usage the most primitive and poverty-stricken part of the peasantry [1954:337].

Although the social system is still subjectively perceived as consisting of two corporate groups, these perceptions are increasingly phrased in terms of class indicators. Behavioral patterns derived from an order of prestige based upon the dichotomy between superior and inferior cultural groups are more and more derived from a hierarchy in which the "haves" excel the "have-nots." Mestizos, although they have not abandoned references to "inditos" and "naturalitos," frequently speak of Indians in class terms–"la gente humilde" (the humble people) or "los pobres" (the poor). Such designations are totally in agreement with the peasant's self-conception; "somos todos humildes y pobres" is their open statement of fact (we are all humble and poor). Mestizos also realize there is considerable overlap in socioeconomic position between the two groups, and poor Mestizos and Indians are often designated by the same status term–"peasant." Most people do not mind being known as peasants. "Peasant" is primarily the occupational status of poor farmer and is used interchangeably with "agricultor" by ejidatarios and small-scale proprietors. Since most poor farmers are also Indian, the term has subtle ethnic connotations. Poor Mestizos who have lived in town for several years and manage small stores or work as artisans are often referred to as peasants because of their known Indian origin. They are the most vociferous denigrators of the Indian, who often surpasses them economically and has the minimal satisfaction of owning his own home and possessing inalienable rights to a piece of land.

Just as Indians regard themselves and are regarded as the "clase humilde," "clase baja" (lower class), or "los pobres," Mestizos identify and are identified with the "clase media" (middle class). Although there are considerable differences in standards of living within each status group, the Mestizos associate the clase humilde with stark misery, while the Indians characterize the middle class as "those who live well." Both classes also distinguish themselves from the "clase alta" or "clase rica" (the upper class or the rich), a group found only in the metropolis.

Within the middle class, people recognize three status levels, based primarily on economic criteria (wealth and occupation), and secondarily on such factors as education, family background, and individual worth. It is not surprising that when "progress" is conceptualized in personal terms of improving one's economic situation–"earning one peso, and then trying to earn two"–and living better, status distinctions should also be expressed as "los ricos," "los que estan más o menos" (those who manage), and "los que van con el dia" (those who live from hand-to-mouth). Los ricos are distinguished principally by their capital assets; they are people with money in the bank, properties (land and houses), and commercial establishments. Their assets are valued at a minimum of 100,000 pesos and they are envied for their financial security and the independence mobilized by this security. They are the "doers" of the town, having participated in public office, organized civic affairs, and aroused community spirit. They are considered knowledgeable because of their practical experience culled from a lifetime of hard work, and are successful examples of the frequent statement, "la persona que mas sabe, mas gana" (the person who knows more earns more). Men with professional titles, although they do not possess the capital assets characteristic of the elite, are included in this group. Teachers, public accountants, and doctors are respected for their long years of formal education and evident literacy. This class has also expanded to include several men who "never made much money," but live well and are descended from old town families. They hold an anomalous position among the elite because of their selfless and continual devotion to town affairs. To the other townsmen, their *palancas*–their influence with outsiders–is an obvious advantage, as long as these contacts are cultivated with decency and honorableness.

Although the local ricos constitute a *rural* elite, they think of themselves as distinctly urban. Even the well-to-do merchant who may be the only person "de razón" in one of the interior ejido villages lives at a level which he believes is shared by middle-class residents of Mexico City. He, too, has traveled to Europe, displays tourist trinkets in his sitting room as evidence of his worldliness, furnishes his home with coordinated "sets," entertains with sophisticated appetizers and desserts and expensive liquor, owns the latest kitchen appliances, is intensely interested in camera equipment, owns a car or at least a truck, buys his clothes in Mexico City or Toluca, reads La Prensa or Excelsior, and sends his children to college.

The rural elite feel they live in the provinces, not in the country, while the town-based elite are the most susceptible to "city sickness." Harris's observation of town-country relations in Brazil, in which "the uninformed visitor to Minas Velhas can find no quicker way to alienate himself from the townspeople than to confuse life in the interior (a vida do sertão) with life in the country (a vida do campo)" (1956:144) is equally applicable to San Felipe. Wealthy townspeople know that if a stranger walked into their homes, he would think he was in Mexico City; women wear slacks only when they go on picnics and regret that they do not live in the country where they could wear slacks every day. Wealthy townspeople consider even the most successful merchants who reside in the country *rancheros.*[40] Rancheros are famous for their niggardliness. They fry their eggs on a dry skillet to save shortening; they might invite one to be a godparent out of esteem, yet they are also motivated by "interests." Luis López was invited to be the godfather of a young bridegroom from San José and merely expected to give the couple an extravagant gift; he soon found himself contracting the *mariachis* (band) and orchestra at the specifications of the parents, buying flowers in Toluca, and later transporting them to the village. He recalled his experience with this family when he spent a night in San José:

> We were reduced to talking about the weather.
> "It's cold."
> "Yes, it's very cold," I answered.
> "It's very windy."
> "Yes, it's quite windy . . . are the girls in school?"
> "No, they used to be with the nuns in Toluca."
> By then it was eight o'clock and the conversation had ended. What was I going to do at 8:00 P.M.–there wasn't even a book around. So I went to bed early. The bed looked great until I got under the covers. A swirl of dust escaped from the bedding and a horrible odor like dead hens permeated the blankets. I thought I would die. I woke up at 5:00 A.M. because I couldn't breathe, ran out of the house and down to the truck where I napped for two hours before returning to San Felipe. I did say good-bye to the family and never returned. The girls are in the store all day and let an Indian girl run the house; the food she prepared–a huge plate of soup with unidentifiable things floating on top–I wouldn't give to the dogs. And the sheets hadn't been changed in years. That's life in the country. And these people are really something! The godmothers are going to be in long dresses–one wrong step and the dresses are ruined. Do they think they live in Toluca?

As one moves down the status hierarchy, the pertinent characteristic of those considered *más o menos* is their basic decency; they are the *gente decente*. They may not have servants in their homes, a sitting room, a television or a refrigerator, but they have steady incomes of at least 1000 pesos monthly from such diverse sources as small businesses, corn crops, government jobs, a small inheritance, or a pension. They, themselves, do not expect to drastically improve or change their situation, but they have aspirations for their children; they want their children to have a basic primary-school education and a skill, and they will skimp and sacrifice so that one or two can become a professional. They are hard workers and have little patience with those who exist from hand-to-mouth. These people must eke out a living from a small piece of ejido land, a tiny shop, artisanship or brief stints as an unskilled laborer on public projects. They, too, are often blamed for their own poverty; their vices and their laziness are seen as impediments to a decent life.

Not everybody agrees about the status placement of particular persons. San Felipe is a small town where residents generally know each other's business, but perspectives differ. To those below, los ricos appear to be a solidly united impenetrable club in which intermarriage is a natural occurrence. Yet it is precisely these families that keep to themselves, entertain themselves, and reinforce family ties through compadrazgo because they do not wish to be obligated to outsiders. And intermarriage is a fortuitous event in which prominent families are forced to socialize when their children marry over their objections. Dissensions, aversions and incompatibilities are lost in the shimmer of a status position that obscures all but the reality of unavoidable wealth. Los ricos, on the other hand, may think that certain people have "nothing to live from" when, in fact, they might be quite *decente*, living what others think is a strict moral life and striving to improve their economic situation.

While prestige is contingent primarily upon monetary factors, it is also dependent on an evaluation of one's honorableness. People are respected and treated accordingly not only because they are wealthy, but also because they have conducted themselves honorably. A man of modest economic means, although he may never receive as much esteem as wealthier townspeople, will be considered respectable if he is a good family man, a dedicated and honest worker, and does not drink excessively. He will not be respected if he thinks he is better than everybody else, is self-centered, or has casually fathered illegitimate children throughout the town; a woman who gossips viciously, strikes her children or parents, or is openly promiscuous will never be respected. If a man belongs to los ricos and has acted dishonorably, he will be accorded respect because of his wealth, but he will have no real prestige. Don P., for example, is one of the richest men in town; people defer to him publicly although they do not consider him a respectable person. Every action undertaken by him to reach his present level of wealth was accomplished through fraud and guile. He made his fortune as a money-lender; he cajoled his sister-in-law out of investments. His small cantina does an extraordinary business; the townspeople believe he is spiking the drinks with drugs because the peasants collapse in a stupor upon leaving the premises. Making money is a fine goal as long as it is done with some integrity. Veritable prestige is a status held by ten men at the most; they are the genuine "dons" of the town and are respected by both townspeople and villagers. Don Ernesto, for example, has conducted his life according to his own high principles of integrity and taught his children to adhere to the same standards. He loves the town and has served not only as municipal president, but throughout his life; he has collected funds for civic projects and seen the projects through to completion. He has repeatedly represented the town on regional committees. When he does not have a good word for somebody he remains quiet. He is familiar with municipal and parish archives and versed in town history and lore; he is a prolific writer of town speeches. He offers advice without a trace of egoism and is totally admired by villagers because he gives them legal aid when the "local judge" dismisses them curtly from the town hall.

At the bottom of the prestige hierarchy are los pobres, who receive no respect because they are both impoverished and ignoble (dishonorable). The criteria of "honorableness" is of vital importance in ascertaining why ethnic factors continue to obscure class factors. Historically, the Indians were defined as those without morality and identified by blatant cultural indicators

> which, due to their historical importance in the region, subsume and impose themselves upon all other factors of stratification. While it dichotomizes social relationships, ethnic stratification diminishes the importance of the socio-economic scale or continuum based on quantitative indices. This is true to such a degree that many Indians and Ladinos share the same socio-economic level without the disappearance of ethnic stratification [Stavenhagen 1970b:263].

Although Indians may no longer exhibit the most obvious cultural characteristics and may have risen on an economic scale, they continue to be defined by moral stereotypes which impede the relinquishing of ethnic identification. For

—photo by B. L. Margolies

Don Ernesto López

Mestizos, who live predominantly in town, it is a truism that one must be careful in the outskirts and take heed in the interior; unlike townspeople who are generally "very honorable," the others are without integrity. It is unlikely ethnic stratification will disappear as long as stereotypic definitions obfuscate reality; yet class factors take precedence when the Mestizo can personally evaluate the moral worth of individuals. He must be able to judge one's level of prestige by the same criteria that are his reference points for fellow Mestizos. The Indian, then, in order to be identified, defined and adjudicated as Mestizo has a triple burden.

He must, of course, improve his standard of living, ceasing to show the most palpable evidence of poverty. The Indians are los pobres, but they do not unequivocally share the same level of poverty. Indians may be stoical regarding their poverty, they may be frank about their impoverishment, but they do not value poverty. Service's statement that the peasant's "experience and that of his ancestors, is that consistent application to his work would be expected to maintain him in the status in which he was born but with no chance of enhancing it" (1954:124) would be clamorously disputed in San Felipe. The "Indians" consider themselves farmers and ejidatarios as opposed to acasillados, the status which most eloquently expresses the life style of their parents. They feel that life is better than it was a generation ago and will continue to improve. Indians are not interested in maintaining "traditions" or the socioeconomic indices of their predecessors whom they characterize as "backward," "closed" and "ignorant." Their prime goal is the improvement of their economic position—"overcome the customs we had and the situation we find ourselves in." This has been accomplished by expanding into traditionally Mestizo occupations—artisanship and commerce—and through wholesale migration, both as laborers to Mexico City and braceros to the United States. While there are villagers from the interior who cannot afford a bed and subsist on a diet of nopales, chile, quelites and tortillas, there are also villagers who have refurbished their homes by adding rooms and windows, furnished them with wardrobes and kitchen sets, own bikes, radios, sewing machines, record players, and even stoves. They eat three meals a day including a large dinner in the afternoon; their children are given few responsibilities in the home and enrolled in school. People feel they have the obligation to leave their offspring more than three donkeys and a cuartillo of maize.

The Indian must also modify the obvious cultural characteristics generally associated with his ethnic status. He must maintain a "decent" face, looking and talking like a Mestizo; those elements which are not functional in a Mestizo world must be renounced. Yet genuine cultural distinctions do not necessarily have to be abandoned. Lower-class Mestizos of recent Indian origin participate in orthodox town fiestas, but according to the compañía system; they prepare the same festive foods as the Indian. They may not openly consult an herbalist, but they doctor themselves with herbs for the vaguely defined illnesses of *susto* and *los aires*; they hold the same beliefs regarding "hot" and "cold" foods and malevolent vapors, and practice similar dietary restrictions during the two-month period preceding childbirth. Lower-class Mestizos when contemplating marriage make their intentions known through the services of a go-between, although they might present the bride's family with a homemade cake rather than a basket of bread and fruit. They also retain the joint household pattern when sons marry, yet they will never be mistaken for Indians. As long as one maintains a façade and claims that the Indian belongs to another race, one is assured of Mestizo respectability.

Although an Indian may have prestige and be respected in his own residential community for participation in municipal government or the compañía system, he will receive no respect from Mestizos unless he moves in town networks. He must live in town or near town and have constant reference to the town through work or residence in order to build a reputation as an individual worthy of respect. If he has lived in town for several years, conducted himself with propriety, and participated at least passively in town social networks, his origins will be remembered and occasionally verbalized, but he will be treated as a Mestizo, while his children will be considered "born Mestizos." If he retains his residence in one of the barrios but works in town, holding an occupational status which has not been discriminately associated with ethnic status (comerciante as opposed to tallador), he will be evaluated by class criteria; his ethnic identification will be confused by Mestizos, but his children, too, will be respected as Mestizos. Basilio Marcos, for example, is considered Indian because of his known ability to speak Mazahua; his sons are evaluated as "ejido people" and "small comerciantes." Because they "live more in the town than in Tunal," they are considered "civilized" people, although descended from others who were "more backward." Their ethnic status is uncertain, but their young children neither identify nor are identified as Indians.

In less than one generation, there has been a considerable realignment of ethnic lines according to class relationships. The majority of Mestizos do not feel themselves threatened by the Indian's changing ethnic status, and the few who raise the doubtful specter of "race" interpret this concept in cultural terms. The Mestizo distinguished himself on the basis of cultural superiority–he led a "civilized" life. The Indians, just as peasant populaces elsewhere (Moss and Cappannari 1962; Silverman 1966) were "uncivilized." The Mestizo still clings to his ethnic prejudices, while at the same time acknowledging that through education, occupational diversification, urban experiences, and higher standards of living, the next generation may see the disappearance of the Indian.

POSTSCRIPT

Historical change occurs when the expected renewal of conditions and circumstances from one moment to the next is not completed but altered. The pattern of renewal is recognized but it is distorted; it is changed.

–George Kubler [1962]

When one returns to San Felipe after an absence of several months, familiarity is the prime sensation, yet there are also notable disparities–new street lights blotting the skyline, a recently laid atrium floor, discordant colors of freshly painted houses, the absence of one's favorite stores which could not survive a season of drought, and new families optimistically expecting that life would be better than in their former towns. What had happened since I left? "Nothing," the people say, "there is no progress in San Felipe del Progreso, everything is the same." In comparison with the general *movimiento* (animation) of Mexico City, the construction of an impressive Zócalo in Toluca, the facilities of Olympic City, the phenomenon of hippie invasions for hallucinogenic trips in Oaxaca, and man's conquest of the Moon, San Felipe has not changed.

Upon visiting the barrio of La Cabecera to call on the mother of a newborn infant, I found her bemused and distressed. During her pregnancy and birth, she had been under the care of her mother-in-law and an aged midwife. They insisted that she swaddle herself tightly in an old rebozo. I found her with the rebozo shoved carelessly to the edge of the bed. She had just been checked by the doctor who chided, "what do you mean by swathing yourself, what do you mean by using a swathe!" She happened to agree with the doctor who she felt was obviously competent. But then mother-in-law arrived, spied the abandoned belt, and rebuked her for removing it. She wearily put the belt back on, only to remove it again before the doctor's next visit. Although the doctor had given her a lesson in hygiene, she did not want to quibble with her mother-in-law. The doctor felt that these people would never change.

If one takes a more periscopic perspective, the local society has scarcely been moribund. Change is measured by San Felipeños in palpable terms–the long expected termination of a community project, a new house, an unusually plentiful crop, a more satisfying diet, a new pair of shoes, children growing to maturity, birth and death. Yet they also realize that change is generational and sequential rather than cyclical. Although memory does not revert to a caste system stoked by Criollo-Spanish machinations condoned through governmental indifference, it does extend to a period in which peonage was the life condition most people were born into. The hacendados and the Mestizo townspeople who reveled in their presence were the authorities of their regional demesnes. Peons were theoretically free and could leave the estate at will, but for what—a stint in the mines which would leave one impaired with silicosis, a menial job in the city where conditions were equally bad if not worse, or a living eked from stony parcels abandoned by the hacienda. It was a revolution that simulated agrarian unrest, but it was the revolutionary government that finally translated these demands into land distribution, to institutionalize its bases of legitimacy. The peasant, as far as he is concerned, now possesses the three basics for a rural life—his own house, his own land (or rights to land), and his own food supply—necessities which his parents lacked; empirically, he is correct when he says his life is better than that of his parents. He believes that hard work is more important than luck, but unlike townsmen, he relies on God rather than on "political palancas." Many townspeople actually do have palancas and at least the possibility of successfully manipulating them on occasion, but the peasant does not have such opportunities. The peasant is more and more evaluated in class terms and is not paralytically stigmatized as an Indian, but this does not relieve his patent fears—fear of harvest failure, fear of the consequences of illness, and fear that his most tangible savings, his animals, will dwindle. He knows that these fears can be alleviated and when he claims that the government ignores him, his lack of confidence is justified. Thus he prays to God, his only alternative, because he himself will probably die as a farmer; yet he does not have the same expectations for his children. His children would be fools if they were to follow exactly in their father's footsteps. Rather than being out of tune with a more open society, the peasant, overexpectantly perhaps, has aspirations for his children which belie his actual circumstances.

Although Foster has emphasized the "openness" of Mexican society, in the sense that peasants have been invited "to come into the nation" and partake of its "support, services, and opportunities" (1967:350), the so-called problem of peasant villages is not their static state perpetuated through non-disposable cognitive orientations, but their *exclusion* from the benefits of this wider society because they have been no more than "invited in."

Someone or more accurately, some group, must always bear the blame for such a problem. Occasionally the government is blamed and occasionally the rural elite, but because they are both more powerful and vocal than the peasant, the peasant is the most popular culprit,[41] despite recognition of the historical-social determinants of his "assumptions." It is therefore easy to claim, as Avila has, that faltering growth "can be traced to personality traits of the people themselves" (1969:177). According to this proponent of growth-retarding factors, these personality traits consist of a pastiche of "old beliefs and traditions deeply rooted in their character" (1969:177). Avila then concludes that sentimentalism, pleasure, ignorance, fear of being thought either lazy or ambitious, stubbornness, etc., are examples of nonpecuniarily-oriented behavior which should not be associated with "irrational behavior, because in the scheme of values of the villages they embodied accepted norms" (1969:178). Although Foster explains how easy it is for "economic man" to accuse others of being "irrational," he popularized the "fundamental factor" theory of retardation:

> . . . we must put at or near the top increasingly outdated assumptions about the conditions that govern life. The ideal man of traditional society is no longer ideal in a changing world. The personality characteristics inculcated in him in childhood and by his experiences, which enabled him to function successfully in a relatively static society, now are an enormous drag, a heavy weight which most people are as yet unable to shed. The ideal man of earlier years, who still is the prevailing type, finds himself bewildered and confused by present conditions; in the new world he is increasingly a misfit [1967:350].

His students also insist on "the persistence of a social structure validated by a conservative ethos that impedes major changes" (Nelson 1971:131). Other writers have since whitewashed their appraisals, but they have not yet abandoned them. Cancian states this mellowing tendency with lucidity:

> Ideas about peasant irrationality have virtually passed out of the scientific vocabulary and have become exclusively a part of the public and political domain; to almost all scientists interested in agricultural development, all men are now rational. But the practical problems that originally brought on the notion of irrationality have not disappeared, and the old labels have been replaced among scientists by the more subtle distinction between those who respond to economic variables and those who are tradition-bound [1972:199].

Viewing the "peasant problem" in its proper context instead of reverting to culture syndromes does not, as Liebow stated, "reduce the magnitude of the problem, but does serve to place it in the more tractable context of economics, politics and social welfare" (1967:223).

I can think of no statement more symptomatic of the peasant as problem than the following reference to the "disinherited": "they possess fine human qualities and what they require is that all of us be a little more just, a little more compassionate, so that with them, we can build in all the country, with all the indigenous tribes, the future grandeur of Mexico" (Ideario 1970:160). This rhetoric is so persuasive that it has successfully and perniciously nourished peasant expectations for the past generation. Since the completion of the Agrarian Reform–in its original sense of land distribution–not one systematically applied program has impinged on the farmers of San Felipe with the intention of a more equitable participation in national development. As one townsman stressed, "having lived in the rural zone, you are aware of our problems, and the good and bad as in all situations. You shouldn't depict us as Oscar Lewis has–you have to remember the disquiet in the provinces, of people who are trying to get ahead." As long as the problem remains in the countryside, the pattern of lifting oneself up by the bootstrap method will probably continue. The expression "integral agrarian reform" has lost its significance. It has been used year after year and regularly appears in the newspapers, but it still has not arrived in San Felipe. Today it is a political adjective. The revolutionary government extols the peasant who now, as in 1910, occupies the lowest level of Mexican society. Stale ideologies have coalesced, forming part of a demagogic repertoire manipulated by a political system to insure continuity and evade basic structural changes which might threaten its stability.

APPENDIX I
CHRONOLOGY

National		*Local*	
1810 to 1821	War of Independence.		
1857	New Constitution prohibits Church ownership of real estate for nonreligious purposes and requires the distribution of common lands.	1850 to 1890	Village common lands distributed and sold to speculators. Formation of large, landed estates.
1862 to 1867	The French Intervention and imposition of Maximilian as emperior.		
1876 to 1911	Dictatorship of Porfirio Díaz.		
1883 to 1894	Alienation of public and communal lands.		
1910	Francisco Madero calls for free presidential elections and the restitution of communal lands in the "Plan of San Luis Potosí."		
1911	Emiliano Zapata leads revolutionary activity in the state of Morelos, demanding "Death to the Hacendados." Madero elected president.	1911	"Bandits" attack haciendas.

National		*Local*	
1913	General Victoriano Huerta assassinates Madero and assumes presidency.	1913	Hacendados attend district meeting where they are assured of Huerta's support.
	Revolution intensifies: Venustiano Carranza calls for restoration of Constitution of 1857 and joins forces with Alvaro Obregón.		Munitions distributed by the government for the armed defense of haciendas.
	Zapata continues southern thrust, demanding the restoration of communal lands in the "Plan of Ayala."		
1914	Carranza enters Mexico City and takes control. His reactionary regime is characterized by internecine warfare.	1914	Carranzistas loot haciendas.
1916	National Agrarian Commission formed, making token land distribution.		
1917	New Constitution. Article 27 calls for land distribution and delineates the functions of public and private property.	1917	Hacendados receive more arms from the government.
1920	Carranza assassinated. Obregón controls country through a puppet president.	1920	Peasant unrest.
	Free villages allowed to apply for land.	1921	San Antonio Mextepec receives land expropriated from the hacienda of Tepetitlán.
1923	Plutarco Calles, Obregon's candidate, elected president.	1925 to 1930	Large tracts expropriated from Tepetitlán.
1927	Obregón elected president.		
1928	Obregón murdered.		Violent confrontations between peons and hacendados.

1928 to 1934 — Calles rules through puppet presidents.

1934 to 1940 — President Lázaro Cárdenas sponsors large-scale land distribution.

1939 — Unión Nacional Sinarquista formed.

1940 — Juan Almazán loses elections to Avila Camacho, the official party's candidate.

1930 to 1935 — Hacendados try to save estates through semi-legal sales and gifts.

1936 to 1938 — Increasing expropriations from other haciendas.

1938 — Ejidatarios begin invading land still belonging to the estates.

1939 — The peon Mateo Sánchez appointed municipal president.

1940 — Muncipal authorities denounce hacendados as subverters and enemies of agrarian reform.

Hacendados join reactionary Sinarquista party.

1941 — Martial law imposed and federal troops occupy municipality.

1943 — Land distribution completed; formation of 84 ejido communities.

Most hacendados leave municipality and others begin litigations to protect their remaining properties.

APPENDIX II
THE AGRICULTURAL CYCLE

What anthropologists refer to as the agricultural cycle is a series of procedures for the farmer, each involving a discrete number of tasks and tools, each vulnerable to haphazard occurrences that might jeopardize their final cumulative outcome. The agricultural cycle is primarily a maize cycle. Maize is the only crop that is planted by all farmers on a yearly basis; even under extenuating circumstances when the probability of producing a healthy harvest is minimal, the farmer will plant at least one of his milpas in maize. The maize cycle is similar to the cycle practiced during the colonial period by the Indians and continues to be labor-intensive. During the last thirty years, however, several innovations have been accepted and popularized–innovations once utilized exclusively by the hacendados in the production of commercial crops.

Preparation

The agricultural cycle begins in November, shortly after the completion of the harvest, with the preparation of the soil. Fields are plowed lengthwise to break up the old furrows and uproot the turf. The first plowing, the *barbecho*, is carried out with a yoke of oxen and the *arado extranjero*, a plow with a wooden handle and beam, a single iron moldboard, and a steel share. The ideal condition for the barbecho calls for moist soil unless the land is of top quality; because of the general absence of irrigation, the first barbecho follows the harvest, when the soil is dry, yet still malleable. Over the winter months, the earth hardens to a thick, heavy crust and before the second barbecho, the farmer must either irrigate his fields or wait for the first gentle rains. During the early part of March, those with tierra de riego irrigate their fields by digging shallow ditches to divert the flow from the main canals. Working with a broad-bladed stick or a metal shovel, the farmer waters the entire field by repeatedly turning the soil over. Farmers with "nonirrigated land" cannot proceed to the second barbecho until enough rain has fallen to soften the soil. Once the furrows are demolished, the field is plowed a third time (*doblado*) to kick up and loosen the soil. Subsequently, the earth is given a final pulverizing and levelled (*rastreo*). With his oxen and *rastra*, a wooden harrow-like instrument, the farmer moves up and down the field until he is satisfied with the consistency of the earth. In the few cases where a tractor is employed, the farmer can doblar and rastrear simultaneously, but if he depends on animal traction, he must do these steps separately.

The preparation of the fields is completed by plowing furrows. The *surcado* is the only step in which the once common wooden plow is still employed. The *arado de país* or *arado criollo*, as it is locally known, has an iron share and differs from the extranjero in the absence of a moldboard. Many farmers no longer bother to replace their wooden plows and simply use the arado extranjero after removing the moldboard. Furrowing involves two steps, *rayar* and *cruzar*. The field is first plowed lengthwise and then crosswise. Distances between furrows are determined by the width of the yoke and vary from fifty to eighty centimeters; the resulting checkerboard pattern facilitates both sowing and weeding. Presently, the tendency is to eliminate cross-plowing; when the farmer is pressed for time due to delayed rains or when he plans to use one of the planting methods in which furrowing and planting are done simultaneously, cross-plowing is ignored with impunity.

Sowing

Occasionally a farmer will contend that sowing during the period of a waning moon is unlucky and one must wait for the full moon of a new month, yet most farmers are essentially pragmatic in arranging their planting schedules. The ideal planting period ranges from the third week of March to the beginning of April, that is, following several brief showers but before the full rainy season. Farmers will often wait as late as the end of April for rain, the last feasible date for a full growing season.

A variety of planting methods are known. Several are "traditional" and have been practiced continuously since pre-conquest times; others, of recent (twentieth century) origin, have been proven efficacious. Despite the longer historical continuity of some planting methods, there is no correlation between traditional practices and "traditional farmers." A farmer may vary his practices from one year to the next or he may try different methods for each of his plots. His preferences are determined by any number of conditions: climatic fluctuations, the size of his parcel, soil consistencey and quality, momentary financial circumstances, access to irrigation, secondary occupational obligations, and the availability of family members.

The plow has completely replaced the aboriginal digging stick in the preparation of the soil, but sowing is still accomplished through the indigenous methods of *pala* and *tapa pie*. Both require separate and prior furrowing, and are labor-intensive, time consuming, and relatively inexpensive. Pala takes its name from the *pala de sembrar*, a sturdy tool of evergreen oak. An adaptation of the aboriginal *espeque*, it is not only a digging stick with a metal tipped point at one end, but can also be turned over and used as a shovel. The farmer loosens the soil with the blade; then he flips the pala over. Holding himself erect, he grasps it with both hands and thrusts the tip deeply into the soil. He works his way down the furrow, followed by an *echadora* who kneels down and places several seeds precisely in the center of the hole. She, in turn, is followed by another farmer who covers the hole by repeatedly slapping the face of the blade against the ground. Rarely is it necessary for the planting party to work in unison; since the field has been previously crossplowed and everyone knows exactly where the seeds are to be placed, planters generally scatter, shift sites and working partners,

MAIZE CYCLE
(Production Time per Hectare)

Process	*Number of Days*	
Preparation		
Barbecho I	3	
Barbecho II	3	
Riego	2-5	
Doblar	3½	
Rastrear	3	
Surcar		
Rayar	2	
Cruzar	2	
Sowing		
Pala	2	(20 workers)
Tapa pie	1	(10 workers)
Embudo	1½	(3 workers)
Cultivation		
Escarda I	1½-2	
Escarda II	2	
Tablón	1	
Desyerbar (weeding)	4	
Harvest		
Despunte	2-3	
Cosecha (harvest)	2-3	(12 workers)
Cortar Rastrojo (cutting stalks)	2	
Transporte maíz, rastrojo (transportation)	5	

and vary tasks. Pala always involves a large group. An average planting party consists of twenty to twenty-five workers and includes in-laws, parents, siblings, cousins, nieces and nephews, two or three hired laborers, and assorted children. Planting is frequently accomplished with excessive conviviality–swigs from the pulque jug, joking, good-natured shouting–and numerous rest breaks to stretch one's limbs. Yet despite the esteem with which the pala method is regarded, it has steadily declined in popularity. Farmers, particularly younger men, are devoting more and more time to their secondary occupations and are unwilling to join work parties of others who have helped them. Pala persists, however, precisely because it is so effective. Wherever the wooden plow is still in use, pala is the proper planting complement; as long as farmers rely primarily on rainfall, the pala de sembrar will continue to be the most functional instrument for pulverizing the soil during a dry year.

Tapa pie is the most popular sowing method and is considered rapid, economical, and almost as secure as pala. It requires humid, semi-soft soil and is effective in both irrigated fields and those seasonally watered fields which have received adequate precipitation. Tapa pie has totally superseded pala in irrigated fields. Here, more favorable conditions have enabled the farmer to eliminate the meticulous and onerous planting stick without prejudice to his crop. Although furrowing and sowing cannot be done simultaneously by tapa pie, the farmer's attitude is, "hacerlo de un solo golpe" (do it in one stroke). He accomplishes the two steps at the same time by eliminating crossplowing and dividing plowing and planting tasks among his work party. As the plowman makes the furrow, the planters–men, women and children–follow in his path. Carrying his seeds in a makeshift receptacle–a sombrero, a shawl wound about the waist, or a metal pail–the planter makes a crude hole with his foot, drops in three or four seeds, covers the hole with the same foot and impacts the earth with his other foot. The pala de sembrar is used as an accessory to break up any remaining clods of earth. Tapa pie is less laborious than the pala method; consequently, the work party is much smaller. A farmer prefers to ask a neighbor for help, a man who is also his compadre and his associate in festive activities. As one farmer put it, "this way I don't have to spend any money; I help him and he helps me." Between the two farmers and their respective families, a plot can be sown easily in one day. The host is obligated to compensate the work party with pulque and a picnic lunch of tortillas and greens, and to reciprocate with equal labor. Despite an expressed preference for hiring labor, many farmers have come to rely on the yearly attendance of the same compadre. Since the ejidos are often a two- or three-hour walk from the residential site, laborers cannot be depended on to come that far.

A variation of tapa pie, practiced when the rains are late, is *a rabo de buey*. Similar to broadcasting, the seeds are simply deposited along the furrow and then covered by a second plowing. It is believed that the resultant deeper planting will provide additional protection during the dry period preceding the heavy rains.

The other planting methods, requiring machinery such as the tractor or seeder, or investment in additional implements like the funnel plow are of recent innovation and are practiced infrequently. The superiority of the tractor is an acknowledged fact, but it is of minimal practicality for most farmers. The tractor, of course, permits extensive cultivation of large, adjoining fields and is owned almost exclusively by ranchers.[42] The seeder also permits extensive cultivation, eliminates large labor requirements, and is less expensive. Widely used by the hacendados, it has practically been abandoned because of its poor results in hard soils. Farmers who previously employed the seeder now plant by *embudo*. Embudo is even replacing tapa pie, although many farmers "lack faith" and still reject it. The embudo is a funnel which is fitted to a specially shaped iron plow, the *arado de embudo*. As with the tractor, one can cut lengthwise furrows and sow simultaneously; embudo also facilitates the application of insecticide. A team of three is required–the *yuntero* to guide the oxen, and two helpers, one to deposit seed in the embudo and the other, insecticide. Because the seed is planted to a shallow depth, the embudo method is successful only when the soil is loose and soft. For the proper use of embudo, one should prepare the field with a tractor. This is rarely done since it is still less expensive to hire a work party than to rent a tractor.

Cultivation

In June or when the corn has reached a height of twenty-five centimeters and several leaves have sprouted, cultivation is initiated with the first *escarda*. Fertilizer is manually applied around each plant and then plowed in during the ensuing escarda. With a double-winged cultivator, the farmer reverses the furrows by pushing the soil against the young plants. His object is to both weed and conserve humidity without causing the putrefaction of the root system. His helpers, family members, remove the remining weeds and expose any plants that have been buried. The process is repeated a month later (the segunda escarda), and occasionally a third time (*tablón*) to aerate the soil. Between escardas and following the tablón the family is occupied in the interminable task of weeding, either with sickles or hoes.

When the tender ears have almost reached their full maturity, the points of the stem are cut (*despunte*), ground, and reserved for fodder. The despunte is done as late in the season as possible because it eliminates the corn's principal nutritional source and hastens the drying process. Some farmers also cut the stalks near the base and pile them, along with loose leaves and stubble, into a pyramid (*mogote*). The mogote is reinforced by binding it with the stems of wild flowers and serves effectively as a repellent against late rains and resultant decay.

Harvest

When the corn is relatively dry, generally by mid-October, it is harvested. Regardless of the size of the farmer's property or his financial circumstances, the harvest is a manual operation; it is also the most arduous of the agricultural processes. Farmers work together in large groups or if feasible, will hire a harvest party. Each harvester is responsible for a set number of furrows and works with a *pizca*, a pointed husking tool of wood or bone. The *pizcador* opens the leaves enveloping the corn ear, inserts the pizca between the bottom of the cob and the husk, twists the ear loose, and places it in his *ayate*, an ixtle shoulderbag. When the ayate is full, he empties it into a *costal*, a henquin sack with a capacity of seventy kilos. The costales are then carried, by means of a tumpline, to the edge of the milpa; at the day's end, they are transported by burro, horse-drawn wagon, or truck to the house site.

If the stalks had not been previously arranged into mogotes, they are cut with a machete during the harvest and stacked into bundles which are left to dry. They are later transported to the house and piled into a rick to serve as forage. On completion of the harvest, the corn is carefully examined; loose leaves and stubble are removed and the finest ears (large cobs with even grains) of various classes–white, yellow, blue and mixed–are selected and set aside for the next season's sowing. The remainder is stored in a wooden corncrib adjoining the house. Those farmers with old style houses continue to store their corn in the *tapanco* (attic), following a period of outside exposure for thorough drying. Once dry, the corn is shelled as needed.

APPENDIX III
MUNICIPAL BUDGET: JUNE 1970

Revenues

1. Praedial
   Properties valued at under 500 pesos are taxed
   12 pesos annually 36.00

2. Sale of alcohic drinks
   Merchants must pay a 5% tax on the sale of alcoholic
   beverages and 6% on the sale of pulque 49.20

3. Bike registration
   18 pesos 270.00

4. Commercial and industrial patents
   All commercial houses and workshops must pay a
   2% tax on income 2,984.10

5. Peddlers
   Although most door-to-door salesmen manage to escape, if
   they are seen peddling their goods, they must pay 2%
   of their sales 160.00

6. Residues
   Fines for tax evaders 332.00

7. Civil registration fines
   5 pesos for each year of late registration of births, deaths,
   and marriages 1,108.40

8. Police fines
   Fines for public drunkenness, disturbing the peace, etc.
   Each day spent in the municipal jail is worth 10 pesos 252.30

9. Reintegrations
   The municipal treasurer is fined if he inadvertently or
   deliberately does not collect the correct amount. This is
   especially effective during the changeover in office, when
   the treasurer still lacks familiarity with the taxes 33.30

10. Sheets of special paper
    Registrants are charged 4 pesos for the value
    of certificates 532.00

11. Certificates
All births, deaths, and civil marriages must be registered and certified by the municipal president; a copy of the certificate costs 16 pesos 2,128.00

12. Civil registration of births
15 pesos. Births and deaths may be registered in several villages but all monies and records must be forwarded to the town hall 5,324.40

13. Civil registration of marriages
30 pesos 652.52

14. Civil registration of deaths
12.25 pesos for children, 28.75 pesos for adults 2,360.00

15. Municipal pound
Pigs, cows and horses are not allowed to roam in town, are confiscated and impounded. The claimants are charged a daily rental of 1-3 pesos depending on the animal 3.00

16. Municipal slaughterhouse
This tax of 10 cents on each kilo of meat is evaded by all except town butchers 141.10

17. Market
1 pesos per square meter 5,141.50

18. Authorization plaques
Each merchant must pay 30-200 pesos annually depending on the size and type of business 850.00

19. Registration cards
Every merchant must register his business every four years at a cost of 1 peso 33.00

20. Public education fund
15% surcharge on all municipal taxes. For example, bike registration will cost 18 pesos plus a 15% surcharge of 2.70. This sum is later transferred to the "Receptoría de Rentas." 2,599.95

21. Donations
These are "voluntary gifts" offered to the treasury for general oversights such as lowered land values, etc 929.00

22. Federal participations
Monies remitted by the federal government and derived from pulque production, beer consumption and forest exploitation 1,292.67

23. Pension deposits
6% of salaries of police and municipal employees 309.90

Total 27,522.34

Expenditures

1.	Presidential gratuities	2,085.00
2.	Police salaries	3,800.00
3.	Treasurer's percentage Rather than a salary, the treasurer receives 10% of municipal revenues	2,752.00
4.	Representation expenses President's expense account	1,000.00
5.	Expenses of municipal offices	1,492.25
6.	Public lighting	1,220.55
7.	Public works Cost of construction materials and workers' salaries	1,845.90
8.	Education Subsidy for secondary school teachers who work overtime. This fund also covers two fellowships for secondary school students of 35 pesos each	500.00
9.	Literacy campaign Salaries of three teachers	720.00
10.	Pensions	390.00
11.	Miscellaneous expenses Banquets, trips to Toluca, etc	6,722.90
12.	Public education–15% surcharge	2,599.96
13.	Municipal tariff–10%	2,245.96
	Total	27,353.73
	May–Balance	64.96
	June–Entries	27,522.34
	Total	27,587.30
	Expenditures	27,353.73
	Balance	233.57

NOTES

[1]The identification of the regional community is based on Arensberg's definition of the community as a "unit minimum population aggregate"–"a structured social field of inter-individual relationships unfolding through time" (1961:250). A network conceptualization of community is used as the unit of analysis since the regional system mediates between the local-national dyarchy. The community comprises the administrative and market seat (*cabecera*) of the municipality, the suburban barrios at the periphery of the town, and the satellite villages, ejidos, rancherías, etc., of the rural zone. As a result of the highly centralized nature of Mexican territorial divisions, the boundaries of this network roughly correspond with the boundaries of the municipality, varying according to the nature of the network, whether political, religious, economic or social. The units within the network are neither complete communities nor self-contained sociocultural systems. With ties of complementarity *vis-à-vis* other units, each unit may be considered isolable only in the sense that they are residential and resource exploiting segments. The concept of region is also employed heuristically (Steward 1955); the region is an open system and does not have inherent boundaries.

[2]A person granted an encomienda, a colonial grant of Indian tributaries and the area occupied by them.

[3]Mexicans of Spanish decent.

[4]This family name has been changed.

[5]A derogatory term applied to native-born Spaniards living in Mexico.

[6]An alcoholic drink derived from the sweet juice of the maguey plant.

[7]These figures are approximations since most informants were unable to calculate land resources with accuracy. In San Onofre, the only hacienda where archives have survived, statistics invariably refer to agricultural productivity rather than to areal extensions of lands devoted to particular crops.

[8]The local designation for all non-Indians, literally "people of reason."

[9]This popular ritual dish consists of boiled turkey and a hot sauce prepared with chiles, nuts, chocolate, raisins, sesame seeds and numerous spices.

[10]All employees, by the nature of being employees, were believed to have disinterested and honorable intentions, and open trusting relationships with their employer.

[11]San Antonio Publo Nuevo, for example, retained communal holdings of 152 hectares: 96 hectares were individually cultivated by 279 families; 14 hectares were classified as "stony and barren"; 42 hectares of forest and grazing lands were shared by the community. San Antonio Mextepec retained 315 hectares: 156 hectares were classified as *tepetate*, a sandy soil of poor quality lacking organic materials; grazing lands amounted to 149 hectares; the remaining 10 hectares were considered cultivable and supported 175 families. In Palmillas, 46 hectares were cultivated by 173 families; 20 hectares were classified as "barren"; the village lacked forest or grazing lands and turned to the hacienda for grazing and gleaning rights (Communal Lands Section, Municipal Archives 1921).

[12]The ejido, a community with inalienable land granted by the government, was the predominant form of land tenure created by the agrarian reform program. Every family of the ejido has usufructuary rights to a specified plot. This plot cannot be divided, rented or sold, and must be worked continually. A commission, elected by the ejidatarios, represents the agrarian community before the nation and is responsible for curbing abuses of the Agrarian Code.

[13]Forest lands were appraised annually and their value recorded, but their area was never included in the inventories. The hacienda would then appear to be smaller than it actually was. The approximate figure of 10,000 hectares was given by the ex-hacendado and corroborated by several ex-administrators.

[14]After the "loss" of 2822 hectares, the remaining 6051 hectares were appraised at $195,982. The depreciation discount amounted to $101,688, resulting in a final value of $94,294. Forest lands were also discounted and within a year, their value dropped from $105,780 to $85,027.

[15]The author does not strictly clarify the composition of the dependent or exploited groups and wavers between treating "internal colonialism" as an indigenous problem and as a national problem. At one point he states that at least 10% of the total population may be considered indigenous (1968:478). Later he states that a minimum of 20% of all Mexicans are indigenous (1969:134). This figure is based upon a redefinition of "Indian," in which criteria other than linguistic (technology, institutions, etc.) are used. Yet in trying to specify the Indian's position in Mexico, the author admits the difficulty of distinguishing many Indians from non-Indians: "We tried to find in the case of Mexico, correlations by Indian–non-Indian regions, without finding significant coefficients, probably because the population which does not speak only Indian tongues, in the proximities of the Indian communities, has conditions of life similar to these" (1969:132). Elsewhere, considering the problem of a neocolonial structure a national one, the author notes that 65% of all Mexicans constitute a repressed group, that is, Indians simply form one sector (aside from poor peasants and unskilled laborers) of a marginal group which is uniformly exploited by the "participating" sectors (1968:480).

[16]The general term for non-Indians in southern Mexico and Guatemala.

[17]The classic characteristics of the indigenous "economy of subsistence" are: primitive technology; total absence of communications; elementary division of labor; low level of production; family productive unit, minimal level of capitalization; institutional redistribution of capital through the mechanism of the civil-religious hierarchy; absence of salaried relationships; use of special purpose money; savings in the form of a subsistence fund; inseparability of economic activities from their social context (Aguirre Beltrán 1967:128-135).

[18]In town, occupations fall into the following categories: commerce (store owners, cattle and grain dealers); civil service (municipal, state and federal); professional; service; artisans; industry (raíz processing); agriculture.

[19]The majority of farmers are *campesinos* (peasants), whether Indian or Mestizo. The peasant, as defined in Mexico, is a farmer who, utilizing his own resources (land and labor), produces both for his own consumption and the market. I prefer not to speak of peasants. "Peasant" is the favored term of rhetorians who consistently employ it in a political context to refer to a "sector." In San Felipe, the "peasant sector" is of secondary importance and both farmers and non-farmers are affiliates. Farmers identify themselves as *agricultores*, not campesinos. "Campesino" is primarily a class term for San Felipeños, meant to identify someone who is very poor, whether or not he is a farmer. It is very often used in a derogatory sense to denigrate a person, upwardly mobile, but with unimpressive origins. Those farmers who have a somewhat larger land base than average are known as ranchers; they may be wealthier than the others, but share the same problems.

[20]The minimum size of seasonally watered fields, originally specified as 4 hectares, was raised to ten hectares in 1949 to alleviate runaway minifundium. This revision of the Agrarian Code had no practical consequences for San Felipeños, whose land had already been distributed.

[21]During the colonial period, the diezmo was a tithe of 10% of the harvest delegated to the Church. In San Felípe, although the term, "diezmo" has remained, the offering is never more than 1 costal or 70 kilos of corn ears.

[22]Whether the merchant's transaction is in tons or sacks of fertilizer depends principally on the fertilizer he lends. Two commercial fertilizers are in general use–Amonitro (ammonium sulfate) and Guanomex (superphosphate of calcium). Amonitro is expensive and is used discriminately; it is sold in sacks varying from 25 to 40 kilos in weight and sells

for 1.90 pesos per kilo. A farmer will rarely use more than 200 kilos per hectare. Guanomex is sold in sacks of 50 kilos at 33 pesos per sack. If a farmer buys a ton, he will be given a discount of 10 pesos.

[23]Municipalities are grouped into districts, but the district has judicial functions only.

[24]The PRI (Partido Revolucionario Institucional) was known as PNR (Partido Nacional Revolucionario) until 1937, and PRM (Partido de la Revolución Mexicana) until 1945.

[25]The ayuntamiento is composed of six *propietarios*: president, *síndico*, first, second and third *regidores, juez menor*, and seven *suplentes*. Each propietario has a substitute, the suplente, with the exception of juez menor who has two suplentes. The first regidor substitutes for the president in his absence, and serves as acting president for three months in the event of his death; the position will then be filled by the first suplente. The síndico is an auxiliary of the Public Ministry and is responsible for forwarding criminal cases to the district judge. Each of the regidores is assigned various commissions–communications, education, electricity, etc. The general secretary, judicial secretary and treasurer, additional members of the ayuntamiento, are appointed by the municipal president. The president also appoints the police commissioner and three policemen for the town. Each village is represented by a municipal delegate and three suplentes as well as a security service of three policemen; these officials are considered auxiliaries of the ayuntamiento and their appointments must be approved by the municipal president.

[26]San Felipe-Ixtlahuaca is only 18 kilometers, whereas San Felípe-Atlacomulco-Ixtlahuaca is 43 kilometers.

[27]Observances consisting of prayers or services on nine consecutive days.

[28]A large clay pot filled with favors, fruit, candy, etc., and covered with crepe paper; it is suspended above the heads of the children who–blindfolded and one-by-one–try to break the pot with a large stick.

[29]Long live Christ the King, the bishop, the priest, the Pía Unión of Pilgrims, the pilgrimage of Concepción; long live Mexico, long live Mexico, long live Mexico.

[30]Nicolas León gives a complete description of the various extant terminologies in "Las Castas de México Colonial." They differ in breadth and are often contradictory.

[31]Parish records indicate that a castizo was the child of mestizo-Spanish parentage, while the morisco was of mulatto-Spanish origin. The more original categories were not explained. According to the various ideal systems, a lobo was a mixture of either indio-negra or salta atrás (morsico-Spaniard with india)-mulata. The significance of coyote was even more confused and was variously designated as a mixture of blanco-india, indio-mestiza, and cuarterón (mulatto-mestiza)-mestiza.

[32]During the Díaz regime, the "castas" were replaced by racial categories and Spaniards, Creoles, mixed races, and Indians were differentiated on the basis of physiognomy, character and temperament, "habits," "customs" and "mode of life." See García Cubas, "The Republic of Mexico in 1896," for a prejudiced analysis of racial groups and race relations.

[33]The synopsis of the lesson on race is based on an eighth grade history class taught in San Felipe.

[34]The similarities betweeen Indian and rural Mestizo groups are summarized in the "Heritage of Conquest" (Tax 1952). Salz (1944) traces the relativistic identification of Indians and Mestizos, while Lewis and Maes (1945) reject cultural criteria, defining Indians on the basis of social necessities of rural communities. More recently, Goldkind (1963) and Stavenhagen (1970a) have compared the culturalistic and structuralist approaches, concluding that an emphasis on distinct cultural traditions, as a criterion of differentiation, is a simplification of the situation since it does not control for rural-urban factors.

[35]As defined by Stavenhagen, an ethnic group is "a social group whose members participate in the same culture, who may sometimes be characterized in biological or racial terms, who are conscious of belonging to such a group and who participate in a system of relations with other similar groups" (1970b:284).

[36]Integration is viewed as a means to national grandeur and was a predominant theme during the presidential campaign. Integration is defined as "the complex of actions through

which the grand part of the population is joined under the consciousness of a single culture, a single language and—the essential—a single nationality" (Ortiz 1970:1).

[37]The upper-class townsman would never condescend to denigrating Indians in public, although at home he might be quite capable of teaching his children proper manners by reminding them not to behave like Indians.

[38]According to national censuses, monolinguism has declined both absolutely and relatively. From 1950 to 1960, the number of monlingual speakers declined from 5558 to 4464 representing 13.5% and 8.5% of the population. In 1970, the absolute number of monolingual speakers was virtually the same—4473—but now represented only .05% of the total population.

[39]By 1970 the rise in bilingualism had leveled off; 32,098 bilingual speakers represented only 37% of the total population.

[40]A person with country manners—unpolished and rude.

[41]Outsiders are generally more vociferous than townspeople in this respect. A typical example is Rural Mission 17 which had a varying reception. Despite their mission to combat poverty, poor health conditions and ignorance, they blamed their difficulties on the fanaticism, superstitiousness, moroseness and apathy of both townspeople and villagers.

[42]Approximately 10% of the farmers rent tractors from the ejido bank for the barbecho. During a dry year, it is the only effective method for preparing nonirrigated lands.

BIBLIOGRAPHY

Aguirre Beltrán, Gonzalo

1967 Regiones de Refugio. El Desarrollo de la Comunidad y El Proceso Dominical en Mestizo América. México, D.F.: Instituto Indigenista Interamericano.

Albornoz, Álvaro de

1966 Trayectoria y ritmo del crédito agrícola en México. México, D.F.: Instituto Mexicano de Investigaciones Económicas.

Arensberg, Conrad M.

1961 The Community as Object and as Sample. American Anthropologist 63:241-264.

Avila, Manuel

1969 Tradition and Growth. A Study of Four Mexican Villages. Chicago: University of Chicago Press.

Beals, Ralph

1946 Cheran: A Sierra Tarascan Village. Institute of Social Anthropology Publication 2. Washington DC: Smithsonian Institution.

Bernal, Ignacio, Roman Piña-Chan and Fernando Cámara

1968 Tesoros del Museo Nacional de Antropología de México. México D.F.: Daimon Mexicana, S.A.

Borah, Woodrow

1954 Race and Class in Mexico. Pacific Historical Review 23:331-342.

Brandenburg, Frank R.

1964 The Making of Modern Mexico. Englewood Cliffs, NJ: Prentice-Hall.

Cámara, Fernando

1965 Rescate etnográfico nacional en México. Vienna, Bulletin of the International Committee on Urgent Anthropological and Ethnological Research 7:99-104.

1966 Race and Class Concepts in the Survival of Indian Culture: A Mexican Research Project. Unpublished manuscript.

Cancian, Frank

1972 Change and Uncertainty in a Peasant Economy. The Maya Corn Farmers of Zinacantan. Stanford: Stanford University Press.

Carrasco, Pedro

1950 Los Otomíes. Cultura e historia prehispánicas de los pueblos mesoamericanos de habla otomiana. México, D.F.: Universidad Autónoma de México. Instituto de Historia No. 15.

IV Censos Agrícola, Ganadero y Ejidal (1960)

1965 Estado de México. México, D.F.: Secretaría de Industria y Comercio. Dirreción General de Estadística.

VI Censo General de Población (1940)

1943 Estado de México. México, D.F.: Secretaría de Industria y Comercio. Dirreción General de Estadística.

VII Censo General de Población (1950)

1953 Estado de México. México, D.F.: Secretaría de Industria y Comercio. Dirreción General de Estadística.

VIII Censo General de Población (1960)

1963 Estado de México. México, D.F.: Secretaría de Industria y Comercio. Dirreción General de Estadística.

IX Censo General de Población (1970)

1973 Estado de México. México, D.F.: Secretaría de Industria y Comercio. Dirreción General de Estadística.

Codice Mendocino
1938 The Mexican Manuscript known as the Collection of Mendoza and presented in the Bodleian Library, Oxford. James Cooper Clark, Ed. and Trans.

Colby, Benjamin N., and Pierre L. van den Berghe
1969 Ixil Country. A Plural Society in Highland Guatemala. Berkeley: University of California Press.

Colín, Mario
1949 El municipio en México. Toluca.
1964 Adolfo López Mateos y Los Mazahuas. Estado de México, Testimonio de Atlacomulco 20.

Cumberland, Charles C.
1968 Mexico. The Struggle for Modernity. New York: Oxford University Press.

Dar poder adquisitivo al campesino, nuestro problema: LE
1970 Excelsior, January 24:1. México, D.F.

Descontento popular en la mayoría de los municipios
1969 El Heraldo de Toluca. September 11:1.

Despres, Leo
1967 Cultural Pluralism and Nationalist Politics in British Guiana. Chicago: Rand McNally.

Durán, Marco Antonio
1967 El agrarismo mexicano. México, D.F.: Siglo Veintiuno Editores S.A.

Erasmus, Charles
1967 Culture Change in Northwest Mexico. *In* Contemporary Change in Traditional Societies. Julian Steward, Ed. Vol. III, Mexican and Peruvian Communities. Urbana: University of Illinois Press. pp. 1-131.

Excelsior
1955 August 17:1. México, D.F.

Fernández Ponte, Fausto
1970 El estado contra el latifundismo, propósito de Echeverría. Excelsior, February 19:1. México, D.F.

Ferreira, Angel
1970a Programa de Echeverría para colonizar las costas con campesinos sin tierra ni trabajo. Excelsior, February 17:4a. México, D.F.
1970b Del existo del trabajo rural depende nuestra prosperidad, dijo Echeverriía. Excelsior, April 12:4. México, D.F.
1970c Mensaje al campesino. Actuén como combatientes revolucionarios: Luis Echeverría. Excelsior, June 5:1. México, D.F.

Foster, George M.
1967 Tzintzuntzan. Mexican Peasants in a Changing World. Boston: Little, Brown.

Friedrich, Paul
1970 Agrarian Revolt in a Mexican Village. Englewood Cliffs, NJ: Prentice-Hall.

Furnivall, J. S.
1944 Netherlands India. A Study of Plural Economy. New York: Macmillan.

García Cubas, Antonio
n.d. The Republic of Mexico in 1896. A Political and Ethnographic Division of the Population, Character, Habits, Customs and Vocations of Its Inhabitants. México.

Geertz, Clifford
1968 Agricultural Involution. The Process of Ecological Change in Indonesia. Berkeley: University of California Press.

Goldkind, Victor
1963 Ethnic Relations in Southeastern Mexico: A Methodological Note. American Anthropologist 65:394-399.

González-Casanova, Pablo
1968 Mexico: The Dynamics of an Agrarian and "Semi-capitalist" Revolution. *In* Latin America. Reform or Revolution? James Petras and Maurice Zeitlan, Eds. Greenwich, CT: Fawcett. pp. 467-485.

1969 Internal Colonialism and National Development. *In* Latin American Radicalism. A Documentary Report on Left and Nationalist Movements. Irving Horowitz, Josué de Castro and John Gerassi, Eds. New York: Random House. pp. 118-139.

Harris, Marvin
1956 Town and Country in Brazil. New York: Columbia University Press.

Hunt, Eva, and Robert Hunt
1969 The Role of Courts in Rural Mexico. *In* Peasants in the Modern World. Philip K. Bock, Ed. Albuquerque: University of New Mexico Press. pp. 109-139.

Hunt, Robert
1969 *Review of* Regiones de Refugio: El Desarrollo de la Comunidad y el Proceso Dominical en Mestizo América. American Anthropologist 71:545-552.

Ideario, Precandidato Luis Echeverría
1970 México, D.F.: Organo teorico y doctrinario del PRI.

Inclán, Luis G.
1966 Astucia, el jefe de los hermanos de la hoja, o los contrabandistas de la Rama. México, D.F.: Editorial Porrua, S.A.

Inicua explotación de 300,000 Mazahuas
1969 El Sol de Toluca, October 4:6.

Iwańska, Alicja
1971 Purgatory and Utopia. A Mazahua Indian Village of Mexico. Cambridge, MA: Schenkman.

La ciudadanía de San Felipe registró a D. Tomás Ordóñez
1969 El Sol de Toluca, September. 4.

León, Nicolás
1924 Las castas del México Colonial o Nueva España. México, D.F.: Museo Nacional de Arqueología, Historia, y Etnografía.

Lewis, Oscar, and Ernest E. Maes
1945 Base para una nueva definición práctica del indio. América Indígena 5(2):107-118.

Lewis, Oscar
1963 Life in a Mexican Village: Tepoztlán Restudied. Urbana: University of Illinois Press.

Ley Federal del Trabajo
1970 Ultimas reformas y adiciones. México, D.F.

Liebow, Elliot
1967 Tally's Corner. A Study of Negro Streetcorner Men. Boston: Little, Brown.

Margolies, Luise
1969 The Rural Elite in a Mexican Municipality. Anthropological Quarterly 42:343-353.

Moss, L. W., and S. C. Cappannari
1962 Estate and Class in a South Italian Hill Village. American Anthropologist 64:287-300.

Nash, Manning
1957 The Multiple Society in Economic Development. Mexico and Guatemala. American Anthropologist 59:825-833.
1966 Primitive and Peasant Economic Systems. San Francisco: Chandler.
1967 Indian Economics. *In* Handbook of Middle American Indians. Vol. VI, Social Anthropology. Manning Nash, Ed. Austin: University of Texas Press. pp. 87-102.

Nelson, Cynthia
1971 The Waiting Village. Social Change in Rural Mexico. Boston: Little, Brown.

Ochoa, Guillermo
1970 Hay 2 Méxicos: el rural y el que come bien: Salvador Zubirán. Excelsior, April 26:1. México, D.F.

Ortiz Reza, Alejandro
1970 Barreras diversas hacen que uno de cada 10 campesinos viva marginado. Excelsior, March 4:1. México, D.F.

Pródigo Reparto de Tierras a Campesinos
1969 El Universal, October 4:6. México, D.F.

Ramírez, Rafael, et al.
1948 La enseñanza de la historia de México. México, D.F.: Instituto Panamericano de Geografía e Historia.
Redfield, Robert
1941 The Folk Culture of Yucatan. Chicago: University of Chicago Press.
Ribeiro, Darcy
1969 Las américas y la civilización. I, La civilización occidental y nosotros. Los pueblos testimonio. Buenos Aires: Centro Editor de América Latina S.A.
Richardson, Miles
1967 The Significance of the "Hole" Community in Anthropological Studies. American Anthropologist 69:41-54.
1970 San Pedro, Colombia. Small Town in a Developing Society. New York: Holt, Rinehart and Winston.
Romero Espinosa, Emilio
1963 La reforma agraria en México. A medio siglo de iniciada. México, D.F.; Cuadernos Americanos.
Rubin, Vera
1960 Discussion of "Social and Cultural Pluralism." *In* Social and Cultural Pluralism in the Caribbean. Vera Ruben, Ed. Annals of the New York Academy of Sciences 83(5):780-785.
Salarios Minimos que regiran en los años de 1968 y 1969
1968 México, D.F.: Comision Nacional de los Salarios Minimos.
Salazar Mallen, Rubén
1969 El Universal, October 4:4. México, D.F.
Salz, Beate
1944 Indianismo. Social Research 11(4):441-469.
San Felipe del Progreso, México
Municipal Archives. 1866-1966.
Parish Archives. 1711-1925.
San Onofre, México
Archives. 1914-1955.
Service, Elman R., and Helen S. Service
1954 Tobatí: Paraguayan Town. Chicago: University of Chicago Press.
Silverman, Sydel F.
1966 An Ethnographic Approach to Social Stratification: Prestige in a Central Intalian Community. American Anthropologist 68:899-921.
Simpson, Lesley Byrd
1967 Many Mexicos. Berkeley: University of California Press.
Smith, M. G.
1960 Social and Cultural Pluralism. *In* Social and Cultural Pluralism in the Caribbean. Vera Rubin, Ed. Annals of the New York Academy of Sciences 83(5):763-777.
Stavenhagen, Rodolfo
1970a Social Aspects of Agrarian Structure in Mexico. *In* Agrarian Problems and Peasant Movements in Latin America, Rodolfo Stavenhagen, Ed. New York: Doubleday. pp. 225-270.
1970b Classes, Colonialism, and Acculturation. *In* Masses in Latin America. Irving Louis Horowitz, Ed. New York: Oxford University Press. pp. 235-288.
Stavenhagen, Rodolfo, et al.
1968 Neolatifundismo y explotación. De Emiliano Zapata a Anderson Clayton & Co. México, D.F.: Editorial Nuestro Tiempo, S.A.
Steward, Julian
1955 "Region"–An Heuristic Concept. Rural Sociology 20:297-298.
Steward, Julian (Ed.)
1956 The People of Puerto Rico. Urbana: University of Illinois Press.
Tamayo, Jorge L.
1962 Geografía general de México. 4 vols. México, D.F.: Instituto Mexicano de Investigaciones Económicas.
Tannenbaum, Frank
1929 The Mexican Agrarian Revolution. Washington DC: Brookings Institution.

Taylor, Paul
1933 A Spanish-Mexican Peasant Community: Arandas in Jalisco, Mexico. Ibero-Americana 4.
Tax, Sol (Ed.)
1952 Heritage of Conquest: The Ethnology of Middle America. Glencoe: Free Press.
Tello, Carlos
1968 La tenencia de la tierra en México. México, D.F.: Instituto de Investigaciones Sociales.
Vera, Fortino H.
1880 Itinerario parroquial del arzobispado de México y reseña histórica, geográfica y estadística de las parroquias del mismo. Amecameca: Imprenta del Colegio Católico.
Vernon, Raymond
1965 The Dilemma of Mexico's Development. The Roles of the Private and Public Sectors. Cambridge, MA: Harvard University Press.
Wagley, Charles
1968 The Latin American Tradition. Essays on the Unity and the Diversity of Latin American Culture. New York: Columbia University Press.
Wagley, Charles, and Marvin Harris
1965 A Typology of Latin American Subcultures. *In* Contemporary Cultures and Societies of Latin America. Dwight Heath and Richard Adams, Eds. New York: Random House. pp. 42-69.
Wolf, Eric R., and Sidney W. Mintz
1957 Haciendas and Plantations in Middle America and the Antilles. Social and Economic Studies 6:380-412.
Wolf, Eric R.
1959 Sons of the Shaking Earth. Chicago: University of Chicago Press.
1965 Kinship, Friendship, and Patron-Client Relations in Complex Society. *In* The Social Anthropology of Complex Societies. Michael Banton, Ed. ASA Monographs 4:1-22. New York: Praeger.
1966 Peasants. Englewood Cliffs, NJ: Prentice-Hall.

www.ingramcontent.com/pod-product-compliance
Lightning Source LLC
LaVergne TN
LVHW090944080826
845145LV00003B/885

* 9 7 8 0 9 8 2 6 7 6 7 1 4 *